Formal and Informal Work

Routledge Advances in Sociology

For a full list of title in this series, please visit www.routledge.com

Formal and Informal Work

The Hidden Work Regime in Europe

Edited by Birgit Pfau-Effinger, Lluís Flaquer and Per H. Jensen

Routledge
Taylor & Francis Group

LONDON AND NEW YORK

First published 2009
by Routledge

2 Park Square, Milton Park, Abingdon, Oxon OX14 4RN
52 Vanderbilt Avenue, New York, NY 10017

Routledge is an imprint of the Taylor & Francis Group, an informa business

First published in paperback 2012

© 2009 Taylor & Francis

Typeset in Sabon by IBT Global.

Library of Congress Cataloging in Publication Data

Formal and informal work : the hidden work regime in Europe / edited by Birgit Pfau-Effinger, Lluis Flaquer, & Per H. Jensen.
  p. cm.
Includes bibliographical references and index.
1. Labor—Europe. 2. Informal sector (Economics)—Europe. I. Pfau-Effinger, Birgit. II. Flaquer, Lluís, 1946– III. Jensen, Per H.
  HD8374.F656 2009
  331.094—dc22
  2008039576

ISBN13: 978-0-415-64786-1 (pbk)
ISBN13: 978-0-415-96469-2 (hbk)

Contents

Part III: Comparative Perspective

Figures

Tables

Foreword

This book presents findings from the research project "Formal and informal work in Europe (FIWE). A comparative analysis of their changing relationship and their impact on social integration" financed by the 5th EU Framework Programme, Theme 1: The challenge of socioeconomic development models for Europe (2002–2005). The overall aim of the FIWE project has been to analyse how the interrelationship between formal and informal work has changed, and how such changes have influenced social integration in European societies such as Finland, Denmark, Germany, Great Britain, Spain, and Poland.

The consortium behind the project was composed of Pertti Koistinen, University of Joensuu, Finland; Per H. Jensen and Jens Lind, Aalborg University, Denmark; Birgit Pfau-Effinger, Universität Hamburg, Germany; Traute Meyer, University of Southampton, Great Britain; Lluís Flaquer, Universitat Autónoma de Barcelona, Spain; and Aleksander Surdej, Cracow University of Economics, Poland. The project was coordinated by Birgit Pfau-Effinger.

Hamburg, June 2008
Birgit Pfau-Effinger

Part I

Introduction to the Approach of the Book

1 The Development of Informal Work in the Work-Welfare Arrangements of European Societies

Per H. Jensen, Birgit Pfau-Effinger, and Lluís Flaquer

INTRODUCTION

In the debate about the future of work, it is common to focus on processes of change within formal employment. However it is not possible to explain the development of the work society only through the development of formal employment; it is important to include different kinds of informal work, the interrelation of informal work and formal employment, and the dynamics of this relationship.

In the last three decades, the development of informal work and its relation to the development of formal employment has been the subject of empirical research and theoretical discussion in many respects:

Two forms of informal work—eldercare and childcare in the family—were identified in the 1970s by feminist research as a main factor contributing to the unequal structuring of labour markets in favour of men and to the disadvantage of women with respect to career opportunities. In more recent discussions, the integrating potential of family-based care has also been stressed (Pfau-Effinger and Geissler 2004).

In the 1980s, forms of informal work, such as voluntary work and new forms of subsistence work, were mainly seen as a new chance to develop an 'alternative' exchange-economy beyond the capitalist market economy (cf. Offe 1982). In another form, this argument experienced a revival in the late 1990s, as state promotion of voluntary work was seen as a possible solution to the labour-market crisis of West-European societies and, at the same time, as a contribution to strengthening the forces of civil society and social integration (Beck 2000; Rifkin 1998).

Another form of informal work is 'undeclared work', or as we call it here, 'informal employment'—market-based, paid work (Williams and Windebank 2001, 3). It has more recently been the subject of academic discussion and political intervention. Its development has often been discussed in relation to problems of social disintegration and marginalization, deterioration of wages and social security, a weakening of worker bargaining conditions, and a loss of taxes for the state (Thomas and Thomas 1994). Therefore it is also seen by the European Union (EU) as a major problem. However, in some recent publications based on empirical studies, it is pointed out that informal employment can also contribute to social integration (Williams 2001; Williams and Windebank 2002; Williams and Windebank 2005).

A characteristic feature of academic discussion and research on informal work is that diverse forms of informal work are most often analysed separately from one another. There have been very few analyses that choose a broader approach and deal with different types of informal work, the ways they interact, and their relationship with formal employment.

In this book, however, the aim is to integrate the study of heterogeneous forms of informal work into a comprehensive approach and, in a comparative perspective, shed light on different kinds of informal work: how the different kinds of informal work are interrelated, and how informal work is related to the formal employment system. We argue that the development of European work societies can only be adequately understood when informal work, and its relationship with formal employment, is included in the analysis. Changes in the informal work sector and its relationship to formal employment were a substantial element in the overall process of the division of labour in European societies. In the last three decades some parts of the informal sector have been formalized, that is, reconstituted and included in the formal employment sector. Other parts, even if not transformed into formal employment, have been the object of welfare-state regulation and at least in some respects formalized (after Geissler and Pfau-Effinger 2005; Pfau-Effinger 2005). Within informal work, there has been a definite trend towards new forms of informal, undeclared work taken by immigrants in private households (Hillmann 2005; Lutz 2002). Those jobs that have remained informal have in part changed their societal meaning to a certain degree. It is the aim of this book to analyse the main features of informal work and the driving factors of their development in a systematic, comparative perspective.

The central questions we aim to answer in this book include:

- How did the relationship between formal and informal work develop in the last decade?
- Under which conditions is work in European societies organized in informal form, and under which circumstances does the same type of work appear as formal employment?
- How can cross-national differences in the size and structures of informal work be explained?

The book presents findings of an international comparative study in six European countries.[1] Four types of informal work were selected for empirical analysis: childcare and eldercare in the private household, undeclared work, and voluntary work.

Care work is defined as support that people give others who need care. We refer here to the theoretical conception of 'social care', after which informal care of children and frail elderly people is embedded in an emotional, physical, mediatory horizontal and reciprocal social relationship involving practical assistance and surveillance (Daly and Lewis 1998, 2000; England 2005; Knijn and Kremer 1997; Lewis 1998). Informal care is based on an ethic and feeling of moral obligation on the part of those providing care, and it is embedded in a close social relation in which both partners become more or less dependent (Deven et al. 1998). Informal care work takes place most often in private households. Informal childcare is mainly provided by parents of the child, but it can also be provided by the extended family. Informal eldercare is most often provided by the spouses or children of frail elderly people. Since the advent of industrial society, the care responsibilities of households have been mainly assigned to women in the form of women's unpaid care work, which in turn contributes to the unequal structuring of labour markets in favour of men and to the disadvantage of women in respect to career changes. More recently the gender division of labour in this field has been gradually changing, if very slowly (Eydal 2005).

Voluntary work is work provided by citizens within civil society in order to support other citizens. Voluntary work can take place as an activity organized by nonprofit organizations and in unorganized forms outside of such organizations within social networks (Ślęzak 2004). Motives behind voluntary work may be altruistic, including a feeling of solidarity with the poor; it may be instrumental, that is, the aim may be to gain new skills and experience; or it may be obligatory, as when a sense of moral, religious or political duty is the driving force (Barker 1993, 28). The voluntary sector is marked by a tremendous complexity, but it is possible to distinguish two major forms of voluntary work in which the motives of the providers differ. Voluntary work may be philanthropic, that is, targeted at the production of classical welfare provision against social risks such as poverty, homelessness, sickness, and so on, or voluntary work may be self-centred or self-expressive, that is, targeted towards leisure activity in the form of sports, culture, and so on (Sivesind et al. 2002).

According to the common consensus on the definition of *informal employment* or *undeclared work*, the term means all remunerated activities that are in principle legal but hidden from the state in that they are not declared to the public authorities, though their declaration is required by the regulatory system of the specific state. Paid work in which the good or service itself is illegal is not included (European Commission 2007, 8; Renooy 2008, 250; Thomas 1992; Williams and Windebank 2005, 83). Thus, informal employment is carried out in a market separate from the formal market, and most often informal employment is considered morally unacceptable (for the acceptance of informal work in Europe, see European Commission 2007, 43ff). Moral and legal condemnations however must take into account that the phenomenon is a supply-driven as well as a demand-driven activity. On the demand side, households and backward or labour-intensive sectors of the economy are the main purchasers of informal work. These actors profit by escaping taxation, social security contributions, and the like. On the supply side, the purpose is to increase the income and prosperity of private households. Different motives, however, may trigger the supply of informal labour. A distinction can be made between 'moonlighting' and 'poverty-escaping' forms of informal work (Pfau-Effinger 2008). Poverty-escaping forms of informal work may be viewed as a struggle for subsistence in a labour market with no job openings and meagre welfare benefits. Undeclared 'moonlighting' is about earning an extra income in addition to the 'ordinary' wage income, or what Parsons (1956) called 'an optimum extra' in his analysis of the entry of housewives into the formal employment system. Whatever the case, undeclared workers are deprived many rights and easily exploited by employers. Thus informal work is connected with problems of low wages and social security benefits, and thereby with a weakening of workers' bargaining position and a loss of income for the state (Thomas and Thomas 1994).

We believe that the question to what degree these activities are organized in an informal form, and to what degree in a formal way, and how this is changing, is of particular relevance for the future of the globalized, postindustrial societies of Europe.

1.1 DEFINITION OF FORMAL AND INFORMAL WORK

Formal work, or *formal employment*, comprises forms of work which are regulated on the basis of the conditions of a legal framework. 'Formal' work usually means the work is carried out on the basis of formal gainful employment, that is, as officially registered employment and for which all necessary tax payments, payments of nonwage labour costs, and so on, are made (see also Bettio and Plantenga 2004, 86).

Formalization can also take place in another way, other than by the integration into formal employment, if it takes place in the context of welfare-state programmes such as childcare given by parents in the context of parental leave, or when care of the elderly given by family members is carried out as registered care in the context of cash-for-care systems and the like (e.g., Ungerson 2005). In this case the informal work is legally regulated and formalized in this respect, without having the character of formal gainful employment. Geissler and Pfau-Effinger (2005) have introduced the term *semi-formal work* for such forms of work.

Informal work includes all activities leading to the production of goods or services for others provided outside a legal framework in the market-based economy, in civil society or by family members. It can be paid or unpaid. Thus informal work can be income-oriented and based on principles of market exchange, or it can be solidarity or community oriented and based on mutual help and moral obligation.

In general the distinction between formal and informal work is a social construction that can take different shapes according to the spatial-temporal context (cf. also Portes 1994; Williams and Windebank 1998, 4). In the definition of eldercare applied to the welfare-state policies of the Nordic countries, for example, eldercare includes all activities that support people in their everyday lives, including physical care, cleaning, shopping, and the like. The definition in the context of the German care-insurance law of 1996 is more restrictive, meaning only physical care (Theobald 2005; Pfau-Effinger and Sakač Magdalenić in this volume; Jensen and Rathlev in this volume). Also, cross-national differences exist in the definition of 'undeclared work': something defined as undeclared work in one country may be evaluated as an expression of kindness to friends in another and not subject to taxation. Of particular importance in the case of Germany, for example, is the relatively high legal tolerance of undeclared work in as far as it takes place in private households and in the context of friendship networks. Such types of paid informal work, which are deemed as being done 'out of sheer kindness', are not defined as 'undeclared work' or prosecuted in Germany, even though a considerable amount of money or pay in kind may be paid for them (see Pfau-Effinger and Sakač Magdalenić in this volume). In Denmark, however, the definition of undeclared work is much more comprehensive and includes any productive activity which is paid for in cash or in kind and is not declared (see Jensen and Rathlev in this volume).

How is informal work linked to what is called the 'informal economy'? Often, these are treated as synonyms. In this case, the typology depends on the different forms of informal work and the societal sphere in which they are provided. But the gain in explanatory power of the concept of 'informal economy' over that of 'informal work' is marginal. For example Gershuny and Pahl (1979) and Renooy (1990) suggest an overall distinction between three different subsectors within the 'informal economy': (a) the 'household economy', which provides goods and services for members of the household (most often) without financial payment; (b) the 'communal economy', which is carried out voluntarily, and which contributes to the production of welfare for society as a whole or for members of the community other than those of the household; and (c) the 'underground economy', referring to work activities directed at gaining income which remains hidden from the authorities.

We argue that there are some problems with this concept of the 'informal economy' (see also Breman 1976; Connolly 1985), for at least the first two of these subsectors are not only based on informal work, but also on other forms of work that are relevant. Concerning the 'household economy', we gain more insight into its specific nature if we consider that within the private households, informal work, formal employment as well as semiformal forms of work can coexist. Treating the private household not as a subsector of the 'informal economy', but as a unity in which different types of work can be provided, opens the possibility that the role of informal work can be analysed in relation to the role of formal employment—and semiformal work—within the private household. A similar argument applies to the 'community economy': In the nonprofit sector, it is important to consider that voluntary work is often only a minor part of the activities of nonprofit organisations. Different from what is for example assumed by Salamon and Anheier (1998), organizations in the nonprofit sector are often strongly dependent on the use of formal employment, as in Germany, and on a combination of formal employment with informal, voluntary work. In the context of social networks in civil society, undeclared work too can be relevant, as Williams and Windebank (2005) have shown, if solidarity-oriented activities in social networks, which are to some extent paid, are taxed in a welfare state, and people do not comply with the tax requirement. It is therefore important, as in the case of the community sector, to include all types of work in the analysis—formal as well as informal—instead of treating informal work per se as just a subsector of the 'informal economy'.

When it comes to the 'underground economy', it is useful to conceptualize it as a broad (including more activities than informal employment) economic sector of not only simply undeclared activities such as undeclared work, but also of different kinds of illegal activities (such as drug-dealing), and those which are illegal in terms of the services or goods produced (see, e.g., Schneider and Enste 2000). 'Informal work' is a specific type of activity within the underground economy. In this book we analyse the ways informal work is used and structured and how it is related to formal work in different sectors of the economy.

1.2 THE RELATIONSHIP BETWEEN DIFFERENT KINDS OF WORK

All of these forms of informal work include activities that can in principle also be organized on the basis of formal employment or in semiformal forms of work.

By and large it is not controversial to assert that there is a close, interdependent relationship between formal employment and informal work. The relationship between them is however not static. Work is distributed differently between formal and informal activities in different countries, and the relationship between formal and informal work, and between different forms of informal work, is constantly changing.

In the debate about the future of work two opposing assumptions predominate: On the one hand, the 'formalization thesis' argues that economic activities are shifting from the informal to the formal sphere, that is, informal work is on the verge of disappearing, not least because the welfare state 'crowds out' informal work (Rostow 1960). On the other hand, the 'informalization thesis' argues that informal economic activities are growing due to globalization and economic restructuring, which are contributing to the decline in manufacturing and the rise of the new service-dominated economies (Sassen 1994). Both theses wrongly assume that formal and informal work are mutually substitutable and that change and transitions follow a one-dimensional, universal logic. The picture is far more complex, as formalization and informalization can take place simultaneously (Williams and Windebank 1998, 31).

Over the last three decades some areas of informal work have been formalized, that is, reshaped and included into the sector of formal employment. This has a special bearing on the case of the extension of public childcare provision, which has promoted the transition from informal to formal employment. This transition has created a new formal care workforce, which has been crucial to the integration of larger segments of women into the formal employment system. A parallel and somewhat contradictory trend is that new social rights have created new 'semiformal' forms of care work, as mentioned above. Thus, care work in the household is no longer in principle unpaid, but paid and subsidized by the state, exemplified for example by the 'income substitute' for parents during parental leave or so-called cash-for-care schemes (Ungerson 2000, 2005; Daly 2000; Pfau-Effinger 2005), which help full-time carers be financially autonomous. Such semiformal forms are a combination of the domestication and formalization of care work. Major parts of care work never ceased to be informal. But gender roles and the content and meaning of care, that is, social constructions positing what 'good care' is all about, are rapidly changing.

The example of care indicates that two processes are taking place at the same time, a formalization of care work, as well as the extension of new semiformal forms of care work. Thus, the issue is not about the relationship between formal and informal work on a scale of 'more or less'. Rather, what is at stake is that the formal as well as the informal economies are changing in character. Formal work is subject to the further development of postindustrial societies, which will change the structure and composition of the formal workforce. The same applies to informal work which is subject to reorganization. Informal childcare, for example, has taken on a new meaning. It has lost its close connection with the moral obligations of mothers in the housewife model of the male breadwinner marriage. Today, instead, it has the character of a temporary life-phase of adults who otherwise are oriented to continuous participation in the employment system and who often associate this period with their aims of self-fulfillment and happiness (Pfau-Effinger 2006).

Voluntary work has also changed from being mainly based on philanthropy to moving towards a kind of work based more on citizens' wish for self-expression.

Moreover, a new type of informal work has been established in the realm of private households in many European countries, based on a 'marketization' of care without formalization. Increasingly, domestic workers are employed to handle the care obligations of private households. This care work, especially in South-European countries, is typically being performed by immigrants in the 'underground economy'. Thus although informal care given by mothers of dependent children and by relatives of elderly people is declining in many European societies, there is a growing demand in the economy for informal female foreign workers to fill the demand of the domestic-care sector.

On the other hand, it should also be stressed that, in some countries, processes of 'informalization' are taking place. This is the argument used, for example, in relation to the field of eldercare in Nordic countries such as Sweden and Finland (Koistinen et al. in this volume). Neither is there a unique trend towards a formalization of care work in the Central and Eastern European countries (Saxonberg and Sirovatka 2006).

Hence it is safe to say that ongoing changes in formal as well as in informal work will dramatically transform the overall system of work in European societies.

The formal–informal relationship is highly complex, and changes in the overall system of work in Europe do not follow a universal course of development. Thus the same kind of factors, such as the degree of the public provision of childcare and the generosity of paid parental leave schemes, can have a different impact on formalization and informalization processes in different countries. The reason for this is mainly that actors do not react to material or symbolic signals in a uniform manner. Some actors are able to make use of day-care institutions—others not. This may be so because different actors in different contexts are endowed with different cultural orientations. If, for instance, women believe that good mothers should take care of their children themselves, they are probably not disposed to leave their children in a kindergarten and enter the formal employment system. Such cultural values and models related to the family differ in specific ways across European societies (see Pfau-Effinger in this volume). Therefore, formal and informal work should be analysed in specific contexts of cultural ideals and values.

1.3 THE THEORETICAL AND METHODOLOGICAL APPROACH OF THE STUDY

The main argument of this volume is based on the assumption that the development of European work societies can only be adequately understood when informal work and its relationship with formal employment are included in the analysis. The relationship between formal and informal work, however, is changing. New combinations of formal and informal work are emerging. Changes in the work system take place at different speeds and, in part, along different developmental paths in different European countries. This calls for a comparative approach, and it is a central aim of the book to contribute to our empirical knowledge of the different developmental trajectories of formal and informal work. Thus, an international comparative perspective is an integrated and central part of this book.

We think that Gösta Esping-Andersen's 'welfare-regime' approach is a useful starting point for the explanation of cross-national differences in the degree to which informal work is used in different European societies, for he has stressed in his work that different welfare regimes act on the basis of differing principles of social justice and the role of the state in maintaining it. However, his assumption of a close theoretical connection of welfare regime and policy of the welfare state towards formal employment and informal work proves problematic. In his argument, differences exist in relation to the degree to which some activities like care work appear in formal or in informal forms, and differences among regime types can substantially contribute to explaining why such differences exist (Esping-Andersen 1990, 1999). This part of his theoretical approach is contestable and, in part, not supported by empirical evidence (for an overview, see Pfau-Effinger in this volume). Rather, it should be assumed that for every 'regime type' there is a certain range of policies with respect to women's gainful employment (Duncan 1998; Pfau-Effinger 2004).

The 'welfare-regime approach' does not seem to be able to integrate a range of diverse forms of informal work, such as voluntary work and informal employment, into the overall theoretical framework.

Moreover, the approach does not take into account that the size and structures of informal work, and its relationship to formal employment, are not simply the outcome of welfare-state policies. The behaviour of individuals and social groups takes place in a broader societal context of cultural values, welfare-state policies, other institutions, and structures of social inequality. Thus the impact of welfare-state policies is modified by other, different cultural institutional and sociostructural factors, and so we argue that only some parts of Esping-Andersen's approach are useful in an explanation. The explanatory framework must be extended, and the broader institutional, cultural, sociostructural, and economic context of each society should be included.

Therefore we use the approach of the *arrangement of work and welfare* which was introduced by Pfau-Effinger (Pfau-Effinger 2001 and in this volume) to identify the specific societal context which shapes the size and structures of informal work and its links to formal employment. The approach is based on the assumption that differences in the size and structures of informal work can mainly be explained in the context of the interaction of cultural values and models, welfare-state policies, labour-market development, family structures, and the role of social actors in the arrangement of work and welfare in specific societies. Such an arrangement can be accepted or contested. Tensions and incompatibilities between the institutions involved, as well as tensions and conflicts among social groups, can lead to change in an arrangement. The 'arrangement of work and welfare' is constituted by the overlapping of, mainly, two different societal arrangements (see Pfau-Effinger in this volume). These are the:

> *welfare arrangement*, constituted of the following elements:

- the level of decommodification of labour, after Esping-Andersen (1990, 1999), and the underlying cultural values;
- the stratifying nature of welfare-state policies, after Esping-Andersen (1990, 1999);
- the 'other side' of the state-citizen relationship, namely the citizens' attitudes towards the welfare state, shown mainly in the strength of the civil society and the degree of trust in the state;

> and the *work and family arrangement*, made up of the following elements:

- welfare-state institutions and policies that are focussed on the family, care, and employment;
- their stratifying nature in terms of gender;
- cultural values and models surrounding the relationship of family, care, and employment.

In this approach, cross-national differences in relation to the size and structures of informal work, and the ways this work is linked with formal employment, can to a substantial degree be explained by the differences in the specific profile of the arrangement of work and welfare in different societies.

1.4 ORGANIZATION OF THE RESEARCH AND METHODS

We selected five different types of arrangement of work and welfare: those of Denmark, Finland, the UK, Germany, Poland, and Spain. These are based on the different types of welfare arrangements in Esping-Andersen's classification: Social-Democratic, Liberal, and Conservative type. Spain represents a different type of welfare arrangement, which Leibfried (1992, 141ff) has suggested calling a 'rudimentary' type of welfare regime—which in his opinion dominates in South-West European countries—instead of the 'conservative welfare regime' as Esping-Andersen assumes. These are states that fulfill only a residual welfare function, similar to that of the Anglo-American welfare states. They rely on traditional supply systems of the subsistence economy and the family, which is the reason they have a large informal sector. Other authors have subsequently characterized this welfare-regime type as a *family/kinship-solidarity regime* (Naldini 2003; see also Flaquer 2000; Flaquer 2002; Flaquer and Escobedo in this volume). We also distinguish a specific *postsocialist welfare state* (Ferge 2007; Arts and Gelissen 2002). The countries we included in the study also represent different arrangements of work and family that are based on differing underlying cultural 'ideal models' of the family: a dual breadwinner/female part-time care-provider model (UK, Germany); a dual breadwinner/state care-provider model (Denmark, Finland); and a dual breadwinner/extended-family care model (Spain, Poland) (see Pfau-Effinger in this volume). The selection of Finland and Denmark, which represent the same welfare arrangement type, and the same type of arrangement of work and family, allow us to make some reflections about differences in the formal-informal relationship within the same type of arrangement of work and welfare.

The knowledge in the social sciences about informal work is much less developed than that about formal work, and the relevant databases are in part still only weakly developed. The methods used for empirical analysis in this book are primarily those of statistical analysis, secondary analysis of international and national representative surveys, and of empirical studies and interviews with users and providers of informal work. As comparative data on informal work is scarce, the book contains an appendix with accessible comparative data of relevance to the research questions raised here.

The research on which the findings are based was organized in five different steps. The first was a statistical analysis of patterns of formal and informal work, using already existing statistical data such as time-budget studies and household panels. The second included analyses of the cultural and institutional framework of informal work and its interrelation with formal employment in the selected countries (Denmark, Finland, Germany, Poland, Spain, UK). In the third, a theoretical framework for the comparative analysis of work-welfare arrangements was elaborated. The fourth comprised fieldwork based on qualitative interviews with households. We wanted to find out the reasons individuals had for taking up formal and informal work, the consequences of it for their life situation, and the possible risks and chances that individuals confront when they combine both types of work. This has contributed to answering questions about whether informal work can help increase social integration, whether it provides options leading to a good quality of life, or to what extent it only has the character of a precarious, insufficient substitute for formal and secure employment. The fifth step was a cross-national comparison of the country results with the aim of explaining cross-national differences in the structure of informal and formal work and includes a discussion of our empirical results in the light of a 'New Work Society'. Moreover, factors in the societal context that can explain differences in the role of informal work for achieving social integration were identified.

Because of the 'hidden' nature of informal work, reliable data, particularly comparative data, are difficult to get. As far as data exist, they are often not based on exact calculations. In part, indirect research methods have had to be used, which produced somewhat vague results.

What methods do we use to compare the relationship of formal and informal work and the contribution of informal work to social cohesion in a cross-national perspective? There are in principle two possibilities. The first is to compare the different variables for all countries step-by-step (which Maurice in 1991 called a 'cross-national comparison'). The approach of the 'arrangement of work and welfare' is however based on a different principle: The idea is to 'contextualize' the analysis, which means to explain the concrete structures of formal employment and informal work, and their contribution to social cohesion, in the context of the specific society. This kind of procedure is what Maurice (1991, 1999), in his proposal for a contextualized societal approach, has called an 'international comparison'.

The findings are therefore presented here for each country separately. Afterwards, the findings of the comparison of the country-specific analyses are presented.[2]

1.5 STRUCTURE OF THE BOOK

In Chapter 2, Birgit Pfau-Effinger introduces the theoretical approach of the 'arrangement of work and welfare', and then the main assumptions about cross-national differences in the size and structures of informal work, and the ways it is related to formal employment, are explained.

Chapters 3 to 8 introduce the results of the central research questions for each country in the study. The outline of the findings in each chapter is structured on the basis of the same set of central questions. The central questions in each chapter are: What is specific to the patterns of informal work in the specific country?; and how can the size and structures of informal work in the country be explained in the context of the arrangement of work and welfare? As far as possible, the chapters refer to a common set of tables with comparative data, attached in the Appendix of the book. Also, the chapters relate to the same theoretical framework: the approach of the 'arrangement of work and welfare'. Each chapter is structured as follows: After a short introduction, the specific features of the arrangement of work and welfare in the country are outlined in a first section. A second section gives an overview of the development of formal employment in the country and of its economic development. In a third section, the development of the four forms of informal work (i.e. family-based childcare; family-based eldercare; informal employment; and voluntary work), their size and structures, and the ways these relate to formal employment is analysed and explained in the context of the specific arrangement of work and welfare in the country. A fourth section concludes the findings by summarizing the specific features of informal work and the ways it is related to formal employment in the context of the arrangement of work and welfare in that country.

The size of informal work is lowest in the two Nordic countries. In Chapter 3, Per H. Jensen and Jakob Rathlev present their results on the size and specific structures of informal work in Denmark. In Chapter 4 the findings for Finland are introduced by Arja Jolkkonen, Riitta Kilpeläinen, and Pertti Koistinen. In both countries, informal work plays only a rather moderate role. However, the share of voluntary work is considerable, even if it is far more common in the field of sports and culture than in social services. The specific size and structures of informal work are explained in the context of the respective arrangement of work and welfare in each of both countries. Both arrangements can be classified as 'social-democratic' welfare arrangements that interact with an arrangement of work and family based on a cultural family model of the dual breadwinner/state care-provider family. However there are also some minor differences, mainly in the field of informal childcare as well as in the proportion of undeclared work occurring. It becomes clear that the differences are mainly based in cultural and institutional particularities of these arrangements in both countries, particularly in the value-orientation the citizens have towards the welfare state.

In Germany, by contrast, informal work plays a relatively prominent role (Chapter 5). There are considerable differences between the West and East of Germany though, with the share of informal work considerably higher in the West. Birgit Pfau-Effinger and Slađana Sakač Magdalenić, the authors of Chapter 5, explain the specific features of informal work in Germany in comparison to those of the Nordic countries and the differences within Germany in the context of the arrangement of work and welfare in Germany, which is based on a conservative welfare arrangement. In West Germany this is combined with an arrangement of work and family that is mainly based on the cultural model of the male breadwinner/female part-time care-provider model of the family. This is a main reason why the share of informal work is relatively high in West Germany in comparison to the other countries. The conservative welfare arrangement of the German welfare state is combined with another arrangement of work and family in East Germany, this based on a dual breadwinner/state care-provider model. Therefore, the share of informal work in East Germany is considerably lower.

Traute Meyer and Graham Baxendale show that for the UK the role of the market in providing activities such as care is less dominant than one would expect in a liberal welfare arrangement (Chapter 6). The size of the sector of informal work resembles the share in the conservative welfare arrangement of West Germany. The family still plays a strong role in the provision of welfare here. The main features of informal work in the UK can be explained by the liberal welfare regime, where a low level of state support is typical, and most citizens have to rely on the market or the family for their welfare. It is also relevant that in the liberal arrangement of work and welfare, the civil society is given an important role. The dual breadwinner/female, part-time, care-provider model is dominant as the main basis of the organization of childcare, so mothers of young children try to balance part-time employment with their unpaid part-time childcare. They do this with the support of market-based solutions and, in part, by using undeclared care work by immigrants in the middle class and through close social networks in the underprivileged classes.

The size of the sector of informal work is greatest in Spain and Poland. As Lluís Flaquer and Anna Escobedo explain in Chapter 7, informal work has long been very widespread, culturally embedded, and socially well accepted in Spain. This is mainly due to a combination of a 'latin-rim' welfare arrangement based on family solidarity and an arrangement of work and family that is based on a cultural model of the dual breadwinner/extended-family care model. Because of the continuing increase in women's labour-force participation, however, the care potential of the female adults in the extended family is decreasing. Together with the scant public provision of care services, this is a main reason that—particularly in Spain since the 1990s—undeclared work performed by immigrants in private households has played a great role in the provision of childcare as well as eldercare. It is mainly used by middle-class households. However there has recently been a strong shift in welfare-state policies towards care, which have to a substantial degree extended social rights and social spending related to care. As a consequence, there is now a relatively strong trend towards the establishment of formal, public forms of care work as well as semi-formal care work in the private household.

In Poland, the amount of informal work has dramatically increased during the transition to post-industrial society, as Alexander Surdej and Ewa Ślęzak show in Chapter 8. As until recently in Spain, informal care work and informal employment—in part overlapping—have played a substantial role in Polish society. This includes the care of small children, even though mothers of young children are already participating to a relatively great extent in full-time formal employment. The main burden of childcare and eldercare in Poland, as in Spain, is still being provided within the framework of the extended family. This is due to the dominance of the cultural model of the dual breadwinner/extended-family care family and a 'hybrid' welfare state that is largely organized as a liberal welfare regime that strongly relies on the family for the provision of welfare. According to the authors,

> the major change which has taken place in Poland since late 1980s can be summarized as a shift in the responsibility for the provision of social welfare from the state to families. The increasing role of informal social care has been indicated as one of the most distinct features of this shift initiated by politicians and policy-makers of different political backgrounds, left-wing and right-wing, conservative and liberal, as well as ex-communists. (see Surdej and Ślęzak in this volume)

However, unlike 'conservative' welfare states like Germany, the Polish family is not supported in this. The number of people providing voluntary work is particularly low in comparison to the other study countries, which is mainly due to the fact that civil society did not play an important role in state socialist society.

In Chapter 9, Birgit Pfau-Effinger, Per H. Jensen, and Lluís Flaquer summarize the findings of the country chapters with respect to the specific size and structures of informal work, and they analyse the findings in a cross-national comparative perspective. They use the approach of the 'arrangement of work and welfare' for their explanations. Moreover, they give an overview of developmental trends in informal work, its relation to formal employment, and in the change in the arrangements of work and welfare that are the driving factors in this development.

Altogether, the book aims to contribute to our empirical knowledge of informal work and its different interrelations with formal work in various European societies; to the further development of the theoretical framework for cross-national analyses of informal work and the way it is related to formal work; and finally, to the development of public policies and social services that can deal effectively with the problems of informal work, but also recognize its diverse contributions to social integration.

NOTES

1. 'Formal and informal work in Europe. A comparative analysis of their changing relationship and their impact on social integration' (FIWE) 5th Research Framework of the EU, October 2003–December 2005. B. Pfau-Effinger, University of Hamburg (Coordinator); P. Jensen, University of Aalborg; L. Flaquer, Autonomous University of Barcelona; A. Surdej, Cracow University of Economics; T. Meyer, University of Southampton, P. Koistinen, University of Tampere.
2. The findings of the interviews with private households regarding the ways they combine formal and informal work will be published separately.

REFERENCES

Arts, W., and Gelissen, J. (2002) 'Three worlds of welfare capitalism or more? A state-of-the-art report', *Journal of European Social Policy* 12:137–158.

Barker, D.G. (1993) 'Values and volunteering', in J.D. Smith (ed.) *Volunteering in Europe*, Volunteering Action Research, No. 2. London: The Volunteer Centre.

Beck, U. (2000) 'Die Seele der Demokratie: bezahlte Bürgerarbeit', in dsb. (ed.) *Die Zukunft von Arbeit und Demkratie*, Frankfurt/M.: suhrkamp, S. 416–448.

Bettio, F., and Plantenga, J. (2004) 'Comparing care regimes in Europe', *Feminist Economics* 10(1):85–113.

Breman, J. (1976) 'A dualistic labour system? A critique of the "informal sector" concept', *Economic and Political Weekly* 48:1870–1876, 49:1905–1908, 50:1939–1944.

Connolly, P. (1985) 'The politics of the informal sector: A critique', in N. Recclift and E. Mingione, (eds) *Beyond Employment. Household, Gender and Subsistence*, Oxford and New York: Basil Blackwell, 55–91.

Daly, M. (1997) 'Welfare states under pressure: cash benefits in European welfare states over the last ten years', Journal of European Social Policy, vo. 7, no. 2, pp. 129–146.

Daly, M., and Lewis, J. (1998) 'Introduction: Conceptualising social care in the context of welfare state restructuring', in J. Lewis (ed.) *Gender, Social Care and Welfare State Restructuring in Europe*, Aldershot: Ashgate: 86–103.

Daly, M., and Lewis, J. (2000) 'The concept of social care and the analysis of contemporary welfare states', *British Journal of Sociology* 51(2):281–298.

Deven, F., Inglis, S., Moss, P., and Petrie, P. (1998) *State of the Art Review on the Reconciliation of Work and Family Life for Men and Women and the Quality of Care Services*, Final Report for the European Commission on Equal Opportunities Unit (DGV), London: British Department of Education and Employment.

Duncan, S.S. (ed.) (1998) 'The spatiality of gender, innovation: *The European Journal of Social Sciences. Special Volume: The Spatiality of Gender*, 11, 2.

England, P. (2005) 'Theories of care', *Annual Review of Sociology* 31:381–399.

Esping-Andersen, G. (1990) *The Three Worlds of Welfare Capitalism*, Cambridge: Polity Press.

———. (1999) *Social Foundations of Postindustrial Economy*, Oxford: Oxford University Press, 13–94.

European Commission (2007) *Undeclared Work in the European Union*, Report: Special Eurobarometer 284, by A. Riedmann and G. Fischer, Brussels: European Commission.

Eydal, G. (2005) 'Childcare policies of the Nordic welfare states: Different paths to enable parents to earn and care', in B. Pfau-Effinger and B. Geissler (eds) *Care and Social Integration in Europe*, Bristol: Policy Press, 153–172.

Ferge, Z. (2007) 'Socialist heritages in a capitalist world-welfare culture in Eastern Europe', in Oorschot, W. van, Opielka, M., Pfau-Effinger, B. (ed.) *Culture and Welfare State Values and Social Policy in Comparative Perspective*, Cheltenham, UK and North Hampton, MA: Edward Elgar.

Flaquer, L. (2000) 'Is there a southern European model of family policy?', in A. Pfenning and T. Bahle (eds) *Families and Family Policies in Europe. Comparative Perspectives*, Frankfurt a.m. and New York: Peter Lang, 15–33.

———. (2002) 'Political intervention and family policy in Europe and the USA: Family policy and the maintenance of the traditional family in Spain', in A. Carling, S. Duncan, and R. Edwards (eds) *Analysing Families: Morality and Rationality in Policy and Practice*, London: Routledge, 84–92.

Geissler, B., and Pfau-Effinger, B. (2005) 'Change of European care arrangements', in B. Pfau-Effinger and B. Geissler (eds) *Care Arrangements in Europe—Variations and Change*, Bristol: Policy Press.

Gershuny, J.I., and Pahl, R.E. (1979) 'Work outside employment: Some preliminary speculations', in *New Universities Quarterly*, vol. 34, No. 1: 120–35.

Hillmann, F. (2005) 'Migrants' care work in private households, or: The strength of bilocal and transnational ties as a last(ing) resource in global migration', in B. Pfau-Effinger and B. Geissler (eds) *Care Arrangements in Europe—Variations and Change*, Bristol: Policy Press.

Knijn, T., and Kremer, M. (1997) 'Gender and the caring dimension of welfare states: Toward inclusive citizenship', *Social Politics* 4(3):328–361.

Leibfried, S. (1992) 'Towards a European welfare state: On integrating poverty regimes into the European community', in Z. Ferge and J.E. Kolberg (eds) *Social Policy in a Changing Europe*, Frankfurt and Boulder, Colo: Campus Verlag-Westview Press, 245–279.

Lewis, J. (ed.) (1998) *Gender, Social Care and Welfare State Restructuring in Europe*, Aldershot: Ashgate.

Lutz, H. (2002) 'Transnationalität im Haushalt', in C. Gather, B. Geissler, and M.S. Rerrich (eds) *Weltmarkt Privathaushalt. Bezahlte Haushaltsarbeit im globalen Wandel*, Münster: Westfälisches Dampfboot, 86–103.

Maurice, M. (1991) 'Methodologische Aspekte internationaler Vergleiche: Zum Ansatz des gesellschaftlichen Effekts', in M. Heidenreich and G. Schmidt (eds) *International vergleichende Organisationsforschung. Fragestellungen, Methodenund Ergebnisse ausgewählter Untersuchungen*, Opladen.

———. (1999) 'The paradoxes of societal analysis. A review of the past and prospects for the future', in M. Maurice and A. Sorge (eds) *Embedded Organizations*.

Societal Analysis Of Actors, Organizations And Socio-Economic Context, Amsterdam and Philadelphia: Benjamins, 15–36.

Naldini, M. (2003) *The Family in the Mediterranean Welfare States*, London and Portland, OR: Frank Cass.

Offe, C. (1984), 'Some Contradictions of the Modern Welfare State', in Claus Offe (ed.) Contradictions of the Welfare State, London: Hutchinson, pp. 147-161.

Offe, C., Hinrichs, K., and Wiesenthal, H. (1982) Arbeitszeitpolitik: Formen und Folgen einer Neuverteilung der Arbeitzeit, Frankfurt and New York: Campus Verlag.

Parsons, T. (1956) 'The American family: Its relations to personality and to the social structure', in T. Parsons and R.F. Bales (eds) *Family—Socialization and Interaction Process*, London: Routledge and Kegan Paul, 3–33.

Pfau-Effinger, B. (1999) 'Change of family policies in the socio-cultural context of European societies', in *Comparative Social Research* 18:135–160.

———. (2001) 'Kontextualisierung der international vergleichenden Analyse von Arbeitsmarktwandel', in P.A. Berger and D. Konietzka (Hrsg.) *Neue Ungleichheiten der Erwerbsgesellschaft*, Opladen: Leske und Budrich.

———. (2004) *Development of Culture, Welfare States and Women's Employment in Europe*, Aldershot: Ashgate.

———. (2005) 'Welfare state policies and the development of care arrangements', *European Societies* 7(2):321–347.

———. (2006) 'Cultures of childhood and the relationship of care and employment in European welfare states', in J. Lewis (ed.) *Children, Changing Families and Welfare States*, Cheltenham, UK and Northampton, MA: Edward Elgar.

———. (forthcoming) 'Varieties of undeclared work in European societies', *British Journal of Industrial Relations* 3.

Pfau-Effinger, B., and Geissler, B. (eds) (2004) *Change of European Work-family Arrangements*, Aldershot: Ashgate.

Portes, A. (1994) 'The informal economy and its paradoxes', in N. J. Smelser and R. Swedberg (ed.) *The Handbook of Economic Sociology*, Princeton and New York: Princeton University Press.

Renooy, P.H. (1990) *The Informal Economy. Meaning, Measurement and Social Significance*, Utrecht: Elinkwijk bv.

———. (2008) 'Undeclared work: A new source of employment?', *International Journal of Sociology and Social Policy* 27(5/6):250–256.

Rifkin, J. (1998) *Das Ende der Arbeit und ihre Zukunft*, Frankfurt/M.: Suhrkamp.

Rostow, W.W. (1960) *The Stages of Economic Growth*, London: Cambridge University Press.

Salamon, L.M., and Anheier, H.K. (1998) Social Origins of Civil Society. Explaining the Nonprofit Sector Cross-nationally. *Voluntas*, 9: 213–248.

Sassen, S. (1994) *Cities in a World Economy*, California, Thousand Oaks: Pine Forge/Sage Press.

Saxonberg, S., and Sirovatka, T. (2006) 'Seeking the balance between work and family after communism', *Marriage and Family Review* 39:1–2.

Schneider, F., and Enste, D. (2000) *Schattenwirtschaft und Schwarzarbeit. Umfang, Ursachen, Wirkungen und wirtschaftspolitische Empfehlungen*, München, Wien: Oldenbourg.

Sivesind, K.H., Lorentzen, H., Selle, P., and Wollebæk, D. (2002) *The Voluntary Sector in Norway. Compositions, Changes, and Causes*, Oslo: Institutt for Samfunnsforskning.

Ślęzak, E. (2004) 'Overview on the discussion and the development of voluntary work and on its relationship to formal work', in B. Pfau-Effinger (ed.) *Review of Literature on Formal and Informal Work in Europe*, Discussion Paper 2 of the Discussion Paper Series of the 5th EU Framework Research Project "Formal and Informal Work in Europe (FIWE)—A comparative analysis of their changing relationship and their impact on social integration", Hamburg, University of Hamburg.

Theobald, H. (2005) 'Labour market participation of women and social exclusion: Contradictory processes of care employment in Sweden and Germany', in B. Pfau-Effinger and B. Geissler (eds) *Care Arrangements in Europe—Variations and Change*, Bristol: Policy Press.

Thomas, J.J. (1992) *Informal Economic Activity*, Hemel Hempstead: Harvester Wheatsheat.

Thomas, R., and Thomas, H. (1994) 'The informal economy and local economic development policy', *Local Government Studies* 20(3):486–501.

Ungerson, C. (2000) 'Thinking about the production and consumption of long-term care in Britain: Does gender still matter?', *Journal of Social Policy* 29(4):623–643.

——. (2005) 'Gender, labour markets and care work in five European funding regimes', in B. Pfau-Effinger and B. Geissler (eds) *Care Arrangements in Europe—Variations and Change*, Bristol: Policy Press.

Williams, C.C. (2001) 'Tackling the participation of the unemployed in paid informal work: A critical evaluation of the deterrence approach', in *Environment and Planning C: Government and Policy* 19:729–749.

Williams, C.C., and Windebank, J. (1998) *Informal Employment in the Advanced Economy. Implications of Work and Welfare*, London: Routledge.

——. (2001) 'Beyond profit-motivated exchange. Some lessons from the study of paid informal work', *European Urban and Regional Studies* 8(1):49–61.

——. (2002) 'The uneven geographies of informal economic activities: a case study of two British cities', *Work, Employment and Society*, 16(2):231–250.

——. (2005) 'Refiguring the nature of undeclared work: Some evidence from England', *European Societies* 7(1):81–102.

2 The Approach of the 'Arrangement of Work and Welfare' to the Cross-National Analysis of Formal and Informal Work

Birgit Pfau-Effinger

INTRODUCTION

In this book we analyse the 'hidden work regime' of European societies. Our analysis includes the amount and structures of informal work, the interrelation between different forms of informal work, and the relationship between informal and formal employment. Four main areas of informal work are examined in-depth: family-based childcare; family-based eldercare; informal employment and voluntary work.

The aim of this chapter is to introduce the theoretical framework of the analyses in the book. It may help us answer questions such as: How is it possible to explain cross-national differences in the amount and structures of informal work and the way it relates to formal employment? Under what conditions does specific work appear in informal forms? Under which circumstances is the same work found as formal employment? How can cross-national differences in relation to the amount and structures of informal work be explained?

2.1. THE 'WELFARE-REGIME' APPROACH: EXPLANATORY STRENGTHS

2.1.1. The 'Welfare-Regime' Approach

In the early 1990s sociological discourse gained new impetus from the influential works of Scandinavian resource theorists such as Gøsta Esping-Andersen and Walter Korpi, in which the connections between welfare-state policy and gainful employment on the one hand and informal work on the other play an important role. Here the book *The Three Worlds of Welfare Capitalism* by Esping-Andersen (1990) met with a tremendous response. Its author investigates how welfare states in Western industrial society influence the structures of social inequality and the nature of formal employment in society. It also provides a framework for the analysis of why specific work appears in informal forms. The question in this chapter is whether this approach can provide an adequate framework for the explanation of cross-national differences in the amount and structures of the forms of informal work that are included in this study.

According to Esping-Andersen, various 'welfare regimes' can be identified in which the state—in different ways and with different objectives—intervenes in the market and steers the social distribution of resources and the amount of formal employment. The differences are due to the fact that policy orients itself to the specific principles on which each welfare state is based. These welfare regimes can be distinguished on the basis of three criteria: the quality of social rights, their effects on the structures of social inequality, and the way state, market, and family are related.

According to this theory, welfare states differ substantially with regard to the quality of social rights as indicated by the degree of the decommodification of labour in a society caused by welfare-state policies. Esping-Andersen refers here to the degree to which individuals are enabled by the social security provided by the welfare state to secure their livelihood by means other than gainful employment, 'the degree to which individuals, or families, can uphold a socially acceptable standard of living independently of market participation' (1990, 37).

The extent of decommodification of labour, as Esping-Andersen argues, affects the conditions under which individuals have to sell their labour, the level of wages, the welfare and security of workers, and the opportunities workers have for organizing themselves collectively in their own interest. The outcome of welfare-state policies in relation to social stratification is another expression of the differences between welfare regimes. Finally, welfare states also differ in relation to the degree to which women participate in formal employment, and whether childcare is mainly provided by state institutions, by the market or in the form of informal work within the family (see also Esping-Andersen 1999).

On this basis Esping-Andersen (1990, 1999) differentiates between the social democratic, the conservative-corporate, and the liberal welfare regime. The *social democratic* welfare regime, which according to the author can be found especially in the Nordic countries, is characterized by universal social citizen rights and a high degree of decommodification.[1] It typically tends to promote a smoothing out of social inequalities. This type of welfare-state policy—the Swedish welfare state is the prototype for Esping-Andersen—is based on the idea that men and women should both be fully integrated into gainful employment and that the state is primarily responsible for the production of social welfare. Hence the welfare state provides a wide range of social services. It thereby also becomes one of the most important employers of women. A prerequisite for the realization of this type of welfare state is the heavy taxation of incomes. As this requires the participation of the middle classes in the political consensus, welfare-state benefits are provided at a qualitatively high enough level to also meet the demands of the middle classes. In the *conservative-corporate* welfare regime on the other hand—

which in the approach of Esping-Andersen (1990) is typical especially of continental Western Europe, for example, West Germany, Austria, and France—the state plays an important role in the distribution of welfare, and decommodification is an important policy element. In contrast to the Scandinavian welfare regimes, however, social policy is not oriented to the principles of solidarity, nor tries to level social inequalities, but rather tends to reproduce the existing structures of vertical inequality. Accordingly, the entitlements to benefits from the social security system vary with the size of income. The family is of particular importance for the production of social services. Government transfer payments and services come into effect only when the family is unable to generate these goods itself. At the same time, the gainful employment of women is not promoted: The state does not provide any special services supporting the entry of mothers into the employment system. This restriction of employment creates a fundamental problem: For Esping-Andersen, a relatively small part of the population has to generate the wage and salary income that is to also secure the livelihood of the population who are not gainfully employed.[2] It is important to consider that a substantial part of those parts of the population who are not gainfully employed—mainly mothers of small children and family or relatives caring for vulnerable elderly people—are providing informal work (Esping-Andersen 1999).

The *liberal* model of the welfare state, realized especially in the Anglo-American countries, is based on liberal ideals of the 'free play of market forces' as the best guarantee of fair distribution. Here the state interferes as little as possible in the market and maintains the commodity character of labour to a large extent. The function of the state in this welfare regime is a more residual one: a cushion against the worst effects of poverty. Here the degree of decommodification is particularly low, and all adult individuals are generally compelled to provide for themselves through gainful employment. The benefits granted by the social security systems are relatively low level. With this policy, as Esping-Andersen argues, liberal welfare regimes reinforce the existing structures of social inequality. A special policy of the promotion of women's gainful employment—for example, by providing an extensive supply of public kindergartens—is not strived for, as here 'concepts of gender matter less than the sanctity of the market' (Esping-Andersen 1990, 28).

Esping-Andersen's principal explanation for the differences between the various welfare states is that social democracy's capability to form class coalitions varied historically in different countries (Esping-Andersen 1990).

What can we conclude from this approach in relation to cross-national differences in the amount and structures of informal work? One would expect that the *social-democratic* welfare state is supplanting all forms of informal work related to the provision of welfare by transforming these into formal employment. These forms include informal childcare and eldercare, and voluntary work—at least in the social sector. On the other hand, if we follow the argument of neoclassical economists (e.g., Schneider and Frey 2000; Schneider and Enste 2000), one would expect that the population will not comply if taxes and social security contributions are comparatively high, as they are in social-democratic welfare regimes. Therefore we would expect a large amount of undeclared work in this type of welfare state, by which people aim to circumvent paying taxes and social security contributions. The *liberal welfare state* on the other hand, according to the 'welfare-regime' approach, leaves the provision of welfare mainly to the market. One would therefore expect childcare and eldercare there to be mainly provided through formal employment in market-based enterprises, at least as far as the middle class is concerned. Lower-income groups might be obliged to rely on social networks and voluntary work. On the other hand, it can be assumed that the amount of undeclared work is small, for if taxes and social security contributions are modest, people may not need to avoid them through informal forms of employment. We could also expect that in the *conservative welfare regime* the share of informal work provided within the family to be particularly great. One would also expect that the amount of voluntary work, at least in the social sector, to be relatively large. On the other hand it could be assumed that the share of undeclared work is medium-sized, for the taxes and social contributions are at a medium level by comparison.

Leibfried (1992, 141–142) has suggested adding the *rudimentary type of welfare regime*, which in his opinion dominates—instead of the 'conservative welfare regime' as Esping-Andersen assumes—in South-West European countries. These are states that fulfill only a residual welfare function, such as the Anglo-American welfare states. They rely on traditional supply systems of the subsistence economy and the family, which is the reason that they have a large informal sector. Other authors have subsequently characterised this welfare-regime type as a *'family/kinship solidarity regime'* (Naldini 2003; see also Flaquer 2000, 2002; Flaquer and Escobedo in this volume). Because this regime type mainly relies on mutual support within the family and social networks, one would expect that the sector of informal childcare and eldercare, as well as of voluntary work, to be large. We would assume the share of undeclared work to be low, on the other hand, if we complied with the explanatory approach of the neoclassical economists.

More recently another argument has stressed that the *postsocialist welfare states* are also different in regard to their main principles of social security and the provision of care. However it is contestable whether these welfare states really constitute a specific *postsocialist-regime* type, or are simply variations of Esping-Andersen's regime types (Ferge 2007; Arts and Gelissen 2002).

2.1.2. Discussion of the 'Welfare-Regime' Approach

Esping-Andersen's approach in any case contains an important idea, namely that welfare states act on the basis of differing 'principles' (or perhaps 'cultural values') and therefore have an impact on the proportion of formal employment in society, as well as on how much work is provided informally within the family. Nevertheless, some objections to his theory can be raised.

Although Esping-Andersen's typology of welfare states is convincing, his assumption that the general principles of welfare-state policy he identifies are linked to a respective specific policy towards informal work and women's participation in gainful employment does not seem entirely plausible. It is difficult to see why basic cultural principles of a policy that attaches particular value to the decommodification of labour should be logically linked to the degree to which work is provided formally or informally, and to which women are integrated into formal employment. A discrepancy between the general principles of welfare-state policy, and policy regarding women's labour-force participation in gainful employment, is evident in the development of, for example, the Norwegian and the French welfare state. In Norway, a society where welfare-state policy corresponds to the social-democratic regime, policy was not oriented to the idea of full employment of women and comprehensive public childcare provision until well into the 1990s (Leira 2002; Ellingsaeter 1999). In France, according to Esping-Andersen (1990, 1999), the general cultural principles that policy has been based on in recent decades correspond to a significant extent to those of the conservative welfare regime. With respect to women's labour-force participation and the societal organization of childcare, however, France resembles much more a social-democratic welfare state (see also Daune-Richard 2005; Fagnani and Letablier 2005). Hence his close theoretical connection of welfare regime and the policy of the welfare state towards formal employment proves problematic. It should be assumed, rather, that for every 'regime type' there is a certain range of policies affecting women's gainful employment (Duncan 1998; Pfau-Effinger 2005a).

The theory also puts unwarranted emphasis on the working class and its history in the sociohistorical explanation of the differences between welfare states. If cross-national differences in the policy of welfare states towards formal and informal work, women's labour-force participation, and the provision of childcare and eldercare are to be explained, it does not suffice to analyse the development of the welfare state only as the result of conflicts and negotiation processes between the state, employers, and employee representatives, but also as the result of negotiation processes in relation to the *arrangement of work and family* in society. Moreover as Pfau-Effinger (2004a, 2004b) has shown, cross-national differences in relation to the societal organization of childcare are in part rooted in historical differences among cultural models of the family, which can themselves be, in part, explained by differences in the historical role of the urban bourgeoisie.

Another strand among proposed welfare-state typologies is based on the 'gender'-related policies of welfare states. Jane Lewis and Ilona Ostner

(1994) developed a concept for the classification of welfare regimes from the gender perspective on the basis of the feminist critique of the resource-theory approach. The basis of their classification is welfare-state policy with respect to women's position between family and employment system. Their typification is oriented on the extent to which the family model of the male breadwinner marriage is developed in a society. Lewis and Ostner assume that the male breadwinner marriage, with a dependent wife doing unpaid work and dependent children, are elements of the welfare state that vary in degree from country to country; this has consequences for mothers' labour-force participation and the organization of childcare (Lewis and Ostner 1994, 1). The main consequence is in how women are treated, not only as mothers but also as gainfully employed persons. On this basis the authors distinguish between welfare states with strong, modified, or weak male-breadwinner orientation. The classification depends on the relation between the public sphere of paid work and the private sphere of unpaid caring and on the assignment of men and women to these two spheres, as well as on the role the welfare state plays in assuming tasks of social care. The authors cite a number of examples to show how variations in the degree to which policies result from the male breadwinner model cause differences in the welfare states' gender policies.

This approach, though providing important starting points for the development of a theoretical model for an explanation of the differences in the institutional frameworks of female gainful employment, is limited in its scope to welfare-state policy. The existing behavioural patterns of women are regarded as the result of welfare-state policy, whereas the question of the influence of other institutions and cultural values and notions is not pursued any further. Also, it should be asked whether the male breadwinner model is indeed the underlying pattern for gendered division of labour in European societies, as this approach assumes. I have shown that, in some countries, the family is not organized on the basis of the male breadwinner model, and in some of these countries that model has never even been relevant as an actual family form or cultural family model (Pfau-Effinger 2004b). Therefore restricting welfare-state policies to variants of the 'male breadwinner model' is too narrow. Lewis (with Giullari 2005) has suggested speaking more generally about state policies supporting an 'adult worker model' of the family. However, that approach is restricted to the sphere of welfare-state policies and does not deal with the ways other factors besides welfare-state policies influence behaviour.

I argue at this point that the amount and structures of informal work are not simply an outcome of welfare-state policies. The behaviour of individuals and social groups takes place in a broader societal context of cultural values, welfare-state policies, and other institutions such as the labour market and the family, and the structures of social inequality. The impact of welfare-state policies is modified by such factors.

This is a reason that discrepancies can exist between the provision of childcare by the welfare state and parents' actual demand for childcare. This kind of discrepancy can arise when the state is still oriented towards a more traditional family model, so state policies do not sufficiently take into account changes in the cultural orientation of a majority of the population.

To conclude: the available theoretical approaches to the relationship of welfare-state policy and formal employment and informal work contain important points for a theoretical framework suitable for cross-national comparative research on the social integration of men and women. They allow a differential examination of the policy of the welfare state with respect to both types of work. But they do not suffice for an explanation of cross-national differences in size and structures of informal work. It is often implicitly assumed that welfare-state policy directly determines the behaviour of individuals and that the aggregate behaviour is the result of welfare-state policies. Hence it is frequently argued that institutional constraints are responsible when some jobs in society end up as informal work instead of as regular employment. Instead, what we need is a more comprehensive, differentiating theoretical approach to the way welfare-state policy affects the behaviour of individuals and social groups. This approach should posit that the impact of welfare-state policies can be modified by cultural values, other institutions, and social structures and acknowledge that, in similar welfare-state contexts, people may behave in different ways.

2.1.3 The Approach of the 'Arrangement of Work and Welfare'

In this section, I introduce a theoretical approach that explains cross-national differences in the size and structures of informal work and its relationship with formal employment and the behaviour of individuals and social groups by which these structures are produced.

This theoretical approach refers to the tradition of approaches to cross-national comparison which are based on the idea that we need to 'contextualize' social research (see Maurice 1999; Pfau-Effinger 2004a; Bang, Jensen, and Pfau-Effinger 2000). It is assumed here that social phenomena (as in our case, informal work and the relationship to formal work) can be explained in the specific context of interrelations between institutions, cultural values, social structures, and the field of social actors in a specific country. That means that a specific causal relation may exist in one country but does not necessarily play a role in another.

The *arrangement of work and welfare* is defined here as the specific field of interrelations between cultural and institutional factors and social structures, with regard to the way work and welfare are organized in a society, and how they are interrelated. Informal work, and its relationship with formal employment, are both embedded in this context.

It is assumed that the arrangement of work and welfare is the result of conflicts, negotiation processes, and compromises of social actors in an earlier period of time. Different kinds of social actors contribute to its restructuring or change. An arrangement is based on dominant cultural ideas to which the institutions and social actors refer. Because of its cultural references an arrangement is usually, at least to some degree, coherent, though within an arrangement contradictions and time lags can develop. Such contradictions at the level of the cultural and/or social system, or conflicts between social actors, can be the basis for change of the arrangement. During processes of change new contradictions and time lags can develop (Pfau-Effinger 2004a).

The amount and structures of informal work and the ways they are linked with formal employment can be analysed and compared crossnationally in the context of the arrangements of work and welfare in European societies. Similarities and differences between countries in the way the relationship of formal and informal work and the role of informal work for social cohesion are shaped, are explained here by the complex— and often also contradictory—interplay of culture, institutions, social structures and social actors, and the 'profile' that it has in specific countries or groups of countries.

Using this approach in this book, we perform a comparative analysis of the factors that can explain the size and structures of informal work and the ways it is linked with formal employment, as well as analysis of the influence of cultural factors and the ways these interrelate with other factors. 'Culture' is defined here as the 'system of collective constructions of meaning by which human beings define reality. It includes stocks of knowledge, values, and ideals—in sum: ideas'. Cultural values can be seen as 'switches' on the pathways along which interests influence the actions to be taken, as has also been argued by Lepsius (1990, 31). Such collective constructions of meaning are produced and reproduced by the social practices of social actors, and can be the subject of conflicts, negotiations and compromises between social actors, with cultural change as a result. These theoretical assumptions refer to the theories of Max Weber (1976, 1988), David Lockwood (1964), and Margaret Archer (1995). The approach is not normative, as it leaves space for cross-national variations in the ways such arrangements are shaped, and in how informal work is manifested and structured.

I argue further that the differences in the patterns and social significance of informal work can mainly be explained by the characteristics of two 'subarrangements', which contribute substantially to the shaping of the respective arrangement of work and welfare and the ways these interact:

- the welfare arrangement, and
- the arrangement of work and family.

The concept of the *welfare arrangement* starts with Esping-Andersen's 'welfare-regime' approach and takes over two of the three criteria he uses for his classification of welfare regime: the extent of decommodification of labour, and the stratifying nature of the welfare state. Accordingly, it is specifically related to the ways the relationship between employers and employees is modified by the social security system, and the redistribution connected with it. Each type of welfare arrangement is based on a specific set of cultural values dealing with the general role of the welfare state in society and its relation to its 'social citizens', redistribution, and what is 'just'. Therefore the quality of social rights, the generosity of benefits, and the coverage of welfare-state provision can all differ between welfare regimes. The concept as it is used here leaves out policies towards and regulation of women's employment and the organization of care.

Moreover, the concept of the welfare arrangement is more comprehensive than Esping-Andersen's welfare-regime approach. For it is not restricted to welfare-state policies and the ways the welfare state constructs the relationship of the citizens towards the state as 'social citizenship'. It also includes the relationship that these social citizens themselves establish with the welfare state. This 'other side' of the arrangement is shaped by the degree of trust that citizens have towards the state, the degree to which they organize themselves vis-à-vis the state in civic organizations, as well as by their attitudes towards the role of the welfare state. The concept of the 'welfare arrangement' therefore relates to a mutual relationship of actors, institutions and organizations on both sides—the side of the welfare state and that of the social citizens. On this basis, a *welfare arrangement* (for more details see Pfau-Effinger 2005a) is a constellation of actors, institutions, structures, and welfare culture which interact with each other and with welfare-state policies. Actual welfare arrangements are the (temporary) result of conflicts, negotiations, and compromises between social actors.

The *work and family arrangement* is the other main element of the theoretical framework. It refers to the arrangement in society that surrounds the family and care, and how this is linked with the system of formal employment in society.

The particular arrangement of work and family in a society comprises the specific configuration of institutions, social structures, socioeconomic factors, and constellations of actors that refer to the relationship of family and work. Welfare-state institutions and policies that are focussed on the family, care, and employment, and the cultural values on which these are based, are one central element of the arrangement. It is assumed that it provides the main conditions that are influencing the size and structures of informal work as far as it relates to childcare and eldercare. Moreover, it is assumed that values and cultural models (*Leitbilder*) regarding the relationship of family and work contribute an explanation of the ways the structural relationship between family and work—and how the actual practices of social actors and their gender specificity in this context—develop. In their ideas and interests, individuals connect, on the one hand, to cultural values and models and, on the other, to the institutional and sociostructural framework. Our approach stresses particularly that in order to achieve an adequate explanation, the interaction of different factors in the specific societal context should be taken into account (Pfau-Effinger 2004a; 2005).

It is my argument that arrangements of family and work can be comparatively analysed and classified by the dominant *family models* upon which they are based. Such cultural models of the family include cultural values regarding different elements in the family structure which relate to: (a) the relationship of family members with the employment system, (b) the adequate sphere(s) for the upbringing of children, and (c) the adequate gender division of labour within the family. It is possible that one specific family model is dominant in a society, or that different family models coexist or compete. Family models can be contested between different types of actors and are subject to change. According to my classification model, in European societies at least six family models, which have survived or newly emerged since the middle of the 20th century, can be distinguished (Pfau-Effinger 1998, 2004a):

- In the *family economy model*, men and women work together in their agricultural or craft business, and both have important roles in the survival of the family economy. Children are regarded as elements of the family economy and are therefore expected to work in the family business as soon as physically able.
- The *housewife model of the (male) breadwinner family* is based on the assumption of a general separation of 'public sphere' and 'private sphere', and on complementary fields of work and action for both genders: The husband is primarily responsible for work in the 'public' sphere, where he provides for his family through gainful employment; the wife is primarily responsible for the private household, including childcare, and is financially dependent on the husband. This arrangement is based on a cultural construct of 'childhood', according to which children require special care and extensive individual support. Care and support are first and foremost regarded as the responsibility of private households. Complementary to this concept is the cultural construct of 'motherhood', according to which it is mainly the task of the mother to raise children and care for them in the private household.
- The *male breadwinner/female part-time care-provider model* rests essentially on the vision of full integration of women and men into paid economic activity. However, within this model it is expected that women, as mothers, may interrupt their gainful activity for a few years, after which they combine employment and responsibility for

childcare through part-time work until their children are no longer considered to require particular care.

- The *dual- (part-time) breadwinner/dual- (part-time) care-provider model*, in which it is considered desirable that both parents be employed part-time and share a part of the childcare between themselves, entails that part of the childcare is entrusted to an outside institution.
- The *dual-breadwinner/external care model* posits that, in principle, all women as well as men should be employed full-time and that childcare is essentially the responsibility of institutions outside of the family. In the majority of countries with this model, the state is seen as primarily responsible for organizing access to these services.
- The *dual-breadwinner/extended family care model* is one in which extended family networks are mainly seen as responsible for family care. This notion is related to the family form of the 'complex family household' (Flaquer and Escobedo in this volume). In addition to the children's parents, other adult relatives reside in these households and are expected to contribute to childcare. Accordingly it is not expected that the welfare state should provide childcare to a significant extent.

I propose that differences between the dominant family model/s in different societies contribute to a substantial degree to explaining cross-national differences in the ways childcare—and to some degree also eldercare—is set up. Using the findings of a comparative study of Germany, Finland, and the Netherlands, I (Pfau-Effinger 1998; 2004a) have shown that cultural differences, along with family policies and labour-market structures, are crucial to an explanation of cross-national differences in the labour-force participation of women, particularly when they are mothers. Saxonberg and Sirovatka (2006), analysing the historical origins of post-communist family policies, found that the legacy of policies dating back to the cultural values regarding the family in precommunist days have the greatest impact on an explanations for the differences (also Saxonberg and Szelewa 2007).

Within an arrangement of work and family in a society, different family models can be particularly relevant. In West Germany and East Germany, for example, two distinctly different family models have remained dominant up to the present day. This is mainly due to the different developmental paths of the two countries after World War II (Pfau-Effinger and Geissler 2002). It is important not to regard the classification as static, but rather to also consider the processes of change that take place within such an arrangement. The ways in which new cultural models, having developed at a given time in the population, are dealt with is strongly influenced by the conflict and negotiation processes taking place in the arena of the social actors.

Modern postindustrial societies can be classified on the basis of the *welfare arrangement* typology on one hand, and on the basis of their specific *arrangement of work and family* on the other. The types of welfare arrangements and the types of arrangements of work and family can vary in different ways between European societies. According to the main assumptions of the approach of the 'arrangement of work of welfare', the size and structures of informal work, and its relationship to formal employment can to a substantial degree be explained by the specific profile of the welfare arrangement, as well as by the underlying cultural values. Moreover, it can be explained by the specific profile of the arrangement of work and family characterized by the dominant cultural model of the family on which it is based. Also important is how both types of arrangement interact in the specific society. Together these then form the main part of the framework for explaining cross-national differences in the structures of informal work and the behaviour of individuals and social groups by which these are produced. As mentioned, it is important to remember that these different types of arrangements can be contradictory in themselves, or contradictions may exist in the ways the welfare arrangement and the arrangement of work and family frame the behaviour of individuals and social groups in relation to informal work and formal employment.

2.2. EXPLANATION OF CROSS-NATIONAL DIFFERENCES—MAIN ASSUMPTIONS

Without a doubt, the 'welfare regime' typology devised by Esping-Andersen contributes to explaining cross-national differences in relation to the degree to which specific types of work in European societies are manifested as informal or formal work. We expect that differences between welfare states related to the 'level of de-commodification', and the outcome in relation to social stratification, together with the level of trust of the citizens towards the welfare state, contribute to explaining the degree to which people escape to undeclared work, either as employers or as employees. We further assume that in welfare arrangements with a lower level of decommodification, and which are met with a relatively low degree of trust by the population, people tend more to escape to undeclared forms of paid work compared to other types and that in welfare arrangements of a relatively high level of decommodification, and which are trusted relatively highly by the population, people are more prepared to comply with tax regulations and less apt to circumvent payment of taxes and social security contributions by establishing undeclared work relationships.

One might assume that strong welfare states are supplanting voluntary work, when one applies Esping-Andersen's approach. For strong welfare states, such as the social-democratic regime type, tend to offer comprehensive public social services. However, we argue here that the 'other side' of the arrangement—the traditions of self-organization of the citizens in civil society—should also be considered. We expect that cross-national differences in the size of voluntary work can indeed be substantially explained by differences in such traditions.

Furthermore we find that the specific profile and cultural basis of the arrangement of work and family, and the cultural family model/s on which it is mainly based in a society, as well as the degree to which the welfare state supports the dominant model/s, are particularly important to an explanation of cross-national differences in relation to the amount of informal and semiformal childcare and of how women combine formal employment with childcare. And such differences can also contribute to explaining why eldercare is accomplished in different ways in different societies, even though childcare and eldercare can, to some degree, be organized in different ways within a single society.

NOTES

1. The concept of 'social rights' comes from the theory by T.H. Marshall (1992) on the historical development of citizenship. In this theory the history of modern societies is seen as a process in the course of which people have been able to extend their basic rights to individual rights towards the welfare state. Feminist researchers have used Marshall's theory in part as a foil to articulate inequalities and injustices in the rights of women and men that result from the special situation of women in many countries, that is, that their main responsibility is for caring tasks (see also esp. Lister 1997; Siim 2000).
2. The catch of this regime is that there is an inherent conflict of distribution between the employed and the unemployed.

REFERENCES

Archer, M.S. (1995) *Realist Social Theory: The Morphogenetic Approach*, Cambridge: Cambridge University Press.

Arts, W., and Gelissen, J. (2002), 'Three worlds of welfare capitalism or more? A state-of-the-art report', *Journal of European Social Policy* 12:137–158.

Bang, H., Jensen, P., and Pfau-Effinger, B. (2000) 'Gender and European welfare states: context, structure and agency', in S.S. Duncan and B. Pfau-Effinger (eds) *Gender, Economy and Culture in the European Union*, London and New York: Routledge.

Daune-Richard, A.-M. (2005) 'Women's work between family and welfare state: Part-time work and childcare in France and Sweden', in B. Pfau-Effinger and B. Geissler (eds) *Care Arrangements in Europe—Variations and Change*, Bristol: Policy Press.

Duncan, S.S. (1998) The Spatiality of Gender, *Innovation: The European Journal of Social Sciences*. Special Volume: The Spatiality of Gender, ed. by S. Duncan, 11,2: 119–128.

Ellingsaeter, A.L. (1999) 'Dual breadwinners between state and market', in R. Crompton (ed.) *Restructuring Gender Relations and Employment. The Decline of the Male Breadwinner*, Oxford: Oxford University Press.

Esping-Andersen, G. (1990) *The Three Worlds of Welfare Capitalism*, Cambridge: Polity Press.

——. (1999) *Social Foundations of Postindustrial Economies*, Oxford: Oxford University Press.

Fagnani, J., and Letablier, M.-T. (2005) 'Social rights and care responsibility in the French welfare state', in B. Pfau-Effinger and B. Geissler (eds) *Care Arrangements and Social Integration in Europe*, Bristol: Policy Press.

Ferge, Z. (2007) 'Socialist heritages in a capitalist world—welfare culture in eastern Europe', in Oorschot, W. van, Opielka, M., Pfau-Effinger, B. (eds) *Culture and Welfare State. Values and Social Policy in a Comparative Perspective*, Cheltenham, UK and Northampton, MA: Edward Elgar.

Flaquer, L. (2000) 'Is there a southern European model of family policy?', in A. Pfenning and T. Bahle (eds) *Families and Family Policies in Europe. Comparative Perspectives*. Frankfurt a.m.and New York: Peter Lang, 15–33.

——. (2002) 'Political intervention and family policy in Europe and the USA: Family policy and the maintenance of the traditional family in Spain', in A. Carling, S. Duncan, and R. Edwards (eds) *Analysing Families. Morality and Rationality in Policy and Practice*. London: Routledge, 84–92.

Leibfried, S. (1992) 'Towards a European welfare state: On integrating poverty regimes into the European community', in Z. Ferge and J.E. Kolberg (eds) *Social Policy in a Changing Europe,* Frankfurt and Boulder, CO: Campus Verlag-Westview Press, 245–279.

Leira, A. (2002) *Working Parents and the Welfare State. Family Change and Policy Reform in Scandinavia*, Cambridge: Cambridge University Press.

Lepsius, R.M. (1990) *Interessen, Ideen und Institutionen*, Opladen: Westdeutscher Verlag.

Lewis, J., and Giullari, S. (2005) 'The adult worker model family, gender equality and care: The search for new policy principles and the possibilities and problems of a capabilities approach', *Economy and Society* 34(1):76–104.

Lewis, J., and Ostner, I. (1994) *Gender and the Evolution of European Social Policy*, Working Paper 4 of the Centre for Social Policy Research, University of Bremen.

Lister, R. (1997) *Citizenship. Feminist Perspectives*, Hong Kong: Macmillan.

Lockwood, D. (1969) 'Soziale Integration und Systemintegration', in W. Zapf (ed.) *Theorien des sozialen Wandels*, Köln/Berlin: Kiepenheuer & Witsch.

Marshall, T.H. (1950) 'Citizenship and social class', reprint in T.H. Marshall and T. Bottomore (1992) *Citizenship and Social Class*, London: Pluto Press.

Maurice, M. (1999) 'The paradoxes of societal analysis. A review of the past and prospects for the future', in M. Maurice and A. Sorge (eds) *Embedded Organizations. Societal Analysis of Actors, Organizations and Socio-economic Context*, Amsterdam and Philadelphia: Benjamins, 15–36.

Naldini, M. (2003) *The Family in the Mediterranean Welfare States*, London & Portland, OR: Frank Cass.

Pfau-Effinger, B.. (1998) 'Gender cultures and the gender arrangement—a theoretical framework for cross-national comparisons on gender', *Innovation: The European Journal of Social Sciences*, Special Issue, ed. by S. Duncan 11(2):147–166.

——. (2004a) *Culture, Welfare State and Women's Employment in European Societies*, Aldershot: Ashgate.

——. (2004b) 'Historical paths of the male breadwinner family model—explanation for cross-national differences', *British Journal of Sociology* 55(3): 377–399.

——. (2005a) 'Welfare state policies and the development of care arrangements', *European Societies* 7(2):321–347.

————. (2005b) 'Culture and welfare state policies: Reflections on a complex inter-relation', *Journal of Social Policy* 34(1):1–18.

————. (forthcoming) 'Varieties of undeclared work in European societies', *British Journal of Industrial Relations* 47(13).

Pfau-Effinger, B. and Geissler, B. (2002) 'Cultural change and family plicies in East and West Germany', in A. Carling, S. S. Duncan and r. Edwards (ed.) Analysing Families: Morality and Rationality in Policy and Practice, London, New York: Routledge.

Pfau-Effinger B., and Geissler B. (2005) *Care and Social Integration in European Societies—Variations and Change*, Bristol: Policy Press.

Saxonberg, S., and Szelewa, D. (2007) 'The continuing legacy of the communist legacy', *Social Politics: International Studies in Gender, State & Society* 14(3): 351–379.

Saxonberg, S., and Sirovatka, T. (2006) 'Seeking the balance between work and family after communism', *Marriage and Family Review* 39(1/2): 319–341.

Schneider, F., and Enste, D. (2000) *Schattenwirtschaft und Schwarzarbeit: Umfang, Ursachen, Wirkungen und wirtschaftliche Empfehlungen*, München, Wien: Oldenbourg: Wissenschaftsverlag.

Schneider, F., and Frey, B.S. (2000) 'Informal and underground economy', in O. Ashenfelter *International Encyclopedia of Social and Behavioral Science*, vol. 12 Economics, Amsterdam: Elsevier Science Publishing Company.

Siim, B. (2000) *Gender and Citizenship. Politics and Agency in France, Britain and Denmark*, Cambridge: Cambridge University Press.

Weber, Max (1976) Wirtschaft und Gesellschaft. Grundriß der verstehenden Soziologie. 5th edition, Tübingen: J.C.B. Mohr (Paul Siebeck).

Weber, Max (1988/1920) Gesammelte Aufsätze zur Religionssoziologie I, Tübingen: J.C.B. Mohr (Paul Siebeck).

Part II

Formal and Informal Work in the Diverse Arrangements of Work and Welfare in European Societies

3 Formal and Informal Work in the Danish Social Democratic Welfare State

Per H. Jensen and Jakob Rathlev

INTRODUCTION

The Danish welfare state is often described as a prototypical Social Democratic welfare state. In a Social Democratic welfare state, 'organised power is deliberately used (through politics and administration) in an effort to modify the play of market forces' (Briggs 1961) by guaranteeing individuals and families an income in case of social risks such as sickness, old age, unemployment, etcetera, and to ensure that all citizens 'without distinction of status or class are offered the best standards available in relation to a certain agreed range of social services' (op.cit.), such as hospitals and care services for children and elderly. A Social Democratic welfare state is, however, very costly. This calls for an effort to 'maximize revenue income', which can best be 'done with most people working' (Esping-Andersen 1990, 28) and by minimising the scale of undeclared work. Thus, Social Democratic welfare states require relatively high (formal) labour-force participation rates. Accordingly, a special feature of the Danish labour market is the very high labour-force participation rate among women (Table 4.1, Appendix)—higher than that in any of the other countries included in this book.

As to the feminisation of the (formal) workforce, most countries showed similar initial conditions in the early 1960s. In 1960, for instance, female labour-force participation rates were slightly higher in Germany (33.6) and the United Kingdom (29.6) compared to Denmark (28.0) (cf. OECD 1995). In Denmark the tendency of integrating women into the workforce was initiated in the early 1960s, when a number of interrelated factors caused the female participation rate to increase rather rapidly, and it has been rising ever since. During the 1960s high demand for labour and low unemployment coincided with the emergence of the service economy. A high proportion of the jobs created in the service economy were produced in the labour-intensive public service and care sector in areas such as childcare, eldercare, education, healthcare, and the like, that is, areas offering jobs which were accessible and attractive to women. Care work was taken over by the welfare state but remained to a considerable degree women's work—now carried out as paid employment (Siim 2000).

The massive growth in public welfare services financed by taxation has served to reduce informal or voluntary work in the child and eldercare sector. An extensive coverage of high quality and affordable public care services has had some crowding-out effect on informal or voluntary care work, which is in accordance with the Social Democratic welfare-state policy that social needs should ideally not be met through private charity networks or the market. A large public sector, however, has not had a crowding-out effect on voluntary work as such: The volume of voluntary work in Denmark is as high as in any of the other countries analysed in this book. Voluntary work, however, has a different nature in Denmark, where it does not consist of private charitable giving but rather is concentrated around sports, culture, and leisure activities. This clearly demonstrates that state involvement in the labour market and civil society does not curb the voluntary energy and initiative (Oorschot and Arts 2005; Kumlin and Rothstein 2005). The Achilles heel of the Social Democratic welfare state is, however, that it is primarily financed through progressive and individual taxation, which makes undeclared work relatively appealing. This may actually contribute to an explanation of the relatively high frequency of undeclared work in Denmark. Large-scale tax evasion would undermine the economic foundation of the Social Democratic welfare state, and tax fraud has therefore been contained. On average the duration of undeclared work is short: about four hours per week, and it is not a primary income source for particular segments on the labour market. Rather, in Denmark undeclared work is primarily moonlighting or an 'optimal extra': that is, most often done to supplement the income of an ordinary full-time job, and/or on the basis of friendly turns.

The aim of this chapter is to describe and explain the specific pattern of formal and informal work in the Danish Social Democratic welfare state. To do this, first we give an overview of the arrangement of work and welfare in Denmark. Second, we show how the economy and formal employment changed fundamentally between the 1960s and 1990s. This is followed by an in-depth analysis of the development path of informal work. The focus is on child and eldercare, undeclared work, and voluntary work. The final section discusses the specific context of the work-welfare arrangement in Denmark.

3.1. THE ARRANGEMENT OF WORK AND WELFARE IN DENMARK

Citizenship-based universalism, high standards, emphasis on social services, and individual and progressive taxation are some of the main features of the modern Danish welfare state. The Danish welfare state constitutes what has been termed a Social Democratic welfare-state regime (Esping-Andersen 1990) or an institutional welfare state (Titmuss 1974), each of which helps 'individuals achieve self-fulfilment' (Wilensky and Lebeaux 1958,

140). The Social Democratic welfare state maintains a policy of emancipation from traditional forms of subordination, such as class, gender, etcetera, and it helps to create independent and autonomous individuals. From a gender perspective the welfare state has been characterised as a women-friendly welfare state (Hernes 1987; Borchorst and Siim 2002).

In the Danish Social Democratic welfare state, social expenditures are relatively high (Table 1.1, Appendix), which helps promote economic and social equality. The Gini coefficient, as a measure for inequality in income distribution, shows that in 2000 Denmark had the most even income distribution within the EU-25. There is hardly any doubt that the equal income distribution in Denmark is an outcome of the redistributional efforts of the welfare state. The risk-of-poverty rate *before* social transfers in Denmark is about the highest in Europe, whereas the risk-of-poverty rate *after* social transfers is the lowest in the EU-25 area (excepting Sweden).

Large central governments and a high degree of state involvement in the market and in civil society are alleged to destroy intermediate institutions and mutual trust (e.g., Fukuyama 1995). This assertion however does not seem to apply to the Danish experience. In Denmark one finds a very high degree of mutual trust combined with a high level of trust in public institutions. Compared to the other countries discussed in this book, trust in the national parliament, courts and legal system, and educational system are very high in Denmark (Tables 3.1–3.5, Appendix). The reason for this may be that Denmark has been free of any authoritarian political tradition. The state was built on popular support from below (Goul Andersen and Hoff 2001), and as social movements have shaped the welfare state in their own image, this has of course nurtured confidence in the state.

The modern Danish welfare state was founded during a period of full employment in the 1960s and early 1970s, and this was paralleled by the entry of women into paid employment, which was preconditioned by what has been termed 'the activation of the entire social protection system' (Barbier and Ludwig-Mayerhofer 2004). That is, the welfare state was designed to increase the size and quality of the labour force. During the 1960s and 1970s, day-care institutions were provided by local governments; the taxation system was changed, emphasising progressive and individual taxation; and the individual—not the family—became the basic social unit with regard to social provisions in cash and kind. All these measures facilitated individualisation and the entry of women into paid employment, and once women had entered, active and passive labour-market policies helped keep women in the labour market. For instance, most women entered the labour market on a part-time basis. To prevent these part-timers from resuming their roles as housewives, from the late 1960s on, the government enrolled them in the unemployment benefit system. The importance of the insurance against part-time unemployment has since declined. Between 1985 and 1995 the number of part-time insured fell from 214,000 to 88,000.

The entry of women into the labour market coincided with deindustrialisation, which in Denmark did not primarily take place in the fast-food and other private service industries. Rather, deindustrialisation led to the fast growth of the public service sector, especially in labour-intensive welfare and caring institutions. As women have often favoured jobs connected with taking care of people, the new jobs created have been suited to this disposition. The result is, however, that gender segregation has become visible when comparing the public sector and the private sector. A majority of women were—and still are—employed in the public sector.

Another feature of the public-service sector as compared with the private-service sector is that the public-service sector offers relatively high wages and a high degree of job security to low-skilled workers. This is due, among other things, to the higher level of unionisation in the public-service sector than in the private-service sector. The degree of unionisation in Denmark among women is among the highest in the world. In 2000 overall unionisation was at 80 per cent for men and 83 per cent for women; in the public-welfare sector, unionisation was at about 90 per cent (Madsen 2000).

As women have become economically independent of a male breadwinner, gender relations have changed dramatically and weakened the male-breadwinner model. Thus, it is safe to say that the family structure in Denmark has moved from a 'housewife model of the (male) breadwinner family' to a 'dual breadwinner/dual carer model' (Pfau-Effinger 2004). Many couples cohabit without being married, and the divorce rate is high. More and more adults are living alone. In 2007, about 43 per cent of all households were composed of one adult (with or without children) (cf. Danmarks Statistik 2007).

The entry of women into the labour market also has had a profound impact on women's self-image and identity and their attitudes towards their position in society in general. In 1965, 82 per cent of Danish women could fully agree with the statement that 'Married women should not work, if the effect is that a man becomes unemployed'; only 19 per cent could agree with the same statement in 1987. In 1965, 80 per cent of Danish women could fully agree with the statement that 'It is the task of the housewife to take care of the children and do the housework'; whereas only 26 per cent could agree with the same statement in 1987 (Togeby 1989). These changes in attitudes clearly demonstrate that women's role perception has changed radically between the 1960s and 1980s. In the 1960s women considered themselves assigned to a marginal or subordinate position in the labour market vis-à-vis the male breadwinner. By contrast, since the late 1980s (most) women have considered themselves to be on an equal footing with men, both with regard to wage labour and the division of housework. What took place could be described as a kind of 'cultural revolution', which meant that women came to believe that the struggle for jobs and career was not reserved for men but was just as much *their* struggle. Perhaps we can say, to borrow loosely from Bourdieu (1977, 91–92), that the *habitus* of women changed from primarily being centripetal, that is, oriented towards the 'house, full of food, utensils, and children', to becoming increasingly centrifugal, that is, oriented towards the market (production and circulation of goods), politics, and so on.

Initially, the integration of women into the labour market was intended to meet the great demand for labour in a situation of near full employment. The expanded use of female labour, however, was only one out of several options for meeting the challenges of the labour market. Other options were, for instance, to make use of immigrants or foreign 'guest workers' or to introduce or increase the use of technology (cf. Kamerman and Kahn 1978). Denmark, however, clearly chose the 'female labour' rather than the "immigrant worker' path. In the late 1960s immigration expanded, but its magnitude remained modest, and even today the percentage of foreign-born and noncitizens in the total population is among the lowest in western countries (Dumont and Lemaître 2005).

The high (formal) labour-force participation rates in Denmark correspond to a very strong work orientation. Table 3.1 shows that the work orientation in Denmark is much stronger than in any of the other countries included in this book.

In part, the strong work orientation in Denmark may be explained by specific traits of identity formation: In Denmark, the labour market plays a central role in bringing about personal well-being and a sense of belonging to the community. In part the prevalence of good-quality working conditions in Denmark, greater than in the rest of EU-15 except for Sweden, may be very important, as it helps to account for differences in motivational patterns (Gallie 2003, 2007). The great number of good-quality jobs in Denmark came about largely with a recomposition of the workforce that took place in the 1990s. As shown by Goul Andersen (2007), during the 1990s the number of unskilled jobs started disappearing at a rather fast rate, and the upgrading of qualifications by means of active labour-market policies 'proceeded at an even higher speed'. In effect, today the proportion of unskilled workers on the Danish labour market is relatively low.

Table 3.1.   Attitudes to Work, by Country and Sex: Proportion of Population Who Are in Agreement with the Following Statement, 'I would continue working even if I did not need the money any more', 2003

	Denmark	Finland	Germany	UK	Spain	Poland
Men	65.9	40.9	48.7	42.5	32.1	53.3
Women	68.2	44.2	54.6	53.7	43.2	54.4

Source: Torres et al. (2006).

3.2. DEVELOPMENT OF FORMAL EMPLOYMENT
AND ECONOMIC CHANGE

Between 1960 and 2007, the Danish population increased from about
4.6 million to about 5.5 million. Simultaneously, the Danish economy
has undergone radical structural changes. The proportion of employers and self-employed has decreased; and industrial employment has followed the same trend as in most other countries: a declining primary
sector, an almost unchanged or slightly declining industrial sector, and
a fast-growing service sector—especially the public-service sector, which
began to expand in the 1960s and 1970s. Changes in the employment
structure were facilitated by active labour-market policies initiated in
the early 1960s, which helped workers become occupationally and geo-
graphically mobile.

Active labour-market policies could not counteract the emergence of
high and persistent unemployment rates between the mid-1970s and late
1990s. Unemployment peaked in 1993 with an OECD-standardised unemployment rate of 9.6 per cent. After 1993 and into the late 1990s, unemployment rates declined significantly and have remained at very low levels
during the 2000s. Thus, Denmark has recovered quite convincingly from
the unemployment crisis. Today, as in the 1960s, Denmark experiences a
situation of near-full employment.

Since the early 1970s, the supply of labour has increased more or less
independently of the demand for labour. The unemployment crises of the
mid-1970s to the mid-1990s had no discouraging effect on flows into the
labour market. Between 1960 and 1990 labour-force participation rates
grew constantly, from 71.2 to 84.1 per cent. Growth in the labour force
peaked in 1990. Between 1990 and 2007, overall labour-force participation rates declined from 84.1 to 76.5 per cent. The decline in labour-force
participation rates since the 1990s coincides with recovery from the unemployment crisis.

Aggregate labour-force participation rates of course tend to conceal different dynamics and development paths: While the participation rates for
women have been increasing, the rate for men has been decreasing, and
these overall tendencies have combined with lower participation among
older workers due to early exit/retirement, and lower participation among
prime-age groups due to disability and unemployability, with the result
that, in 2005—with historically low unemployment rates—the number of
('full-time') welfare recipients in the total population between 18 and 66
years of age was 23 per cent (Danmarks Statistik 2007).

Growth in labour-force participation rates for women accelerated in the
early 1960s. Between 1960 and 1990 the female labour-force participation
rate increased from 43.5 to 78.5. Initially, part-time work functioned as a
bridge towards the full labour-market integration of women. In 1978, 45 per
cent of all working women were part-timers. Gradually, however, women

replaced part-time work with full-time employment. In 2001, only about 21 per cent of all women were working on a part-time basis. The reverse trend is true for male workers. The number of part-time working men is increasing. In 2001 about 9 per cent of all male workers were working part-time. In part the increase in the part-time work of men may be explained by an increase in the enrolment of young people in higher education, and by the fact that most students work part-time (Goul Andersen and Jensen 2002).

Changes in the female labour-force participation rate have meant that it has become more common for mothers with young children to be active in the labour market. The labour-force participation rate of women with children 0–2 years of age is 71.4 per cent and 77.8 per cent for women with children 3–5 years of age (Table 4.4, Appendix). These figures clearly demonstrate that small children do not hinder the labour-force participation of women and that women with small children have become a fully integrated part of the workforce. Neither do working mothers moderate fertility. Danish fertility rates are among the highest in Europe. In 2006 the fertility rate in Denmark was 1.85.

In accordance with collective agreements, around 1990, a normal working week for full-time employees was gradually reduced from 40 to 37 hours. The formal reduction in working time by 3 hours has, however, not resulted in a general reduction in the average working time, as the average working hours for full-time employed only decreased by about one hour from 1980 to the end of the 1990s. The formal reduction has been modified by the fact that more people are working more hours than the norm. Average work time in 2000 was 40.2 hours for full-time employed men and 37.9 hours for full-time employed women. Average work time for part-time women was 21.9 hours and for part-time men, 13.2 hours. Since 1979 each wage earner has been entitled to 5 weeks holiday per year. In effect, the total amount of work per capita has not changed between 1990 and 2001. In 2001 the estimated annual average working hours per capita (workers age 15–64 years) was 1,125 in Denmark. As expected, the work effort is greater in Denmark than in Germany (967 hours) and Spain (1,068 hours), but a bit below the high workload in the liberal welfare state United Kingdom (1,220).[1]

3.3. MAIN FEATURES OF INFORMAL EMPLOYMENT

Formal employment is likely to affect (and be affected by) the structure and dynamics of unpaid care work, informal employment, and voluntary work. In relation to child and eldercare, the Danish dual-breadwinner/dual-carer model has been preconditioned by public provision of care services for children and elderly citizens. Informal care plays a minor role, and the share of informal care work in Denmark is small in comparison with the other countries included in this book. Denmark may be therefore characterised as a 'public-care' society.

Measured by its share of GDP (Table 8.1, Appendix), the volume of informal employment or undeclared work in Denmark is medium-sized in comparison with the other countries included in this book. Still, the structure of undeclared work in Denmark differs from that in the rest of the countries. The frequency of informal employment is high (a high proportion of the population is engaged in undeclared work), but the average duration of that undeclared work is relatively short.

The voluminous welfare state in Denmark has left very little room for charitable activities. Still, the quantity of voluntary work in Denmark is not markedly different than that in any of the other countries in this book. In 2004, 35 per cent of the adult Danish population (age 16–85) participated in unpaid voluntary work and did so on average 129 hours per year (Boje and Ibsen 2006, 235). The nature of voluntary work has some specific characteristics in Denmark: It is concentrated around sports, culture, and leisure activities rather than on charity.

In the following sections the aim is a more in-depth analysis of the dynamics and the significance of unpaid care work, informal employment, and voluntary work in Denmark.

3.3.1. Policies, Patterns, and Explanations with Respect to Family-based Childcare

Two options are open in reconciling the demands of motherhood with wage work: generous maternity leave arrangements, or public provision of high-quality childcare institutions. Among the Scandinavian Social Democratic welfare states Denmark has been an outlier when it comes to reconciling the demands of motherhood, childcare, and wage work. Norway and Sweden choose the path of generous maternity-leave arrangements, but Denmark has—since the early 1960s—followed a path of using public childcare institutions (Leira 1992). Historically, maternity leave in Denmark has been short, and coverage by public day-care institutions has been high. Other things being equal, the Danish path helps to preserve women's close contact with the labour market and their human capital investments during maternity.

The Danish path of public childcare was not a calculated or premeditated political choice. Rather, day-care institutions grew more or less anarchistically from below in the mid-1960s as a combined effect of the needs of working mothers, local labour markets, and employers. In Denmark the municipalities bear the main responsibility for day-care institutions, and such institutions are financed by local taxes. The municipality finances about 75 per cent of all operations, as well as the expenses of housing, maintenance, and the like, whereas the parents must finance a part up to a maximum 25 per cent of all operation expenses. On average, the charge for a child of 0–2 years of age is about €350 monthly and €200 monthly for a child age 3–6. Most municipalities grant a reduction (or sometimes, provision free of charge) to low-income families and to families with more than one child enrolled in a day-care institution. Once the Danish path was formed, the interest of parents and social movements concentrated on issues of fees, the number of children per nursery teacher, and the numbers of day-care places, as until recently the waiting lists have been rather long.

3.3.1.1. Welfare-state Policies and Institutional Framework

A process of the formalisation of childcare started in the 1960s and has accelerated ever since, reaching its climax in 2004, when a new law introduced a general care guarantee which obliges municipalities to provide public day-care facilities for all children above 6 months of age. If the municipality is not able to comply with this, it must cover all costs for a day-care place in a different municipality, or cover the costs for privately organised day care, or pay the parent for taking care of his/her own child. In effect, the expenditures (Table 1.3, Appendix) and coverage of formal childcare provision in Denmark are much greater than those of the other countries included in this book. In 2006, 63.2 per cent of all children 0–2 years old and 96 per cent of all children 3–5 years old were enrolled in a day-care institution (Danmarks Statistik 2007). Opening hours of day-care institutions allow mothers to work on a full-time basis. In 1996, 75 per cent of all mothers with children age 0–6 years were working full-time, that is, more than 36 hours a week (Christoffersen 1997). On average, full-time working mothers with children 0–2 years old work 39.5 hours a week, and mothers with children 3–6 years old work 37.6 hours a week (Bonke and Meilbak 1999).[2]

Moss (1990, 2) has argued that different motives may underlie the formation of day-care institutions. These are (a) to support the integration of mothers into the labour market; (b) to improve the welfare and good functioning of families; and (c) to improve the quality of life, welfare, and development of children. All three motives are present in Danish day-care institutions. As mentioned, opening hours allow full-time employment of working mothers, and the institutions are staffed with highly skilled and trained kindergarten teachers who are able to stimulate the cognitive capacities of children. To become a kindergarten teacher requires 3½ years of full-time study.

As stated, the provision of childcare services rests with the municipalities. Historically this has caused huge regional differences in its realisation, although the care guarantee of 2004 has tended to equalise childcare provision among municipalities. Still, the nature of childcare differs among municipalities. The municipality may freely choose whether it should concentrate childcare spending on day-care institutions or publicly recognised child-minders. In general, Social Democratic-governed municipalities tend to choose the day-care institution model, and liberal- (or conservative-) governed municipalities choose the child-minder model. Economically it is advantageous for the municipality to provide childcare in the form of child-minding because child-minding does not require building public institutions, infrastructure, and so on. Furthermore, child-minders, unlike kindergarten teachers, are not required to be educated.

Although the coverage of day-care institutions is relatively broad, the quality of the maternity-leave arrangements has historically been relatively poor. Until the early 1980s women had the right to take a maternity leave of 4 weeks prior to birth and 14 weeks after. Subsequently the maternity leave scheme was supplemented with paternity and parental leave schemes. The paternity leave (2 weeks) must be taken within 14 weeks after the child is born. The parental leave scheme can be taken by one of the parents or by both. In total the parental leave is 32 weeks, and parental leave can be taken until the child is 9 years of age. This means that the whole or parts of the parental leave can be saved until the child is age 9. For instance, the parents can save eight weeks and go on a four-week family adventure trip when the child is age 8.

3.3.1.2. The Particular Extent and Structure of Informal Childcare

A relatively large share of informal childcare is provided for very young children by parents within the family household. Parents take care of their children themselves on a full-time basis during maternal, paternal, and parental leave. When these leave arrangements terminate, care responsibilities are delegated to public authorities. Most mothers return to work full-time.

Previously, working mothers relied somewhat on relatives and grandparents for childcaring purposes. Between 1965 and 1989, however, the proportion of children between age 0–6 years who were cared for by their grandparents fell from 11 to 5 per cent (Christoffersen 1997). At present this kind of childcare is a very marginal and uncommon phenomenon. Thus, in general the extent of informal childcare is very small in Denmark compared to that of the other countries included in this book.

The formalisation of childcare has more or less functioned as an employment machine. In 2005 about 74,000 persons—about 2.7 per cent of total employment—were employed full-time in childcaring institutions. The move towards more and more formalised childcare in Denmark has coincided with the formation of a genuine dual-carer model. Compared with other European countries, Denmark has the most equal distribution of men and women in the amount of time spent on housework (Lausten and Sjørup 2003, 18). Danish women spend more time away from home while working than women in other countries, and they also spend comparatively less time on housework. Correspondingly, Danish men spend less time away from home while working and are more active in housework than men in other European countries. Nevertheless there is still a gender-based difference with respect to housework in Denmark. If we look at all adults who have children (of all ages) in their household, men spend 1 hour per day on childcare while women spend 1½ hour per day. The proportion of women who take their children to childcare institutions and leisure-time activities is also greater than the proportion of men who do—32 per cent versus 23 per cent.

3.3.1.3. Family-based Childcare—An Explanation

The extent and the patterns of family-based childcare in Denmark are the combined effect of economic change, welfare-state policies, and changing cultural orientations. Economically, the Danish labour market was marked by shortage of labour in the early 1960s, which gave rise to a new, demand-driven opportunity structure for women. Women grasped and made use of the new opportunities, which in turn affected the functioning of the family. These new tendencies—facilitated by the formation of high-quality day-care institutions which helped to crowd out 'private childhood'—nurtured new cultural orientations towards the dual-breadwinner/dual-carer model, promoted women's right to participate in the labour market, and emphasised gender equality with respect to the distribution of household tasks in the family. The idea that the housewife is essentially responsible for running the home and that good mothers must take care of their children themselves ('private childhood') has definitely come to an end. Attitude data in relation to the family and mothers' employment clearly show that the acceptance and support of working mothers is far higher in Denmark than in the other countries analysed in this book. In comparison to those countries, a rather small proportion of people in Denmark believe that 'a pre-school child is likely to suffer if his or her mother works' (32.4 per cent) or that the 'family life suffers when women have a full-time job' (29.1 per cent) (cf. Table 7.1, Appendix).

3.3.2. Policies, Patterns, and Explanations with Respect to Family-based Eldercare

As in most other European countries the Danish population is ageing, and the proportion of people above the pensionable age of 65 is growing. In the Danish Social Democratic welfare state all citizens above age 65 are entitled to a universal tax-financed pension, which in principle makes older people economically independent of wage work, relatives, and private charity.[3] In addition, the welfare state assumes responsibility for frail older people in the form of home help or residential care. In effect, less and less eldercare is provided in private households on an unpaid basis.

3.3.2.1. Welfare-state Policies and Institutional Framework

In Denmark, the municipalities are required to provide eldercare in a magnitude corresponding to the needs of their older citizens. For the care of older citizens who are not fully capable of taking care of themselves, two options are open: home help and residential or 'old people's homes'.

The municipality is obliged to offer 'home help', that is, personal care and assistance with practical tasks in the private home to people who have reduced functional capacities (physical or mental). Even when the elderly person lives with a partner or family members, the municipality is still obliged to provide adequate home help. The local authorities decide whether a person is entitled to help at home and for how many hours per week. Thus home help is not an unconditional social right. The municipality has a considerable degree of autonomy to judge what one is actually entitled to, and there are differences between municipalities as to the extent and coverage of home help. But once home help has been granted in the form of 'permanent' home help, the municipality will normally bear all costs associated with it, that is, in general home help is then free of charge. In the case of short-term delivery of home help, recipients—especially better-off older people—are most often expected to pay for part of the services.

The municipalities (in cooperation with the regions or counties) are also expected to provide the necessary number of 'residential home and/or old-people's home' places for people who have suffered a considerable loss of function and are therefore in need of extensive care. A distinction can be made between 'residential homes' and 'old-people's homes', mirroring the degree of loss of functional capacity. In residential homes, the aim is to offer conditions which resemble a 'normal' home, just as the intervention of staff is minimised to the extent possible. Old-people's homes by contrast totally organise the living conditions of the residents. Residents must pay part of their residence costs out of their pension.

3.3.2.2. The Particular Extent and Structure of Informal Eldercare

Generally speaking, in Denmark, eldercare does not take place in families or as informal care. This is the result of historical developments since the early 1960s which have caused dramatic changes in family structures. In 1962, 18 per cent of older people over the age of 70 lived with their children. In 1988 the figure was only 4 per cent (Christoffersen 1997). Today it is extremely uncommon for adults to share their homes with their (old) parents or relatives. It is equally rare that frail elderly are cared for by neighbours or friends, and even spouses are not expected to care personally for one another. Thus, private eldercare has been more or less crowded out by the welfare state. By 2006 about 75,000 older citizens were living in publicly financed residential or old-people's homes; 200,000 older people in 2004 were receiving home help. In 2005 the total population of 70+-agers was about 570,000.

Until 2002, home help was strictly a public matter and was provided exclusively by the municipalities, and staff were public employees. More recently a 'cash-for-care'-like scheme has been implemented. As of 2002 a person who has been granted home help can freely choose to make use of the municipality or a private contractor. The private contractor is then paid by the municipality. So far however only a small part of the home help has been taken over by private firms.

In 2005 about 100,000 persons—about 3.7 per cent of total employment—were employed full-time in the eldercare sector, and in 2001, total public expenditures on old-age benefits in kind amounted to 1.75 per cent of GDP in Denmark (Table 1.4, Appendix). This figure has no equal with any of the other study countries in this book: In 2001, Finland spent 0.85 per cent of GDP on old-age benefits in kind; Germany 0.19; the United Kingdom 0.45; and Spain 0.21.

3.3.2.3. Family-based Eldercare—An Explanation

Several factors must be taken into account in explaining the extent and patterns of informal eldercare. One is that welfare-state policies have established comprehensive eldercare provisions. Thus, there is extensive coverage and availability of home help and residential care or old people's homes. Furthermore, the Danish family has developed into a genuine nuclear family, weakening traditional kinship relations (cf. Parsons 1951), which is intertwined with new cultural orientations. In Denmark 32.2 per cent of the population think that a parent should move into an old people's home or a nursing home when the parent can no longer manage to live on his or her own, whereas only 8.9 per cent think that 'I or one of my brothers or sisters should invite my father or mother to live with one of us' (Table 7.2, Appendix).

3.3.3. Policies, Patterns, and Explanations with Respect to Informal Employment

In Denmark, 63.5 per cent of all costs of social protection in 2004 were financed by individual taxation (the rest is financed by the social security contributions of employers and employees); the same figure for EU-15 was 37.5 per cent (Eurostat 2007). The financing formula in Denmark is rather atypical, and a major gap in tax revenue, if it occurred, would threaten the Social Democratic welfare state. This is probably why the Danish tax authorities employ a broad definition of informal employment: They define informal employment as all kinds of productive activities which are not declared, and where both the practitioner and the purchaser gain some sort of economic advantages in the form of savings on individual and/or value-added tax. The definition does not distinguish between payment in cash and payment in kind or whether informal employment is organised as friendly turns (e.g., you helping a neighbour fix his bicycle, and he mows your lawn while you are on holiday). In principle, payments in kind and friendly turns must be declared on the tax form.

3.3.3.1. Informal Employment—Regulation and Institutional Framework

Informal employment is illegal and is punished if discovered. An employer hiring informal workers will be punished with a fine or prison term of up to 1½ years, and an informal worker will also be fined or—in the most severe cases—imprisoned. Danish tax authorities, however, turn a blind eye to nondeclared income under €140 per year, and the overall risk of getting caught is very low. A survey conducted in 2005 shows that 83.8 per cent of the Danish population believe the chances of being detected are 'rather low' or 'very low' (Nyt fra Rockwool Fondens Forskningsenhed 2006, 3).

Since the early 1990s informal employment has been subject to considerable attention from Danish politicians who have tried to combat the phenomenon in several ways. First, the levying and monitoring system at the disposal of the tax authority has been improved significantly (Mogensen 1998). Second, the tax authority and customs, in cooperation with the Directorate of Unemployment Insurance, police, and municipal authorities, have carried out high-profile raids on restaurants, bars, kiosks, construction sites, etcetera, trying to uncover undeclared work. Third, several information campaigns against fraud and informal employment directed at the general public have been launched; in 2004 for instance, a so-called *fair play* campaign tried to spread the message that it is un-solidary and illegal to perform undeclared work. Fourth, the welfare state has tried to limit the informal employment opportunities in, for instance, the private cleaning sector. In 1994 a new programme (the home-service programme) began providing a public subsidy to private companies producing services for households such as cleaning, gardening, walking dogs, and so on, and the subsidy meant that private purchasers could buy legal cleaning at the low price of the illegal product. This programme, however, was scaled down in 2000. Nonetheless it is generally believed that the combined effect of the various measures has diminished the inclination to carry out undeclared work (Mogensen 2003).

3.3.3.2. Main Features of Informal Employment

The magnitude of informal employment is for obvious reasons very difficult to monitor and quantify. In Denmark *The Rockwool Foundation Research Unit* carries out most of the research on the shadow economy. The Research Unit has been inspired by the Austrian economist Friedrich Schneider, but has not been able to reproduce Schneider's results on the size and development of informal employment. According to the Research Unit, informal employment has since the mid-1990s generally been decreasing, and this tendency has strengthened over the last five years. Between 2001 and 2005 informal employment fell about 26 per cent from 207 to 153 million hours, which equaled 3.8 per cent of GDP in 2001 and 3.0 per cent in 2005 (Nyt fra Rockwool Fondens Forskningsenhed 2006). Compared to the other countries included in this book, the informal economy in Denmark is medium (Table 8.1, Appendix).

The distribution of undeclared work across the different production sectors has been relatively stable during the last twenty years. Most informal activities are carried out in building and construction and in service sectors such as cleaning, hairdressing, gardening, etcetera (Mogensen et al. 1995; Pedersen 1998, 2003). Previously, informal employment was unequally distributed among regions, with the greatest concentration in the western part of the country. Today, however, such regional disparities have more or less evaporated.

As to the kind of people who perform undeclared work, the following characteristics are particularly evident: First, the frequency of informal employment is high among young people (among these a large percentage are students), that is, those between 18 and 29 years of age. Second, skilled workers and craftsmen in particular are engaged in informal employment. Third, informal employment is also structured by gender. More men than women perform informal employment. In the most recent years however, informal employment frequency has been declining among men and increasing among women. This new trend coincides with the scaling down of the home-service programme in the early 2000s. Fourth, the frequency of informal employment among the unemployed is much lower than among ordinary employees, but the hours that an unemployed person works in informal employment are much more than those of people in ordinary employment. Fifth, illegal immigrants and foreigners without working permits are all doing informal employment if they are working at all. This is mainly the case in the hotel, restaurant, and building and construction sectors. The extent of this is not known, but the building and construction trade union estimated in 2002 that this informal employment amounted to around 1,500 full-time jobs annually. Most probably this number has risen in recent years, as Denmark has experienced a building boom.

The typical user of informal workers is a well-paid and busy person below 40 years of age living in a single-family house, and he or she employs informal labourers because it is cheaper than the formal alternative. As to informal workers, they are mainly driven by two motives: moonlighting or as a means to avoid poverty. Most probably moonlighting is the predominant form of informal work in Denmark. At least several indicators point in this direction: First, an overwhelming share of informal activities is carried out on the basis of friendly turns (Pedersen 1998, 93). Second, the average amount of hours per week spent on informal employment in 2004–2005 was four hours and eight minutes (Nyt fra Rockwool Fondens Forskningsenhed 2006). Still, more and more hours are worked by ever fewer persons, which seem to indicate that the amount of informal employment as poverty alleviation is increasing. Immigrants are more often than (native) Danes involved in informal employment on a more or less full-time basis. Therefore as a general statement we can assume that native Danes and immigrants perform undeclared work for different reasons. For Danes moonlighting is probably the most common motive, whereas immigrants perform informal employment to have any job at all.

3.3.3.3. Informal Employment—An Explanation

There is hardly any doubt that high marginal taxes (which make tax fraud lucrative) in Denmark contribute to the prevalence of informal employment. In 2007, marginal taxes were 42.9 per cent for an income up to about €37,000; 49.2 per cent for incomes between €37,000 and €44,000; and 63 per cent for incomes above €44,000. Still, high marginal taxes may not play as important a role in undeclared work as is often assumed. In Poland and Spain, where marginal taxes are relatively low, the incidence of informal work is much higher than in Denmark. Nonetheless the high marginal taxes in Denmark may have helped make undeclared work, culturally, somewhat more justifiable. On a scale of 1 to 10, where 1 is totally indefensible and 10 is totally justifiable, on average the acceptance of making use of undeclared work was 3.9 in 2004 (Nyt fra Rockwool Fondens Forskningsenhed 2006).

Other factors which may have furthered informal employment are the scaling down of the home-service programme, the fact that Denmark did not apply a buffer period after EU expansion to avoid a possible major inflow of cheap labour from new member-states, and the deteriorating tax-payer ethic of the Danes since the 1980s (Goul Andersen 1998)—although their tax behaviour is relatively ethical in comparison to that of the inhabitants in the other countries included in this book (Jensen 1995, 65ff.). In general however, Danes may actually be happy about paying taxes. A survey conducted in October 2007 shows that 73 per cent of the population would prefer improvements in welfare services rather than a tax reduction, 22 per cent would opt for tax relief, and 5 per cent did not know (Mandag Morgen, no. 45/2007).

The extent of informal employment has declined since the mid-1990s and especially after 2001. Most likely this can be explained as a result of the public authorities' enhanced surveillance measures, which have increased the risk of discovery of those doing informal work or employing informal workers. Another important factor is that a change in the employment structure has reduced the actual opportunities to employ or work informally. In 1997 only 24 per cent of all Danes reported that they had opportunities to do so (Clement 2001). Thus, the coming of a highly regulated service economy seems to affect the extent of informal employment. For instance, few publicly employed nursery teachers are offered informal employment.

Simultaneously, high minimum wages and generous unemployment benefits may make informal employment less attractive. Furthermore it is indisputable that the dramatic decline in unemployment has contributed to the reduction in informal employment. Still, immigrants bear the major burden of unemployment, and that may explain the different patterns in informal employment among (native) Danes and immigrants. Danes are moonlighters, whereas immigrants work informally to escape poverty, not least because welfare benefits have been reduced in Denmark since 2001.

3.3.4. Policies, Patterns, and Explanations with Respect to Voluntary Work

In all-encompassing Social Democratic welfare states, the voluntary engagement of citizens plays a relatively small role in the provision of welfare in cash or kind, and voluntary organisations in Denmark do not offer their services in areas already covered by public welfare services (Henriksen and Ibsen 2001). Accordingly, most Danes believe that care is the responsibility of the national or local welfare state. Only 2.3 per cent think that the provision of childcare should be provided by voluntary associations, and only 1.8 per cent hold this opinion with respect to eldercare.

3.3.4.1. Regulatory Framework and Policies Towards Voluntary Work

The Danish welfare state had matured by the 1960s and 1970s, and voluntary work began to get the reputation as being something, though well-intentioned, not requiring any professional expertise and therefore not representing a serious contribution to the solution of social problems. During the 1980s, however, a new discourse emerged; it propagated a positive view of voluntary social work and voluntary organisations as active participants in Danish social policy. Voluntary institutions began to be subsidised by the state—a financial support which has been increasing for the last ten to fifteen years. The aim was not to replace public welfare services by voluntary organisations, but rather to stimulate the development of alternative or supplementary initiatives which would reach the most vulnerable (drug addicts, prostitutes, etc.) who have turned their backs on the public welfare system.

A large share of voluntary workers in social-policy-oriented voluntary organisations often work formally full-time. By contrast, voluntary workers in culture, sports clubs etc., most often work a few hours part-time and are (however infrequently) rewarded with a tax-free amount of money paid by the sports club subsidised by the municipality and covering such expenses as travel, training suits, and so on.

3.3.4.2. Characteristics of Voluntary Work

It is difficult to measure more precisely the extent of voluntary work. Several surveys seem to indicate that the number of voluntary workers has been increasing sharply since the early 1980s and that around 40 per cent of the population today is engaged in voluntary work. Compared to that of the other countries in this book the share of the population participating in voluntary work is about medium.

Voluntary work is spread over numerous voluntary activities and various sectors of society, but we can distinguish three main activity sectors (Koch-Nielsen and Clausen 2002):

- sports, culture, and other leisure-time activities;
- church, elderly, youth, and other social activities;
- politics, labour unions, and similar activities.

In Denmark, voluntary work is primarily performed in sports, culture, and similar activities: 44 per cent of all voluntary work is done in this sector of society. Twenty eight per cent of voluntary work is carried out in politics, labour unions, etcetera; 28 per cent is occupied with traditional charitable activities. Compared to the other countries included in this book it is quite striking that in Denmark charity is the least common area of voluntary work.

The typical volunteer worker is male, age 30–49, has higher education, is employed full-time, has children, and lives in a small town or rural area. Voluntary work is not primarily done by people who have the most leisure time, but by those who are already very active with their jobs and families. Gender differences are not so marked when it comes to the frequency of participation, but men tend to commit more hours than women. Another gender-specific feature is that, though men are more inclined than women to do voluntary work when employed full-time, women are more inclined than men to do voluntary work when employed part-time. These gender differences may be explained by the distribution of household tasks. Women still do the largest share of household work.

In a Nordic study, Ulla Habermann (2001) made a survey of the motives for doing voluntary work and found that personal ideals are the main driving force behind enrolment in the voluntary sector. For example, most volunteer workers agree with the following statement: 'It is important to help others'. Another attraction is the opportunity to learn from interaction with other people and from working on specific tasks. Furthermore, voluntary work fosters personal identity because, when volunteering, people see themselves as useful and active. Career motives only play a very small role.

3.3.4.3. Voluntary Work—an Explanation

The Danish Social Democratic welfare state encourages voluntary activities, and the activity level is relatively high, most of the activities are outside the scope of social policy. The welfare state has to a large extent crowded out charitable activities, and Danes generally think that voluntary organisations should not be involved in providing childcare or eldercare. Still, voluntary work is recognised as an important part of social life, especially in areas such as culture, sports, etcetera. A new kind of welfare mix has developed in recent years: a strong welfare state and a strong civil society, where the role of voluntary organisations is to organise all sorts of cultural and leisure activities.

This new pattern can be explained by a combination of 'the social arena' and 'the life cycle' approach (Jeppsson-Grassman, 1993; Anker and Koch-

Nielsen 1995). These theories argue that people enter various social arenas at different stages in life. Those most interested in sports clubs and other leisure activities, for instance, are parents with children age 5–18. When children start to play football, at age 5–6, most often there is no coach, which puts pressure on parents to volunteer as football trainers. This helps to explain why the majority of volunteer workers are resourceful males aged 30–50 and that their motive is to help others (along with their own children).

3.4. CONCLUSION: INFORMAL WORK IN THE CONTEXT OF THE WORK-WELFARE ARRANGEMENT IN DENMARK

The relationship between formal and informal work is not a straightforward, zero-sum game. For on the one hand, formal labour-force participation rates in Denmark are very high, and the labour-force participation of women is higher than in other countries discussed in this book; on the other hand, informal work plays more than a minor role, if we compare the magnitude of informal work in Denmark with that of the other countries of this book. Admittedly there is hardly any space for informal childcare and eldercare contributions in Denmark, because the Social Democratic welfare state has more or less completely crowded out these forms of work. But the large public sector has not excluded informal work as such: The volume of undeclared work and voluntary work is at about a medium level compared to that of the other countries analysed in this book.

To explain the particular pattern of formal and informal work we need to look at the interrelations between the welfare state, labour market, social organisation of the family and civil society, and cultural orientation of the Danish population. These various institutions are linked by the overarching idea that labour-market participation and commodification is the golden road to emancipation and individual self-fulfilment. As such, the Danish work-welfare arrangement emerged along the following lines:

- From the late 1960s postindustrialisation materialised as the growth of (and demand for) labour in the public care and service sector where wages (even part-time wages) were relatively high due to the high degree of unionisation, which made it attractive for women to enter the labour market.
- The institutional welfare state has helped to mobilise all segments of the population onto the labour market by means of tax policies, active labour-market policies, part-time insurance against unemployment, etcetera, and—not least—policies liberating women from most care obligations. Denmark has a very wide coverage of public institutional care for elderly people and a childcare guarantee for children over six months of age. In effect, informal care has been crowded out.

- Danish (formal) labour-force participation rates are relatively high (especially for women), even though they are declining for older workers and prime-age males. The increasing labour-force participation of women has fostered new (more egalitarian) cultural orientations and changes in the family structure—not least owing to the feminist movement, which was very strong in the late 1960s and 1970s.
- The family has been relieved of traditional care obligations, and a new cultural model of the family has developed: the dual-breadwinner/dual-carer model. In addition, a single-breadwinner/single-carer model is on the verge of being formed, as about 43 per cent of all households in 2007 were composed of one adult with or without children.
- A new relationship between adults and children has emerged in Denmark. The present generation of children is referred to as the 'curling-generation'; that is, they are compared to a 'curling ball' because their parents sweep all obstacles from their children's paths. If the children want to play sports and there is no trainer, the parents volunteer. This may explain why volunteers are mainly middle-class men in areas such as sports, culture, etcetera, and charitable activities have more or less been crowded out by the welfare state.
- In Denmark the frequency of informal employment is high, and the average duration of undeclared work is short. Moonlighting predominates over poverty-escaping forms of undeclared work. This pattern of undeclared work may be explained by, in the latter case, generous welfare benefits that help reduce the extent of poverty, and, in the former, high individual taxation, which makes tax-free moonlighting more attractive.

Historically, mutual trust and confidence in political institutions have been a precondition to and effect of the good functioning of a Social Democratic welfare society with its voluminous welfare state. Another precondition is that citizens have a very strong work orientation—as in Denmark. A strong work orientation and strong work ethic dampen the incentive to make use of welfare benefits unless they are truly needed. Otherwise the welfare state would be insurmountably costly.

NOTES

1. For measurement and comparability problems, see OECD (2002, 321).
2. Fathers with children 0–2 years of age work 41.9 hours a week; fathers with children 3–6 years of age work 42.4 hours a week.
3. The state pension is composed of a basic amount (about €7900 annually in 2007), a supplementary benefit, and a personal benefit. The supplementary and personal benefits are in principle means-tested. Since the late 1960s however occupational pensions have come to play an increasing role in the overall 'pension package' (see Ploug 2003).

REFERENCES

Anker, J., and Koch-Nielsen, I. (1995) 'Det frivillige arbejde', København: Social-forskningsinstituttet 95:3.
Barbier, J.-C., and Ludwig-Mayerhofer, W. (2004) 'Introduction—The many worlds of activation', *European Societies* 6(4):423–436.
Boje, T., and Ibsen, B. (2006) *Frivillighed og nonprofit i Danmark: omfang, organisation, økonomi og beskæftigelse*, København: Socialforskningsinstituttet 06:18.
Bonke, J., and Meilbak, N.T. (1999) *Danskere på fuldtid—deres faktiske og ønskede arbejdstid*, København: SFI-SURVEY.
Borchorst, A., and Siim, B. (2002) 'The women-friendly welfare states revisited', *Nora* 10(2):90–98.
Bourdieu, P. (1977) *Outline of a Theory of Practice*, Cambridge: Cambridge University Press.
Briggs, A. (1961) 'The welfare state in historical perspective', *Archives Européennes de Sociologie* 2(2):221–259.
Christoffersen, M.N. (1997) 'Spædbarnsfamilien', København: Socialforskningsinstituttet 97:25.
Clement, S. (2001) *Borgerne og lovene II: danskernes forhold til landets love anno 2000*, Aalborg: Aalborg Universitet.
Danmarks Statistik (2007) *Statistisk Tiårsoversigt 2007*, København.
Dumont, J.C. & Lemaître, G. (2005) *Counting Immigrants and Expatriates in OECD Countries: A New Perspective*. Paris: OECD Social, Employment and Migration Working Papers, Delsa/elsa/WD/SEM (2005)4.
Esping-Andersen, G. (1990) *The Three Worlds of Welfare Capitalism*, Cambridge: Polity Press.
Eurostat (2007) Social protection in the European Union. *Statistics in focus: Population and social conditions, 99/2007*, European Community.
Fukuyama, F. (1995) *Trust: The Social Virtues and the Creation of Prosperity*, New York: The Free Press.
Gallie, D. (2003) 'The quality of working life: Is Scandinavia different?', *European Sociological Review* 19:61–79.
———. (2007) 'Welfare regimes, employment systems and job preference orientations', *European Sociological Review* 23(3):279–293.
Goul Andersen, J. (1998) *Borgerne og lovene*, Rockwool Fondens Forskningsenhed: Aarhus Universitetsforlag.
———. (2007) 'The Danish welfare state as 'politics for markets': Combining equality and competitiveness in a global economy', *New Political Economy* 12(1):71–78.
Goul Andersen, J., and Hoff, J. (2001) *Democracy and Citizenship in Scandinavia*, Houndsmills: Palgrave.
Goul Andersen, J., and Jensen, J.B. (2002) 'Employment and unemployment in Europe: overview and new trends', in J. Goul Andersen, J. Clasen, W. van Oorschot, and K. Halvorsen (eds) *Europe's New State of Welfare*, Bristol: Policy Press, 21–57.
Habermann, U. (2001) 'En Nordisk Frivillighed? Om motiver til frivillighed i fem nordiske lande', in L.S. Henriksen and B. Ibsen (eds) *Frivillighedens udfordringer—nordisk forskning om frivilligt arbejde og frivillige organisationer*, Odense: Odense Universitetsforlag.
Henriksen, L.S., and Ibsen, B. (2001) 'Indledning: Udfordrdinger for frivilligheden', in L.S. Henriksen and B. Ibsen. (eds) (2001) *Frivillighedens udfordringer: nordisk forskning om frivilligt arbejde og frivillige organisationer*, Odense: Odense Universitetsforlag, 9–20.

Hernes, H. (1987) *Welfare State and Women Power: Essays in State Feminism*, Oslo: Norwegian University Press.

Jensen, B. (1995) Danskernes dagligdag—Om skatter, velfærdsstat og sort arbejde i Danmark, Viborg: Spektrum.

Jeppsson-Grassman, E. (1993) *Frivilliga insatser i Sverige—en befolkningsstudie*, Stockholm: Statens offentliga utredningar.

Kamerman, S.B., and Kahn, A.J. (1978) 'Families and the idea of family policy', in S.B. Kamerman and A.J. Kahn (eds) *Family Policy*, New York: Columbia University Press.

Koch-Nielsen, I., and Clausen, J.D. (2002) 'Værdierne i det frivillige arbejde', in P. Gundelach (ed.) *Danskernes værdier 1981–1999*, København: Hans Reitzels Forlag.

Kumlin, S., and Rothstein, B. (2005) 'Making and breaking social capital', *Comparative Political Studies* 38(4):339–365.

Lausten, M., and Sjørup, K. (2003) Hvad mænd og kvinder bruger tiden til—om tidsmæssig ligestilling i danske familier, København: Socialforskningsinstituttet.

Leira, A. (1992) *Welfare States And Working Mothers*, Cambridge: Cambridge University Press.

Madsen, M. (2000) 'Ansættelses—og organisationsforhold 2000. Tendenser i lønmodtagernes faglige organisering', *LO-domumentation*, no. 2/2000, 99–121.

Mandag Morgen (2007) no. 45.

Mogensen, G.V. (1998) 'Tax ethics—Danish experience 1980–1997', in S. Pedersen *The Shadow Economy in Western Europe—Measurement and Results for Selected Countries: Appendix 1*, Copenhagen: The Rockwool Foundation Research Unit.

———. (2003) *Skattesnyderiets Historie*, Odense: Syddansk Universitetsforlag.

Mogensen, G.V., Kvist, H.K., Körmendi, E., and Pedersen, S. (1995) *The Shadow Economy in Denmark 1994—Measurement and Results*, Copenhagen: The Rockwool Foundation Research Unit.

Moss, P. (1990) *Børnepasning i de Europæiske Fællesskaber 1985–1990*, Kommissionen for de europæiske fællesskaber, Generaldirektoratet Information, Kommunikation, Kultur. Kvindeinformation Nr. 31.

Nyt fra Rockwool Fondens Forskningsenhed (2006) *Sort arbejde er faldet*, April 2006.

OECD (1995) *Historical Statistics 1960–1993*, Paris: OECD.

———. (2002) Employment Outlook, Paris: OECD.

Oorschot, W. van, and Arts, W. (2005) 'The social capital of European welfare states: The crowding out hypothesis revisited', *Journal of European Social Policy* 15(1):5–26.

Parsons, T. (1951) *The Social System*, Glencoe, Ill.: Free Press.

Pedersen, S. (1998) *The Shadow Economy in Western Europe—Measurement and Results for Selected Countries*, Copenhagen: The Rockwool Foundation Research Unit.

———. (2003) 'Sort arbejde i Skandinavien, Storbritannien og Tyskland', *Nyt fra Rockwoolfondens forskningsenhed—juni 2003*, København: Rockwoolfondens Forskningsenhed.

Pfau-Effinger, B. (2004) Development of *Culture, Welfare States and Women's Employment in Europe*, Aldershot: Ashgate.

Ploug, N. (2003) 'The recalibration of the Danish old-age pension system', *International Social Security Review* 56(2):65–80(16).

Siim, B. (2000) *Gender and Citizenship: Politics and Agency in France, Britain and Denmark*, Cambridge: Cambridge University Press.

Titmuss, R.M. (1974) *Social Policy*, London: Allan and Unwin.
Togeby, L. (1989) 'Da kvinderne gik mod venstre', *Nyt forum for kvindeforskning* 9(3).
Torres, A., Brites, R., Haas, B., and Steiber, N. (2007) *First European Quality of Life Survey: Time Use And Work-Life Options Over The Life Course*, Dublin: European Foundation for the Improvement of Living and Working Conditions.
Wilensky, H.L., and Lebeaux, C.N. (1958) *Industrial Society and Social Welfare*, New York: Russell Sage Foundation.

4 Formal and Informal Work in the Work-Welfare Arrangement of Finland

Arja Jolkkonen, Riitta Kilpeläinen, and Pertti Koistinen

INTRODUCTION

The Nordic countries represent a particular variant of welfare state characterised by the principle of universalism and a strong welfare state. Finland is an example of a social-democratic welfare regime, and a particular variant of the Nordic model, with a relatively generous social security system for pensions and unemployment (Esping-Andersen 1990). The social-democratic welfare arrangement interacts in a relatively coherent way with the arrangement of work and family based on the cultural model of the dual breadwinner/state care-provider (Pfau-Effinger 2004). The Finnish welfare state strongly supports this family model by providing social care services which minimise individuals' dependency on the family and allow women to choose formal employment rather than informal care work. This family model is also promoted by high levels of public childcare and gender neutrality in the tax and benefit systems (Repo 2001).

The institutional and regulatory effects of the welfare state in the field of eldercare differ from those in childcare, but also in eldercare the regulatory power of the welfare state is great, and home help has been redefined as a municipal rather than voluntary service. Before the expansion of welfare services in the 1970s, multiple producers, including local parishes, municipalities, and voluntary organisations provided welfare services for elderly people. Therefore Finnish feminist research argued for the notion of 'the women's welfare state', which refers to the complex ways in which the policies, ideologies, and institutions of the welfare state affect social services, gender divisions in the labour market, and combinations of formal and informal care work. But since the 1990s the curtailment of the welfare state and implementation of the ideas of 'new public management' have altered this main trend and created a welfare mosaic in which a universal welfare state has been infused with neoliberal ideas and led into a redefinition of the role of public sector and a rebirth of services produced as mix of public and private efforts (Wrede and Henriksson 2005).

Our aims in this chapter are to analyse the specific features of informal work in Finland and the relationship of formal and informal work and to examine how these can be explained in the context of the specific work and welfare arrangement of Finnish society. The first part of the chapter describes the arrangement of work and welfare in Finland, after which the main features of the different forms of informal work (family care of children and elderly people, informal employment, and voluntary work) in Finland is analysed. The specific size and structures of informal work in Finland is explained by the interaction of cultural, institutional, and structural factors in the arrangement of work and welfare in Finland.

4.1. THE ARRANGEMENT OF WORK AND WELFARE IN FINLAND

The main characteristics of the Finnish welfare state are as follows (Kuhnle and Hort 2004; Korpi and Palme 2003; Kautto et al. 2001):

- It is based on a high degree of universalism, which means citizens/residents are entitled to basic social security and welfare services of which a significant share is produced publicly.
- There is a relatively high level of redistribution of income, and it is relatively even due to the social transfer system, which is based on two benefits: a flat-rate basic social security benefit, and an earning-related benefit for those who have a work history. The Finnish welfare state, like other Nordic welfare states, also has a comprehensive sector of social services and can be therefore characterised as a 'service state'.
- Specific configurations of the welfare systems are the outcome of the development of a participative political culture, consensus-building and strong local and central government.
- The focus on universal, high-quality education is another particular feature and is also the reason for Finland's top ranking in educational system quality in comparative studies of European countries.
- The Finnish welfare state, like other Nordic welfare states, depends on full employment and is therefore also particularly vulnerable when mass unemployment develops.

The post-war construction of the Finnish welfare state went through two phases: The first was characterised by the establishment and general acceptance of universal population coverage with a flat-rate benefit system. The second phase, from the 1960s on, was marked by the introduction of adequate earnings-related benefits, and hence the maintenance of the income status achieved by a worker while gainfully employed. In the 1980s and especially in the early 1990s the Nordic countries along with other European countries, suffered various economic imbalances and crises which led many observers to doubt the economic viability and fiscal sustainability of welfare states. But critical review of the experiences of Finland, Denmark, and Sweden seem to verify that even after the hardships of the 1980s and 1990s, the Nordic model of social policy remains clearly distinctive and in many respect successful (Kiander 2004). In Finland one of the big challenges was to find a new synthesis between the more flexible use of labour resources, employment, and income security of workers. Achieving this could lead to innovative solutions in economic efficiency and social development and thereby avoid the underemployment and increase in social inequalities typical of the larger European economies, and it seems that the Finnish welfare state has been in this respect successful (Koistinen and Sengenberger 2002).

Welfare-state policies also strongly support the formal employment of mothers and collectivised childcare, which has contributed to domesticating fatherhood (Leira 2002, 9). Since the 1960s social care services have been greatly expanded at the local government level—mainly in the form of kindergartens and institutional or home care and help for the elderly. Also the social right for each child up to age six to public childcare has been gradually introduced. In the 1970s paid parental leave schemes were established and have since become the most generous in the world (Kuhnle and Hort 2004). The main political objective was not to strengthen the role of the housewife, but mainly to react to the 'care crisis' at the end of the 1980s. This crisis was caused by a lack of qualified personnel to effect further expansion of the public childcare system in some urban areas, such as the Helsinki region, and by the fact that municipalities could no longer guarantee the supply of public kindergartens (Joronen 1994; Simonen 1990; Simonen and Kovalainen 1998). Another reason for stagnation of the extension of public childcare services in the 1990s, besides the recession, was the early redefinition of Finnish social policies according to the ideas of 'new public management', which encouraged private initiatives as alternatives to or extensions of public services (Wrede and Henriksson 2005).

Parents have a real choice between public childcare and semiformal family care when their children are small. Altogether, the share of social expenditure for childcare and eldercare is in Finland the second highest among the six countries under analysis. Among the Formal and Informal Work in Europe (FIWE) countries Finland's social expenditure on family and children, as well as on old age benefits, is the second highest in percentage of GDP after Denmark (Tables 1.1–1.5, Appendix 1). Leave rights for fathers were first introduced in the 1970s, and during the past decade father care has been the focus of leave-policy development. However, parental leave has been taken mainly by mothers, the division of childcare and housework in families has remained unequal, and women's position in the labour market is not equal to that of men (Lammi-Taskula 2007; Haataja 2007). Parental leave systems have created a paradox: They support women in combining employment and family life but the amount of women's parental leave has not diminished (Salmi and Lammi-Taskula 2006; Ruuskanen 2007).

These policies of the Finnish welfare state interact with the specific arrangement of work and family based on the cultural model of the 'dual breadwinner/state care-provider family' (Pfau-Effinger 2005). In Finland the housewife model of the 'male breadwinner' family was never dominant at the cultural level, and it was not introduced to any substantial degree into family practice. Rather, until the 1960s, much of the population was based on the social class of free farmers with small farms and was oriented towards a 'family economy' model, according to the typology of cultural family models by Pfau-Effinger (2004).

Seen historically, the exceptional degree of integration of women into male society originates from a time before the idea of a welfare state came into being. At a time when social expenditure in Finland was nearly the lowest in Europe, the country led in the numbers of women at work, political representation, and level of education. It was not until the late 1970s that some other Western countries, notably Scandinavian, caught up. To understand the cultural basis of the arrangement of work and family up to the 1960s, it is necessary to examine its roots in economic and social history. For a long time Finland remained a poor agrarian society with insignificant upper and middle classes. The traditional family model—with the man as breadwinner, the woman as housewife and mother—has never been as strong in Finland as in the earlier industrialised and more pronounced class-societies of Europe. As a backward country, Finland needed women's labour in both industry and agriculture. Also, as it completely lacked 'guest workers', Finland also needed women's labour to effect the dizzying growth of industry and services that took place after the Second World War. Its agrarian structure favoured women's education and their participation in political life, and it created an image of the strong and hard-working woman who was the wife of a peasant or a plywood factory worker (Julkunen 1990, 142).

The care of children and elderly is to a great degree considered the responsibility of the welfare state. This can also be observed in the International Social Survey Program (ISSP 2002) attitude data. Men and women feel that both should contribute to household income and household work and that childcare should be shared equally between spouses. Finns do not feel strongly, as do for instance Poles or Spaniards, that children or family suffer when mothers work outside the household. Finns also feel that best way to care for elderly relatives is to give them enough services at home that independent living can continue as long as possible. If this is not possible, then the alternative is an 'old people's home' or nursing home. This attitude is quite similar to that of Danes, but differs much from attitudes in Spain, where the best option for eldercare seems to be elderly relatives living in the family household and not in nursing homes (Tables 7.1–7.2, Appendix 4).

Even though equality, and gender mainstreaming policies in particular, have explicitly focussed on bringing reproduction to the fore in working life by giving mothers and fathers of small children the right to stay at home on parental leave, and are aimed at adapting working life to family life, these goals seem to conflict with new trends in working life (Brandth and Kvandle 2001). This is quite evident in the case of Finland where the economic recession of the 1990s, the restructuring of labour markets, and reforms of welfare-state provisions have strengthened competition on the labour market. Several studies (Kröger 2005; Salmi and Lammi-Taskula 2007) verify that parents have serious difficulties providing care and reconciling the demands of work and family life.

The question arises whether the deep labour-market crisis that began in the early 1990s initiated a cultural change, with the role of the housewife gaining importance. Actually, the retreat of women into their homes was not regarded as a solution to the problem of unemployment; this would not have been consistent with the logic of the Finnish family model (Haataja 2007; Pfau-Effinger 2004). According to the Gender Equality Barometer 2004, it is self-evident from the perspective of most Finns that 'married women have the full right to work whatever their family situation'. Ninety-four percent of Finnish women and 92 per cent of men agreed with this statement. The male breadwinner role of men, in contrast, is not very popular: The great majority of women (71 per cent) do not agree with the role of men as breadwinners, whereas the proportion of men who object to this role model is not nearly as high (61 per cent) (Melkas 2005, 11–12).

In Finland as well as other parts of Europe there has been a lively discourse about whether changes in welfare-state policies—as a reaction to the deep economic recession—have affected trust in the state, welfare systems, and the citizen's position in society. In general, the trust[1] of Finns in their national parliament has weakened; it is the second weakest among the Nordic countries (the Norwegians have the weakest trust, and the Danes, the strongest). Finns trust more in their courts and legal system than in parliament. This trust is the second highest among the Nordic countries. Their trust in the health care and educational systems is at a high level, and these are priority issues among all parties (Borg 2005; Litmala 2004). In comparison to the other countries studied, the level of trust in public institutions in Finland is among the highest, except for Denmark's. During the times of economic hardship there were remarkable changes in the level of trust in and support for the welfare state. Forma (2002) found that high-income earners became more reluctant to pay the costs of the welfare state and were more willing to introduce cutbacks. There was also some worsening of solidarity between better-offs and worse-offs, but this did not generally affect the legitimacy of the welfare state in the long run. According to results of the latest representative survey carried out in 2006 (Forma et al. 2008), among Finns age 18 to 75, there is strong support for the current welfare-state system. The majority of respondents would not cut social spending even if such cuts led to tax reductions. The majority of respondents would even be willing to pay more taxes if the increased tax revenues were earmarked for health expenditures, pensions, or child benefits.

Finland also has a relatively strong nonprofit sector. Nonprofit organisations are partly treated as supplements to the public welfare system (Ojanen 2005, forthcoming; Niemi forthcoming). In this respect Finland deviates from the classical social-democratic welfare regime. This can be explained in the context of Finnish history: Among Nordic countries Finland was more deeply a class society, and social reforms were accelerated by class struggle. This led to a kind of welfare mix in which municipalities and voluntary organisations took the main responsibility for organising health and social services for families under the care of the municipal social boards (Wrede and Henriksson 2005, 4). On the other hand there was in the society some sound interest in keeping social cohesion in the face of external political and economic pressures. The central ideas and elements of the welfare state were developed by strong social organisations in civil society, which were in great part also established in rural areas. The fact that civil welfare organisations are still relevant in the Finnish welfare state can be explained by the long duration of the dual structure of the Finnish welfare state (Julkunen 1990). Since the 1990s there has been a growing tendency for the government to look for volunteers who can replace public service workers in some fields and to contribute to solving the care deficit in the society.

Informal employment among households in Finland (part-time remodelling, house repair, cash payment to neighbours or relatives for services rendered) is estimated to be small-scale and of short duration. Households' tax-free work that is of a continuous nature by contrast usually concentrates on caring for relatives, which often takes the form of unpaid childcare.

4.2. DEVELOPMENT OF FORMAL EMPLOYMENT AND ECONOMIC CHANGE IN FINLAND

Just as in other countries, in Finland economic growth, increase in productivity development, and overall economic performance are clearly reflected in the demand for labour. Finland seems to be especially sensitive to economic shocks and fluctuations: In the recessions of the 1990s its overall employment dropped even more than in other Organisation for Econmic Co-operation and Development (OECD) countries, but it grew again with the economic recovery. Since the late 1990s, growth has been continuous and among the strongest in the OECD. What was remarkable was the speed at which Finland recovered from the deep economic recession of the early 1990s following the sudden collapse of nearly all trade with the former Soviet Union and other economic shocks. Employment was not only affected by productivity growth, but also by sectoral changes in the economy and regional differentiation in the country. Growth-related structural change enabled the employment of highly skilled workers and offered them better career development and pay. The losers in this game were unskilled and temporary employees who suffered from chronic unemployment and low pay (Koistinen and Sengenberger 2002; OECD 2006).

In 2006 among those age 16–64 the labour-force participation rate was 74.7 per cent and the employment rate was 68.9 per cent, which is above-average for the study countries. Among women the labour-force participation rate was the second highest (73.2 per cent) after Denmark. During the recession years of 1990–1994 the labour-force participation rate declined from 76.5 to 72.0 per cent and employment rate fell even more, from 74.1 to 59.9 per cent (see Table 4.1, Appendix). Especially the share of those less than 30 years of age diminished. It should be noted that, in part, the decrease in labour-force participation was also due to an expansion of the share of students within the respective age groups. To some extent it was also due to a slight increase in the share of women taking parental leave (Haataja 2007). The economic growth and structural change of the last decades has contributed to the growth of jobs at a relatively high level of quality for men as well as women. The increase in private business services and electronic industries since the late 1990s has created job opportunities for educated men, and the growth of public sector services since 2004 has created a demand for women workers. This means that, once again, the growth of the public sector has had a double effect on female employment: It creates women's employment opportunities, and it creates pressure to develop employment-friendly day-care services for families with small children and dependent family members. These structural changes have made women's employment almost identical with that of men, and the employment rate of women is one of the highest in the EU. Also, the labour force in Finland is particularly highly qualified: Around 37 per cent of those employed, and almost 50 per cent of 30- to 39-year-olds have tertiary education (Statistics of Finland 2006). And whereas professional childcare in many other countries,such as Germany, requires that carers have a three-year professional education, in Finland this work partly requires university education.

There are many other reasojns for the high employment rate (67.3 per cent) of women. Because the cultural model of the dual-breadwinner/state-care-provider family is dominant, women, like men, generally orient their labour-market behaviour to continuous full-time employment during their working lives. This is also why both men and women work full-time, and part-time work is relatively uncommon in Finland (Pfau-Effinger 2004). The part-time rate of Finnish women is the lowest (14.9 per cent) among those of the study countries. This behaviour is also supported by other factors, such as the recognition of women's high level of education and partly also the necessity of a double income (European network 2007; Julkunen and Nätti 1999.

Mass unemployment struck Finland in the early 1990s, and in 1994, its unemployment rate was the second highest (16.8 per cent) among the six countries studied. According to Kiander and Pehkonen (1999), the rapid rise in unemployment of the 1990s is mainly explained by the interest-rate shock and the loss of markets in Central and Eastern European countries. Since 1997 Finland has had remarkable and continuous economic and employment growth. It has also been rather successful in reducing its high unemployment rates, though in the shadow of employment's growth, unemployment has remained rather high and persistent (10.4 per cent in 2006; 8 per cent in 2008), and the disparities in the unemployment rate are remarkable. Unemployment has affected a broader cross-section of the population than previously, but disparities by region, gender, age, and education have remained strong.

4.3. MAIN FEATURES OF INFORMAL WORK IN FINLAND

Informal work in general does not play any great role in Finland. The share of informal family childcare for under-3-year-olds is large, but for older children, formal childcare services dominate. Eldercare is mainly provided by public service agencies or in public residential care. Currently there is a slight tendency towards an increase in informal care. Therefore Finland can be characterised as a highly regulated 'public service' society with a large share of formal employment taking place in the public sector. Undeclared work plays a very marginal role and occurs mainly in firms, not in private households. On the other hand, the level of participation in voluntary work is rather high compared to that of other European countries.

4.3.1. Policies, Structure, and Explanation with Respect to Family-Based Childcare

4.3.1.1. Welfare-state Policies and Institutional Framework

In Finland the social welfare, health care, and education authorities administer the services benefitting small children and their families. The welfare state offers a variety of services and provides parents with the scope for a 'real' choice between public childcare and parental semiformal care. It provides support to parents taking care of small children at home. The system of support includes maternity, paternity, parental leave, care-leave, and home-care allowances. Families can receive a home-care allowance for childcare at home until the youngest child reaches age 3, and they receive relatively generous pay for 'semi-formal' family care[2] during parental leave (Publications of the Ministry of Social Affairs and Health 2003). Parents, mothers and fathers, can also 'free' themselves from care duties and be full-time employed, for each child below school age has the right to municipal day care once the parental allowance period (about 11 months) ends. A law guaranteeing all children under school age a place in municipal day care was implemented in 1996. As childcare is a legal right for children under 6 years, unemployed parents can also make use of this privilege. This legal right may be one of the main reasons services to families of small children were not cut even during the recession.

In addition to public-sector services, some organisations in the non-profit sector provide additional childcare services for private households, mainly during times when the public childcare organisations are closed. The best known of these organisations is the Mannerheim League for Child

Welfare, which offers occasional short-term babysitting for families. Households using this babysitting service make a verbal care-agreement with the nanny, so in a sense there is a verbal employment relationship between the two parties. The nannies are doing, in one sense, voluntary work, but there is also a relatively low payment. This payment is taxable income which must be stated on the nanny's tax return (Tommiska 2005).

4.3.1.2. Size and Structures of Informal Childcare

Most families make use of all the publicly supported types of care before their children reach school age, but first children are cared for at home. The carer of small children is in most cases the mother. Mothers of young children choose to use the parental leave scheme only to a limited extent after the end of maternity leave, and for relatively limited periods of time, but altogether in a much larger proportion than do fathers. According to the Family Leave Survey, about half of all mothers stay at home until their child is 18 months old, and more than half do so until their child is 2 years old (Salmi and Lammi-Taskula 2007, 91–92). This is very different from the practice in West Germany, for example, where nearly all women take parental leave, and the great majority takes it for a period of three years, even though it is less generously paid there than in Finland (see Pfau-Effinger and Sakač Magdalenić in this volume). In 2005, 71 per cent of children under 3 years, mostly infants, were cared for at home under the parental allowance or child home-care allowance. About 2 per cent were in private day care with the aid of the private care allowance, 23 per cent used municipal day-care services, and 4 per cent had other day-care arrangements (Ministry of Social Affairs and Health 2006, 13–17). This form of childcare at home, supported by the state in the form of the home-care allowance, could be classified as a semiformal form of care (Geissler and Pfau-Effinger 2005).

Family households in Finland also use some informal care given by relatives or friends. This type of care is usually occasional and based on the exchange of services or small favours. It is especially important to single-parent families and to parents who work shifts (Kröger 2005; Tommiska 2005).

In the context of the privatisation of the public sector and the economic recession of the 1990s, market-based day-care provision has also begun to grow, partly due to a new social benefit, the 'private day-care allowance', which enables parents to purchase services offered on the market. These services are most often provided by self-employed professionals who have left the public care system (Simonen 1990; Simonen and Kovalainen 1998). The growth in market-based day-care services is increasingly related to the needs of labour markets. In order to utilise the full capacity of the labour force, private companies in Finland are providing more and more market-based day-care services for their staff (Parental Leave in European Companies 2007). This kind of expansion of day-care services is reasonable in the context of the full-time employment model of Finland. According to ISSP data (2002), Finnish mothers more often work full-time than do mothers in Germany, Spain, or the United Kingdom. In 2002, 47 per cent of Finnish women who had children under age 7 worked full-time, 15 per cent had part-time work, and 38 per cent were outside the labour market. When the youngest child in the family was over age seven, 77 per cent of mothers had full-time work, 19 per cent part-time work, and 4 per cent were outside the labour market. As of 2008, 19 per cent of all employed Finnish women work part-time. Part-time work for mothers is not common in Finland; they more commonly work full-time or care for children at home on the home-care allowance (Hakovirta and Salin 2006).

The child home-care allowance is paid to all kinds of households with small children, but there are some differences among women as to how long they use it. Mothers employed before the leave return to employment faster than those with no job to return to. Therefore it is reasonable to argue that leave schemes create two categories of women: those with better education and employment status who are able to choose between shorter and longer family leaves, and those who are less educated or are in weaker labour-market positions who do not have such a choice (Salmi and Lammi-Taskula 2007, 91–92).

4.3.1.3. Explanation of the Main Features of Family-based Childcare in Finland

In Finland the share of informal childcare is relatively small because childcare is to a substantial degree provided by the welfare state. However, up to the age of about 1½, many children are cared for by their parents, mainly their mothers, in the family household. Otherwise women participate in the employment system on a full-time basis for nearly their whole working lives.

This behaviour of women, and the specific structures of formal and informal childcare, can mainly be explained in the context of welfare-state policies on one hand, and cultural values related to the family on the other. The welfare state offers a generous and high-quality system of public childcare to which every children has a social right. It also offers relatively generous paid parental leave schemes. At the cultural level, a relatively egalitarian dual-breadwinner/state-carer family model, with lifelong full-time participation of men and women in wage work, is dominant and forms the basis for the arrangement of work and family in Finland. It is based on a long historical continuity of full-time employment of women, including mothers of young children, as research has shown (Haavio-Mannila 1983; Simonen 1990). The especially universalist welfare state promoted women's rights, tending to view women's dependency on the state as less problematic than their traditional dependencies on a male breadwinner, family, community, charity, or employer and thus replaced these with a single dependency on the welfare state (Wrede and Henriksson 2005, 1).

From the institutional point of view there are good reasons to argue that gender divisions are changing, with a greater share of family care for men, and that promising options for reconciling the demands of family and work are emerging. But, in spite of generous welfare-state policies, dual-earner households with small children often face 'rush-hour' situations which make it difficult to cope with the lack of time, increased stress, and other problems of work-life balance (Ruuskanen 2007, 65). This is one reason families also seek out additional childcare services from the voluntary sector. This new kind of volunteering could be seen as one innovative feature in the childcare sector (Tommiska 2005; Kilpeläinen forthcoming).

4.3.2. Size, Patterns, and Explanation with Respect to Family-Based Eldercare

4.3.2.1. Welfare-state Policies and Institutional Framework

Finnish eldercare has gone through several transitions leading to institutionalisation and public-sector interventions in eldercare. The introduction of municipal home care during the 1940s was a remarkable new solution and gave birth to the new activity and profession of the public health-care nurse, who intervenes in private households, helping and counselling people in their care responsibilities. The work of these new professionals was recognised and defined as a social welfare service. In 1950 'municipal homemaking' became regulated by law, but it remained up to municipalities whether to hire homemakers. In the beginning this kind of service was targeted at families in difficulty, but the system was extended to elderly people in the late 1960s, when the Finnish welfare state adopted a more universalistic orientation, which can be seen as a turning point in the institutionalisation of eldercare. Before the expansion of the welfare state in the 1970s there were multiple producers of eldercare, including local parishes, municipalities, and voluntary organisations. This reform meant also the birth of two new professions and a restructuring of the boundaries between professional and informal work. The new care system created a new lower-grade occupation, 'home helpers', and their work was regulated by the municipalities. Unlike homemakers, who were trained at a young age in their jobs, home helpers were adults with backgrounds as housewives. Homemakers provided a more comprehensive social care, and home helpers were intended to replace nonqualified informal care (Wrede and Henriksson 2005, 4–5). Later on this system lost its capacity to respond to new needs and challenges.

Due to the structural and social changes, elderly people in Finland live separately from the younger generations and have residential autonomy; in some cases there is no substantial familial exchange of care. In 1999, 42 per cent of men and 80 per cent of women over the age of 75 lived alone. This structural precondition has increased the need for services and necessitates new arrangements in combining household care and institutional care. The rate of institutionalisation in eldercare has been traditionally high, but since the early 1980s Finnish health-care policy has also aimed at promoting independent living at home and reducing institutional care. Another reason for the institutionalisation of eldercare in Finland is that younger generations have no legal obligations to live with their elderly relatives or provide informal care for them, as they do in South-European countries. Finland is one of the countries where public provision is the commonest way of providing eldercare (Anttonen and Sointu 2006; Noro 1998; Association of Caregiving Relatives and Friends 2008).

Even though the share of institutionalised care for old people in Finland is comparably great, old people do not have any universal right to care services: access to municipal care services is means-tested and in practice always based on professional assessments. Therefore informal help (from children, relatives and spouses) can be considered a primary source of the help and care for elderly people. During the last few years the amount of institutional services to elderly people has even decreased while that of other, informal services has increased, but local authorities still have the main responsibility for providing social care services to older people (Anttonen and Sointu 2006). Local authorities organise residential care as well as home help for the elderly. Alongside municipal services there is a gradually increasing commercial care provision. Those who care for the elderly can apply for a benefit called the home-care allowance that is designed to promote noninstitutional care. Especially in rural areas, neighbourhood help plays an important role in service production for elderly people. It is estimated that the municipalities produce 25–33 per cent of all the help that elderly people receive, and relatives provide the rest (Repo 2001; Vaarama and Hurskainen 1993, 15; Forss et al. 1995, 16).

Despite the long history of the welfare mix in eldercare provision and the emergence of the 'new public management' policies since the 1990s, private businesses produce only a tiny part of Finnish social care, but its share is growing. Small private enterprises increasingly provide home-help services. They have been helped by the availability of tax reductions. Municipal subcontracting has also opened the market to larger companies which have started to operate in all the major fields of social care (Kröger et al. 2003.)

Almost half of the businesses offering home-help services report that cleaning is the service most in demand. After that come cooking, running errands, and assistance with commuting and transportation. Micro-enterprises in the home-help sector also receive requests for temporary childcare, window cleaning, baking, catering at parties, garden work, and regular cleaning. The potential producers of home-help services are municipalities, joint municipal authorities, municipal businesses, organisations, cooperatives, entrepreneurs, or families (Härkki et al. 2000, 16–17).

The 'caregiver allowance' is one form of combining formal and informal solutions. Older people are allowed to look after their grandchildren or elderly relatives for three years at home and have the right to receive a communal care grant for their efforts (Rissanen and Knudsen 2001). By the 1990s the Finnish home-care allowance for carers of elderly people was among the most comprehensive in Europe. However, it only reaches the carers of no more than 2 per cent of the over-65s. The eldercare work done in this framework can be called 'semi-formal care work' (Geissler and Pfau-Effinger 2005). It is mainly performed by relatives, in many cases spouses. As the level of the caregiver allowance is rather low (minimum €234 per month in 2005), the position of caregiver is not tempting. To avoid a new kind of poverty characterised by an increase in low-paid, semiformal care work performed by relatives without social rights and to prevent pay differences arising in home-care services and allowances between municipalities, the Ministry of Social Affairs and Health conducted an inquiry. In it they proposed the expansion of informal care in the health- and social-welfare sector with the aim of integrating it into the formal service structure (Aaltonen 2004). The inquiry also comprised a range of suggestions for developing family care as a way to improve outpatient and home care and to make care given by relatives an important part of social welfare and health services. The proposals included a target date of 2012, with a new law to be introduced in 2006, and responsibility for funding the family care compensation transferred to the state from 2007 to 2009. Municipalities are to continue to be responsible for supporting the new forms of semiformal care work done by family members, and the increase in such services as envisaged by the proposals is to be financed by money currently earmarked for formal services. The proposal also includes a recommendation that framework agreements and recommendations made by labour-market organisations should be implemented to enhance informal care through job alteration leave, reduced working hours, accumulated holiday time under the Annual Holiday Act, overtime leave, remote work, and so forth. If these reforms are implemented, the social rights of informal care-providers, whether family members, relatives, or acquaintances, will be significantly extended and formalised.

4.3.2.2. The Particular Size and Structures of Informal Eldercare

The most obvious difference between Finland and other European countries is in the frequency of providing eldercare. As most elderly people live apart from the younger generations in Finland, the share of family care given is smaller than in many other countriesm and, in most cases, people provide care for their frail elderly parents only temporally at particular life stages. Women and men over age 40 are more involved with eldercare than younger individuals are. Those who do not have children living at home, are widowed, or live alone for other reasons, and those who have flexible working time arrangements or work part-time, seem more likely to provide eldercare (European Working Conditions Surveys 2000, 2001).

Eldercare is in relatively great part provided by public or publicly paid services or in public residential care. However family members are also an important source of support and assistance for elderly people. The role of family members as mediators and representatives of the interests and needs of people in need of care is particularly important. In a system of several service providers and a specialised division of labour between them, organisers and interest-representatives may even play a key role in accessing adequate services (Koistinen 2003). It has been estimated that 70 per cent of all care of elderly people is informal and that there are about 300,000 family caregivers, of which approximately 40,000 are men. Many 'remote' caregivers also provide care for relatives or friends by calling daily or visiting evenings or on weekends. Many of these caregivers are actively engaged in paid work (Reconciling work and family 2005).

The role of nonstate providers for home-help services has remained significant, not in volume but in terms of new initiatives and innovations. Voluntary nonprofit organisations have led to the development of new forms and methods of providing services which tend then to be taken up by central and local authorities. The very idea of home-help services was originally developed within the voluntary sector. Nonprofit organisations have always worked in close cooperation with the public sector. Many of the not-for-profit service providers are also supported by funds from semi-independent associations. In these ways voluntary service provision for older people has become heavily integrated with public provision (Voutilainen et al. 2007, 162).

4.3.2.3. Factors Explaining the Specific Features of Informal Eldercare in Finland

The fact that a comparatively large share of eldercare is provided by public institutions, either in the private household of the person in need of care or in residential care, can mainly be explained in the context of the interaction of the social democratic welfare arrangement with the dominant cultural family model of the dual-breadwinner/state-care-provider family and the cultural values in this family model relating to eldercare.

The welfare state has a major responsibility for eldercare. Public authorities determine and subsidise the costs of eldercare in cooperation with family relatives, but the care itself is organised by nonprofit organisations, private households, and municipalities in combination. Finland is one of those European countries where the public or publicly financed provision of services for the elderly is on a high level. On the other hand it is culturally accepted that there is no legal obligation, or obligation based on cultural values, on the younger generation to take care of the older generations, or on spouses to be the exclusive carers of their frail elderly partners. Citizens are treated socially more as individuals than as members of a family. Generations often live apart from each other, so the possibility of taking part in informal care may be difficult.

However there is still a substantial share of informal or semiformal care work being done by family members. Most informal care continues to take place without any financial support from central government or local authorities, and the coverage of home-care allowance payments is much less than that of home-help services or residential care. For the time being the payments are too modest to motivate anyone to become a carer. In practice, the home-care allowance only seems to encourage relatives to continue the care work they had begun without financial support—just on the basis of the cultural value of family solidarity. In this way the home-care allowance is buffering the demand for formal services. It has been estimated that two out of three persons whose care has been supported under the scheme would otherwise have entered an institution (Kröger et al. 2003, 33).

4.3.3. Size, Patterns, and Explanation with Respect to Informal Employment

4.3.3.1. Informal Employment—Policies and Institutional Framework

Informal employment is not yet a really essential part of Finland's economy, but it seems that its share is growing somewhat. The most significant increase in partially or completely tax-free labour activities has been spawned by the greater prevalence of foreign workers and the recruitment of temporary workers from neighbouring countries. To make collective labour agreements universally valid for foreign temporary workers, too, the government, in cooperation with labour-market organisations, made new laws. Government measures to reduce undeclared work in households have been based primarily on eliminating incentives by lowering the taxation of labour and by making work carried out in households tax deductible (Kaseva 2007).

A nationwide project was launched against the underground economy in 2000 and will continue until 2009. The project's focus is on improving cooperation among various authorities (tax administration, police, and customs offices) in order to tackle undeclared work. It also has the support of the central social-partner organisations and some trade unions. Various other measures have been taken to combat undeclared work in Finland: In the last ten years the government has implemented four programmes to combat the underground economy, and in early 2004 a new underground economy unit was established at the National Bureau of Investigation (Kaseva 2007).

At the household level, the implementation of a 'domestic help credit' in 1997 has been another effective way to reduce informal employment. It allows a personal tax deduction for hiring home help, thus decreasing its costs (Tommiska 2005).

The Finnish Construction Trade Union and Confederation of Finnish Construction Industries have been actively seeking to curb illicit employment in the construction industry. They have agreed bilaterally that companies must demand proof of payment of tax and pension contributions from prospective contractors when they call for tenders. Information about contracts must be delivered quarterly to the tax administration, and electronic pass systems are required for workers and contractors at building sites (Social partners cooperate 2004).

4.3.3.2. Main Features of Informal Employment—What is Specific?

In most sectors of the economy, illegal or undeclared work was not widespread in 2004, but it is assumed that in the context of EU enlargement its share has been increasing significantly in the construction industry and private services. The majority of illegal workers in construction are Finnish nationals, but growing numbers of foreign workers are entering the clandestine labour market. Finland's informal economy is thought to be among the smallest in the EU, accounting for only about 4 per cent of GDP in 2004. In most sectors informal employment is not widespread, but its share is significant in the construction industry. According to available estimates 9–16 per cent (17–23 thousand man-years) of production in the male-dominated construction industry was performed illicitly in 1998. Informal employment is also a major concern in female-dominated sectors, such as in the hotel and restaurant sector, where an estimated 6–9 per cent of production was performed illicitly in 1998, amounting to 21,000 man-years of labour (European Industrial Relations Observatory 2004).

The central organisation of Finnish Trade Unions surveyed its members in 1997 and 2001, which revealed that in 1997 about 9 per cent of those asked were involved in informal employment. The share decreased to 6 per cent (60,000 people) in 2001. The people to whom informal employment had been offered were mostly already employed; such offers were not commonly made to the unemployed. Young men were also targeted more than were women or older men. Immigrant workers are more likely to be offered informal employment such as work on berry farms. During the short berry-picking season there is a sharp rise in the demand for labour in agriculture, but few Finns are attracted by the low pay and strenuous work involved. Therefore seasonal labour is recruited mostly from Russia, Estonia, Poland, and, increasingly, from Asian countries (Suomen ammattiliittojen keskusliitto 2001; Trade Union News from Finland 2001).

4.3.3.3. Explanations of the Specific Features of Informal Employment

Benno Torgler and Friedrich Schneider (2006) have analysed the factors that influence the individual's willingness to pay taxes. They use the term 'tax morale' to indicate individual attitudes towards paying taxes. It is assumed that there is a general moral obligation to pay taxes and a belief in contributing to society by paying taxes. The more involved citizens are in establishing the rules, the stronger their sense of obligation is, and if taxpayers trust state institutions they are more willing to be honest. Trust in the legal system, government, and parliament has a positive effect on tax morale. Finns trust the courts and legal system quite strongly (see section 4.1. in this chapter). This may contribute substantially to explaining the small share of informal employment in Finland. Also, Finns accept undeclared work only with great reservation. On average, the share of Finnish people who say that they find undeclared work absolutely unacceptable is considerably greater than that of people in the other study countries (Undeclared Work in the European Union, 44).[3]

As far as the assumption is correct that undeclared work has increased in Finland in the last couple of years, it can mainly be explained by the increase in migrant labour from new EU member states and by insufficient surveillance and awareness of undeclared migrant work in companies and households. This would support the assumption that periods of economic growth accelerate the increase in informal economy more than do periods of recession, at least in 'social democratic' welfare states. In times of recession the incomes of unemployed people are dependent on and regulated through social transfers, and there is little demand for extra work, but in times of economic boom the demand increases from private households prepared to buy services without paying taxes, and enterprises look for means to motivate employees to work more in the grey economy. In recent years trade unions, the Ministry of Social Affairs and Labour, and the health and safety authorities have put a high priority on attempting to find new ways of monitoring informal employment and especially illegal immigrant labour (Itäkangas 2007; Hirvonen 2007). Tightening surveillance may be a successful method. However welfare-state policies towards migration and the social rights that migrants have are also relevant (Parrenas 2001; Reyneri 2004).

4.3.4. Size, Patterns, and Explanation with Respect to Voluntary Work

4.3.4.1. Policies and Legal Framework

In 2003 there were 10,000 associations in Finland of which 7000 were registered. The association Act oversees the activities of associations and also their voluntary activities. Section 55 of the Occupational Safety and Health Act (23 August 2002/738) also gives some protection to people doing voluntary work; for instance it gives safety instruction in the workplace (Kumppani-lehti 5/2006).

In Finland the nonprofit sector was in a state of noticeable flux during the 1990s. The 1960s and 1970s, the decades of the building of a strong social-democratic, state-centred welfare model, did not offer fruitful ground for voluntary work. The economic depression of the 1990s brought nonprofit work and volunteering more into the focus of public interest. The overall need for social services grew, and the criticism strengthened against the welfare state. The nonprofit sector was more widely recognised as a chance to fill the gaps in service provision which the public sector had created by cutbacks (Yeung 2002).

Sports and recreation are the principal areas of volunteer work, involving almost half of the volunteers. In Finland 24 per cent of all pensioners have done voluntary work for an organisation; 5 per cent of retired men did voluntary work every week, spending almost three hours on it; 3 per cent of the women did voluntary work on average 2.5 hours per week (Niemi 2003; Yeandle et al. 1999, 22–25; Durán et al. 2000, 129).

4.3.4.2. What is Specific with Respect to Finnish Voluntary Work?

Various forms of civic activity have an important role in Finnish society. Voluntary activities are seen as a comprehensive civic activity comprising all kinds of activities such as unpaid voluntary work, rescue services, babysitter services, first-aid groups, youth, cultural, and sports activities, or common neighbourly help. The concept of voluntary work stresses the action of a person. Voluntary work may be done on an unorganised and nonregulated basis as support of others in family networks or other social networks (as in helping a neighbour or elderly relative), or in some organised context, for instance sports or religious associations. The voluntary work carried out in associations is differently regulated, for instance by means of membership (e.g., in sports or political associations) or other rules that associations follow in their voluntary work (Koskiaho 2001).

According to available studies (Ojanen 2005, forthcoming) it seems that men and women participate equally in voluntary activities, but there are differences in the fields of participation. Women participate more in social and caring fields, and men participate more in sports, politics, and trade unions (Ojanen 2005, forthcoming). The average amount of time Finnish people spent on voluntary work in Finland is estimated to be 18 hours per month (Socius-lehti 2004). Voluntary work is more common among higher-income groups, housewives, retired, and elderly people. It is estimated that 37 per cent of Finnish people participate in voluntary work: 30 per cent in sports associations, 25 per cent in health and social services, and 22 per cent in educational settings (for instance, parent associations in kindergartens and schools), which is a relatively large share compared with those of other European countries (Grönlund 2006).

Pensioners are a special group as receivers and contributors of voluntary work. According to the latest Time Use Survey (1999–2000), 33 per cent of pensioners interviewed said they needed help with cleaning, 23 per cent with shopping, and 12 per cent with cooking. The amount of help received increases with age. Whereas only one in ten of those age 65–74 living at home had received cleaning help, one pensioner in four aged 75 or over had been assisted with cleaning or help services. Pensioners not only receive help from others but many of them also give help to other households. According to Niemi (2003) 38 per cent of pensioners had helped a relative, friend, or neighbour during the four weeks preceding the interview. Men and women were almost equally keen helpers. The main recipients of the help were their own children or grandchildren. Every tenth pensioner aged 65 to 74 provides assistance in cooking and equally as many run errands on behalf of other families. The average time a person aged 65 to 74 spends daily on helping a neighbour is 15 minutes—20 minutes for men and 11 minutes for women. The amount of help given decreases with age, when the individual's own need for help increases (Niemi 2003). The most probable explanation for such activity is the fact that nowadays elderly people themselves feel more healthy and wealthy than ever before and have the resources to help others. These generations also remember times of shortages, which may have given them the skills and moral reasons for helping others.

The Equality Barometer has investigated the practice of giving and receiving practical help among households, that is, the existence of unofficial, mutual assistance among neighbours and friends. Women are more active in helping other households in matters relating to illness or infirmity and childcare, and men offer more help with transport, repairs and gardening. Voluntary work is more common in the countryside than in big cities: 44 per cent of people in the countryside participate in some form of voluntary work, whereas one-third of people in the biggest cities are involved in voluntary work (Härkki et al. 2000, 8–9; Grönlund 2006).

In Finland employed women are more involved with voluntary work than are employed men. It is not common for Finns to do voluntary work every day; they do it on a weekly or monthly basis. Finnish men and women participate in voluntary work more than do average European men or women, but there are differences in the frequency of participation (Ojanen 2005, forthcoming).

Finnish men are most involved with voluntary work when they are 65 and over; women are more active when they are younger. Finnish women participate in voluntary work at a younger age than European women on average. The highest proportion of Finnish women doing voluntary work is age 55–64. Finns age 15–24 years are also involved in voluntary work: 39 per cent do voluntary work, mostly in child-, youth-, sports-, or social- and health-related associations. The time spent on voluntary work is 19 hours per month in this age group (Grönlund 2006). According to Ojanen's (2005, forthcoming) results, participation in voluntary and charity work is highest among working women who can influence working time arrangements. One quarter of those who have flexible work hours participate at least monthly in voluntary and charity work. Altogether voluntary work plays a significant role both in supporting the Finnish welfare system and in promoting active citizenship and participation. Voluntary work seems to strengthen social networks among citizens and encourage them to interact further.

The motives for voluntary work change during the life course of individuals; young mothers for instance may spontaneously form baby clubs for the exchange of experiences and to help each other with childcare. The strongest motives for voluntary work are the wish to help and to make social connections. Other motives are a willingness to learn new things and skills and the desire to use one's time doing something important (Yeung 2004; Grönlund 2006).

4.3.4.3. Explanation of the Specific Structures of Voluntary Work in the Context of the Work-welfare Arrangement in Finland

Anne Yeung (2004) has investigated voluntary work in Finland; she thinks one reason for their quite high participation rate in voluntary work is that the country industrialised late, so the old traditions of agricultural life as a community effort are still in the collective memory of Finns. The participation rates for voluntary work are found to be higher in the countryside than in bigger cities.

There is another explanation, one that places the development of voluntary work into the overall context of the developing civil society. During the formative period of the Finnish welfare state and the extension of the third sector, local parishes, voluntary organisations, and informal social work was a very important innovative element for whole social policies. According to one of the founders of Finnish social policy as an academic discipline, Heikki Waris, it is even impossible to understand the rapid development of social policies without considering the active and innovative role played by voluntary organisations and the experts who worked in these organisations (1961, 22).[4]

In the economic recession of the 1990s, which was more severe in Finland than in other countries and caused difficulties in relation to public-sector social policy, the nonprofit sector and voluntary work became very timely issues. They were recognised on a larger plane to be a chance to fill the gaps in service provision created by the budget cuts in the public sector (Kiander and Vartia 1998; Helander and Laaksonen 1999). But surprisingly voluntarism and participation seem to continue even in times of economic prosperity. Reasons for such continuity may lie in the Finns' cultural and social traditions. There is a strong continuity of solidarity and mutual help, and secondly, elderly people are more healthy and active than ever before and so are able to contribute their social capital to the society. This conclusion is very much in line with the other comparative studies suggesting that motivation and structural incentives for volunteering were especially great in the Nordic countries, scant in Spain, and moderate in Germany (Hank and Stuck 2007).

4.4. THE SPECIFIC FEATURES OF FORMAL AND INFORMAL WORK IN THE CONTEXT OF THE WORK-WELFARE ARRANGEMENT IN FINLAND

In Finland informal work in general plays a rather minor role, for work there is mainly organised as formal employment. Finland can be characterised as a highly regulated 'public service' society in which all kinds of care work are organised mainly as formal work in the public sphere, whereas its share in private households is relatively small compared with the same in the other study countries. Childcare is to a large extent organised in public form, even if a considerable portion of children under age 3 are cared for by their mothers as semiformal care work in the context of various parental leave schemes. Public or publicly financed care is also very common in the field of eldercare. The majority of elderly people in need of care receive public care in residential homes or in their private households, though currently there seems to be some increase in informal (household) employment in the eldercare field. As the welfare state was expanding and adopted the principle of universalism in the late 1960s, eldercare became more or less a municipal responsibility. This led to the professionalisation of eldercare and a new division between formal and informal care work. Moreover a considerable portion of the population participates in voluntary work. There is a broad activity of mutual support in civil society, in organised forms in the nonprofit sector, as well as in unorganised forms. It seems that the welfare state is not supplanting voluntary work; by contrast, it seems that the portion of the population involved in such activities is even greater than that of other European countries, particularly those outside the Nordic area (Hank and Stuck 2007).

These specific features of informal work in Finland, and its relationship to formal employment, can to a substantial part be explained in the context of the specific arrangement of work and welfare based on the welfare state with its high level of decommodification and generous rights to social care, which in a relatively coherent way interacts with a work and family arrangement based on the cultural family model of the 'dual breadwinner/ state care-provider' family. It is also based on a long historical continuity of full-time participation of women, including mothers of young children, in productive work in rural areas and expanding industrial regions (Haavio-Mannila 1983; Kaarninen and Markkola 1991; Lahtinen 2007; Pfau-Effinger 2004) and on the early public response of municipalities towards institutionalising social welfare services (Wrede and Henrikson 2005). Accordingly, the family is in the Finnish welfare state not so much treated as a unit of adults and children with mutual obligations, but more as a cohabitation of individuals of different generations with comprehensive individual social rights in the welfare state, which is seen as the institution mainly responsible for the provision of childcare and eldercare. This provision extends to the comprehensive social rights of children up to age 6 to public childcare and of elderly people to publicly paid care services (Anttonen and Sipilä 2005; Kröger 2005). In this context there exists a broad consensus in the Finnish population that public childcare and eldercare must be provided at a level satisfying the demand for quality of all social strata (Anttonen and Sipilä 2005). Trust in the welfare state and public services is in Finland exceptionally high and consistent. Even though the economic hardships of the early 1990s caused the solidarity between better-off and worse-off groups of the population to waver, still the majority of the population seems to be very loyal to the welfare state and even willing to pay higher taxes if the tax revenues are earmarked for health expenditures, pensions and childcare (Forma et al. 2008).

Altogether, the structures of childcare and eldercare can be seen as the outcome of the choices that parents of small children and frail elderly people take between different options of semiformal and formal care. On the basis of the dominant cultural family model, women, like men, orient themselves to continuous full-time employment, so they can opt for high-quality public childcare. Still, half of all mothers stay at home also after the parental leave on the child home-care allowance until the child is 18 months old (Salmi and Lammi-Taskula 2007, 91–92). Some groups of women obviously prefer a period of parental leave over being very quickly employed again. This is different for fathers of young children, whose share in taking parental leave is increasing only very slowly.

The fact that undeclared work plays only a very marginal role in Finland can be explained by the relatively high degree of trust in the welfare state and the generous welfare benefits, which hinder 'poverty-escape' undeclared work from getting established. It also turns out, from analysis of the Eurobarometer data of 2006, that at the cultural level undeclared work is only to a comparatively low degree accepted in the population.

Though it seems that the welfare state is broadly supplanting undeclared care work, this is not the case with voluntary work, which plays a considerable role not only in the fields of sports, leisure, and culture, but also in the sector of social services. The role of nonprofit organisations and voluntary workers as providers of welfare services has gone through several changes as the society has changed. In the context of welfare reforms and policies of cutbacks since the 1990s, social services have developed into a wider institutional matrix which has given new impetus to nonprofit organisations and voluntary work. Nonprofit organisations which undertake voluntary work are partly seen as a supplement to the public welfare system (Ojanen 2005, forthcoming; Niemi forthcoming). This can be explained by the tradition of mutual support in rural areas, as well as by the particular history of the development of the Finnish welfare state, in which civil society has long played a substantial role.

NOTES

1. Finland is not in the ISSP 1998 survey. Some of this missing information is found in the European Social Survey 2002 and World Value Survey 2000 and is used in this analysis.

2. For the term 'semi-formal care work' see Pfau-Effinger 2005.
3. The respondents were asked to use the following scale: '1'means that you find it 'absolutely unacceptable' and '10' means that you find it 'absolutely acceptable'. The average score is 1.9 in Finland, compared with scores of 2.1 to 2.7 in the other study countries. It should be stressed that the data are only to a limited degree reliable, for the number of cases in each country was relatively low.
4. Waris (1961, 22) argued that 'Voluntary work and voluntary organisations . . . helped to defeat the most difficult national diseases like tuberculosis and they created a way for welfare and health service houses to cover the whole country and centralise maternity and child-welfare clinics under the responsibility of qualified nurses and midwives.'

REFERENCES

Aaltonen, E. (2004) *Valtakunnallinen omaishoidon uudistaminen*, Sosiaali- ja terveysministeriön työryhmämuistioita 2004:3, Helsinki: Sosiaali- ja terveys-ministeriö.

Anttonen, A., and Sipilä, J. (2005) 'Comparative approaches to social care: Diversity in care production modes', in B. Pfau-Effinger and B. Geissler (eds) *Care and Social Integration in European Societies*, Bristol: The Policy Press, 115–134.

Anttonen, A., and Sointu, L. (2006) *Hoivapolitiikka muutoksessa. Julkinen vastuu pienten lasten ja ikääntyneiden hoivasta 12:ssa Euroopan maassa*, Helsinki: Stakes.

Association of Care Giving Relatives and Friends (2008), *Care giving in Finland*, http://www.omaishoitajat.com/english.php?p=caregiving (accessed 16 February 2008).

Borg, S. (2005) *Kansalaisena Suomessa. Kansalaisvaikuttaminen Pohjoismaissa ja European Social Survey 2002*, Oikeusministeriön julkaisu 2005. Helsinki: Oikeusministeriö, 3.

Brandth, B., and Kvandle, E. (2001) 'Flexible work and flexible fathers', *Work, Employment and Society* 15:251–267.

Durán, M-A., Bonke, J., Garrido, A., Maruani, M., Angeloff, T., Parista, H., Vaiou, D., Georgiou, Z., Garcia Diez, S., Zambriano, G.P.P, and Pujalte, J. (2000) 'The future of work in Europe: Gendered patterns of time use', in *Gender Use of Time—Three European Studies*. Brussels: European Commission. Equality between women and men, 77–138.

European Industrial Relations Observatory 2004/6, http://www.eurofound.europa.eu/eiro/pdf/eo04–6.pdf (accessed 15 October 2004).

European network of the adult education organizations working on women's employment issues, http://www.women-employment.lt/finland.htm (accessed 14 September 2007).

Esping-Andersen, G. (1990) *Three Worlds Of Welfare Capitalism*, Cambridge: Polity Press.

European Working Conditions Surveys (2000, 2001). London: European Foundation.

Forss, S., Karjalainen, P., and Tuominen, K. (1995) *Mistä apua vanhana? Tutkimus vanhusten avuntarpeesta ja eläkeläisten vapaaehtoistyöstä*. Helsinki: Eläketurvakeskus, 3.

Forma, P. (2002) 'Does economic hardship lead to polarisation of opinions towards the welfare state?', *Journal of Social Policies* 31:187–206.

Forma, P., Kallio, J. Pirttilä, J., and Uusitalo, R. (2008) *Kuinka hyvinvointivaltio pelastetaan. Tutkimus kansalaisten sosiaaliturvaa koskevista mielipiteistä ja valinnoista*, Sosiaali- ja terveysturvan tutkimuksia nro 89, Helsinki: KELAn tutkimusosasto.

Geissler, B., and Pfau-Effinger, B. (2005) 'Change in European care arrangements', in B. Pfau-Effinger and B. Geissler (eds) *Care and Social Integration in European Societies*, Bristol: The Policy Press, 3–19.

Gender Equality Barometer (2004) Publications of the Ministry of Social Affairs and Health. Helsinki.

Grönlund, H. (2006) *Vapaaehtoistoiminnan haasteet tämän päivän Suomessa*, http://www.kansalaistalo.fi/jelli/pdf/Henrietta_Gronlund.pdf (accessed 11 April 2008).

Haataja, A. (2007) 'Parental leaves, child care politics and mothers' employment in Finland and Sweden: A comparison', in R. Myhrman and R. Säntti (eds) *Opportunities to Reconcile Family And Work*, Reports of the Ministry of Social Affairs and Health 16:103–115.

Haavio-Mannila, E. (1983) 'Economic and family roles of men and women in northern Europe: A historical and cross-national comparison', in E. Lupri (ed.), *The Changing Position of Women in Family and Society: A Cross-national Comparison. International Studies in Sociology and Social Anthropology 34*, Leiden: Brill.

Hakovirta, M., and Salin, M. (2006) 'Valinta vai pakko? Kansainvälinen vertailu äitien preferoiman ja toteutuneen työmarkkina-aseman yhteydestä', *Janus* 14:255–271.

Hank, K., and Stuck, S. (2007) *Volunteer Work, Informal Help and Care among the 50+ in Europe*, DIW, Discussion Papers 733.

Härkki, T., Kauppinen, K., and Raijas, A. (2000) *Employment, Family and Community Activities: A new balance for women and men. Finland*, http://www.eurofound.europa.eu/pubdocs/2000/115/en/1/ef00115en.pdf (accessed 12 May 2004).

Helander, V., and Laaksonen, H. (1999) *Suomalainen kolmas sektori. Rakenteellinen erittely ja kansainvälinen vertailu*, Helsinki: Sosiaali- ja terveysturvan keskusliitto.

Hirvonen, M. (2007) 'Rakennusalan harmaa talous', unpublished presentation, 27 February 2007.

ISSP (2002) Family and Changing Gender Roles III. [Questionaire]. http://www.fsd.uta.fi/english/data/catalogue/series.html#issp (accessed 1 December 2008).

Itäkangas, J. (2007) *Harmaan talouden valvonta Suomessa*, http://www.tyo-suojelu.fi/upload/vickiqbb.pdf (accessed 27 September).

Joronen, T. (1994) 'The availability of female labour in the local labour market of Helsinki during the 1980s', in P. Koistnen. and I. Ostner (eds) *Women and Markets*, Tampere: University of Tampere.

Julkunen, R. (1990) 'Women in the welfare state', in M. Manninen and P. Setälä (eds) *The Lady with the Bow. The Story of Finnish Women*, Helsinki: Otava, 140–160.

Julkunen, R., and Nätti, J. (1999) *The Modernization of Working Times. Flexibility and Work Sharing in Finland*, Jyväskylä: SoPhi.

Kaarninen, M., and Markkola, P. (1991) '"vergiss nicht seine wackere Hausfrau . . .": historische Frauenforschung in und über Finnland', in B. Fieseler and B. Schulze (eds) *Frauengeschichte: Gesucht—Gefunden? Auskünfte zum Stand der historischen Frauenforschung*, Köln: Böhlau.

Kaseva, H. (2007) *Article on Undeclared Work from SYSDEM Correspondent*, European Employment Observatory, http://www.eu-employment-observatory.net/resources/reports/FinlandUDW2007.pdf (accessed 12 March 2008).

Kautto, M., Fritzell, J., Hvinden, B., Kvist, J., and Uusitalo, H. (2001) *Nordic Welfare States in the European Context*, London: Routledge.

Kiander, J. (2004) *Growth and Employment in Nordic Welfare States in the 1990s: A Tale of Crisis and Revival*, VATT Discussion Papers 336.

Kiander, J., and Pehkonen, J. (1999) 'Finnish unemployment: Observations and conjectures', *Finnish Economic Papers* 12: 94–108.

Kiander, J., and Vartia, P. (1998) *Suuri lama: Suomen 1990-luvun kriisi ja talouspoliittinen keskustelu*, Helsinki: ETLA B 143.

Kilpeläinen, R. *Pienen lapsen hoiva valinta ja neuvotteluprosessina* (forthcoming).

Koistinen, P. (2003) *Hoivan arvoitus*, Tampere: Vastapaino.

Koistinen, P., and Sengenberger, W. (eds) (2002) *Labour Flexibility. A Factor of the Economic and Social Performance of Finland in the 1990s*, Tampere: Tampere University Press.

Korpi, W., and Palme, J. (2003) 'New politics and class politics in welfare state regress: A comparative analysis of retrenchment in 18 countries', *American Political Science Review* 97:425–446.

Koskiaho, B. (2001) 'Sosiaalipolitiikka ja vapaaehtoistyö', in A. Eskola and L. Kurki (eds) *Vapaaehtoistyö auttamisena ja oppimisena*, Tampere: Vastapaino, 15–40.

Kröger, T. (2005) 'Hoivaköyhyys yksihuoltajaperheissä: kenelle lastenhoito-ongelmat kasautuvat?', in P. Takala. (ed.) *Onko meillä malttia sijoittaa lapsiin?* Helsinki: Kelan tutkimusosasto, 206–232.

Kröger, T., Anttonen, A., and Sipilä, J. (2003) 'Social care in Finland: Stronger and weaker forms of universalism', in A. Anttonen, J. Baldock, and J. Sipilä (eds) *The Young, the Old and the State. Social Care Systems in Five Industrial Nations*. Cheltenham: Edvard Elgar, 25–54.

Kuhnle, S., and Hort, S.E.O. (2004) *The Developmental Welfare State in Scandinavia. Lessons for Developing World*, Social Policy and Development Paper Number 17. United Nations Research Institute for Social Development.

Kumppani-lehti (2006) *Pohjolan epäitsekäs kansa*, 3 May 2006.

Lammi-Taskula, J. (2007) *Parental Leave for Fathers? Gendered Conceptions and Practices in Families with Young Children in Finland*, Research Report 166. Helsinki: STAKES.

Lahtinen, A. (2007) 'Mägde und weibliches Gesinde 1300–1600', in M. Rahikainen and K. Vainio-Korhonen (eds) Arbeitsam und gefügig. Zur Geschichte der Frauenarbeit in Finnland, Berlin: BWV Berliner Wissenschafts-Verlag.

Leira, A. (2002) *Working Parents and the Welfare State. Family Change and Policy Reform in Scandinavia*, Cambridge: Cambridge University Press.

Litmala, M. (ed.) (2004) *Oikeusolot 2004: katsaus oikeudellisten instituutioiden toimintaan ja oikeuden saatavuuteen*. Oikeuspoliittisen tutkimuslaitoksen julkaisuja 201, Helsinki: Oikeuspoliittinen tutkimuslaitos.

Melkas, T. (2005) *Gender Equality Barometer 2004*:11, Helsinki: Ministry of Social Affairs and Health Publications.

Ministry of Social Affairs and Health (2006) *Finland's Family Policy*, Ministry of Social Affairs and Health brochures:12.

Niemi, I. (2003) 'Active or passive ageing?' paper presented at IATUR Conference on Time Use Reseach. Comparing Time, Brussels, September 2003.

———. 'Eläkeläisten taloudellinen ja sosiaalinen aktiivisuus', in P. Koistinen (ed.) *Työn Hiipuvat rajat* (forthcoming) .

Noro, A. (1998) *Long-term Institutional Care among Finnish Elderly Population. Trends and Potential for Discharge*, Research report 87, Helsinki: STAKES.

Occupational Safety and Health Act (2002) No. 758/2002.

OECD (2006) *Economic Survey of Finland 2006*, http://www.oecd.org/document/21/0,3343,en_2649_201185_36546453_1_1_1_1 ,00.html (accessed 14 September 2007).

Ojanen, M. (2005) *Työssäkäyvien osallistuminen vapaaehtoistyöhön ja vanhusten hoivaan eräissä Euroopan maissa*, Sosiaalipolitiikan Pro-Gradu tutkielma, Tampere: Tampereen yliopisto.

——. *Participation of Employed Workforce in Voluntary Work and Informal Care in Seven European Countries* (forthcoming).

Parental Leave in European Companies. Establishment Survey on Working Time 2004–2005 (2007), Dublin: European Foundation of Work and Living Conditions.

Parrenas, R. S. (2001) *Servants of Globalization. Women, Migration and Domestic Work*, Stanford: Stanford University Press.

Pfau-Effinger, B. (2004) *Development of Culture, Welfare States and Women's Employment in Europe*, Aldershot: Ashgate.

——. (2005) 'Welfare state policies and the development of care arrangements', *European Societies* 7:321–347.

Publications of the Ministry of Social Affairs and Health (2003) *Government Resolution Concerning the National Policy Definition on Early Childhood Education and Care* 2003:9.

Reconciling Work and Family Care Giving Project 2002—2005, http://www.omaishoitajat.com/top/index-engl.html (accessed 15 March 2005).

Repo, K. (2001) *WP3 Care arrangements in multi-career families. National report: Finland*. SOCCARE-project, http://www.uta.fi/laitokset/sospol/soccare/report3.1.pdf (accessed 10 October 2003).

Reyneri, E. (2004) 'Immigrants in the segmented and often undeclared labour market', *Journal of Modern Italian Studies* 9:71–93.

Rissanen, T., and Knudsen, C. (2001) *The Child Home Care Allowance and Women's Labour Force Participation in Finland 1965–1998, A Comparison with Norway*, Norsk Institute for forskning om opverks, velferd og oldring, NOVA, Skrifteserie 6/01, Oslo.

Ruuskanen, O.-P. (2007) 'Work-life balance in a European context: What does harmonized time use data tell us?', in R. Myhrman and R. Säntti (eds) *Opportunities to Reconcile Family and Work*, Reports of the Ministry of Social Affairs and Health 16: 63–86.

Salmi, M., and Lammi-Taskula, J. (2007) 'Family policy, labour market and polarization of parenthood in Finland', in R. Myhrman and R. Säntti (eds) *Opportunities to Reconcile Family and Work*, Reports of the Ministry of Social Affairs and Health 16:87–102.

Simonen, L. (1990) *Contradictions of the Welfare State, Women and Caring. Municipal Homemaking in Finland*, Tampere: Acta Universitas Tamperensis ser A, vol 295.

Simonen, L., and Kovalainen, A. (1998) 'Paradoxes of social care restructuring: The Finnish case', in J. Lewis (ed.) *Gender, Social Care and Welfare State Restructuring in Europe*, Aldershot: Ashgate.

Social partners cooperate to tackle undeclared work in construction (2004), http://www.eurofound.europa.eu/eiro/2004/o6/feature/fi0406202.htm (accessed 3 April 2008).

Socius-lehti (2004) *Vapaaehtoistyö meillä yllättävän yleistä*, 8 November 2004.

Statistics of Finland (2006) Labour Force Statistics.

Suomen Ammattiliittojen keskusliitto (2001) *SAK:n jäsenkysely*, Tutkimustietoa 2/2001.

Time Use Survey (1999-2000) Statistics Finalnd.

Tommiska, K. (2005) *Users and Providers of the Informal Work. A National Report for FIWE-project*, Discussion Paper 10, Hamburg: University of Hamburg.

Torgler, B., and Schneider, F. (2006) *What Shapes Attitudes toward Paying Taxes? Evidence from Multicultural European Countries*, Discussion Paper Series, Institute for the study of labour, IZA no 2117.

Trade Union News from Finland (2001) *Six per cent of SAK rank and file have experience of moonlighting*, http://www.artto.kaapeli.fi/unions/archive (accessed 21 September 2004).
Undeclared Work in the European Union (2007) Euro-barometer. Brussels: European Commission.
Vaarama, M., and Hurskainen, R. (1993) *Vanhuspolitiikan tulevaisuuskuvat ja kehittämisstrategiat*, Raportteja 95, Helsinki: STAKES.
Voutilainen, P., Kauppinen, S., Heinola, R., Finne-Soveri, H., Sinervo, T., Kattainen, P., Topo, P., and Andersson, S. (2007) 'Katsaus ikääntyneiden kotihoidon kehitykseen', in M. Heikkilä and T. Lahti (eds) *Sosiaali- ja terveydenhuollon palvelukatsaus 2007*, Helsinki: STAKES.
Waris, H. (1961) *Yhteiskunnalliset muutokset ja kunta*, Helsingin yliopisto, Sosiaalipolitikan laitos, Tutkielmia 16.
Wrede, S. and Henriksson, L. (2005) 'The changing terms of welfare service work: Finnish homecare in transition', in M. Dahl and T. Rask Eriksen (eds) *Dilemmas of Care in the Nordic Welfare State. Continuity and Change*, Aldershot: Ashgate, 62–79.
Yeandle, S., Gore, T., and Herrington, A. (1999) *Employment, Family and Community Activities. A New Balance for Women and Men*, Dublin: European Foundation.
Yeung, A.B. (2002) 'Civil society, social capital and volunteering in Finland. Contemporary trends in the Finnish volunteering, With specific focus on motivation and commitment', paper presented at Fifth International Conference of The International Society for Third-Sector Research (ISTR), Cape Town, July 2002.
———. (2004) *Individually Together: Volunteering in Late Modernity: Social Work in the Finnish Church*, Helsinki: The Finnish Federation for Social Welfare and Health.

5 Formal and Informal Work in the Work-Welfare Arrangement of Germany

Birgit Pfau-Effinger and Slađana Sakač Magdalenić

INTRODUCTION

Scientific discourses that address 'work' as a research subject primarily focus on gainful employment, that is, the sphere of formal work. Informal work has for a long time been regarded as a remnant of precapitalist traditional society which will be eradicated in the ongoing modernisation process of developed societies. We by contrast start with the assumption that the role of informal work is different, that it is the 'other side' to formal employment in modern postindustrial society. We argue here that the development of postindustrial society can be adequately analysed only if the relationship and interaction between formal employment and informal work is studied (see also Chapter 1 in this volume).

Our aim in this chapter is to analyse and explain the particular structure of informal work in Germany. The central questions are:

- What are the specific features of informal work in Germany?
- How can these be explained in the context of the specific arrangement of work and welfare in German society?

Germany has been classified as a 'conservative' welfare regime by Esping-Andersen (1990, 1999), and as a 'strong male-breadwinner state' in feminist discourse, for example by Lewis (1998). Therefore one would assume that the overall share of informal work is large. However, since reunification, Germany exhibits a substantial division with respect to informal work: There is significantly more of it in the West of Germany than in the East. And in the West, substantial change in welfare-state policies towards informal work has taken place in that its formalisation has been strongly supported.

In our first section, we describe the arrangement of work and welfare in Germany. Then we outline the main features of the diverse forms of informal work in Germany—family care for children, family care for elderly people, informal employment, and voluntary work. The particular features of informal work in Germany are explained by the interaction of cultural, institutional, and structural factors in the arrangement of work and welfare in Germany. The chapter ends with a few conclusions.[1]

5.1. THE ARRANGEMENT OF WORK AND WELFARE IN GERMANY

The arrangement of work and welfare is defined here as the complex—and often also contradictory—profile of the interrelations of culture, institutions, social structures, and social actors in a specific region, society, or group of societies (Pfau-Effinger 2001, 2005a, and in this volume). The arrangement of work and welfare in Germany after World War II was characterised specifically by:

- a relatively strong welfare state of a 'conservative' type (Esping-Andersen 1990, 1999);
- the dominance of a housewife model of the male-breadwinner family and the prominent role of the family in the provision of social care (Pfau-Effinger 2004);
- the division between West and East German society which continues to exist even though welfare-state policies after reunification have been mainly dominated by the cultural and institutional setting of West Germany.

Integration into formal employment, from the beginnings of the Federal Republic of Germany and the former GDR, was always the main basis for the social security of individuals. The conservative welfare regime of West Germany was strongly based on employment-based social insurance and in this respect was directed towards the reproduction of the existing hierarchical structures of social inequality (Kaufmann 2004). The social security of those parts of the population that were not integrated into employment, such as married women and children, was derived from the social status of the male head of the household, who acted as breadwinner. Social policy in the former GDR by contrast was directed towards a high level of social equality and full-time integration of women and men into employment. Complementarily, the government had established a comprehensive infrastructure of public childcare provision.

Since the 1990s, welfare-state policies in Germany have gone through substantial change, in part based on a strengthening of economic efficiency and market principles in the social security system and social services. Also, in public discourse about the welfare state, the principle of self-reliance of citizens vis-à-vis the welfare state has been emphasised, and social rights based on the traditional social insurance system weakened (Lessenich 2005; Jensen and Pfau-Effinger 2005). A particularly strong break in continuity took place at the time of the Red–Green government in the first years of the new millennium. In 2005, in the framework of the 'Hartz IV' legislation, unemployment benefits for those unemployed one year or longer were no longer calculated on the basis of their former income level, but cut down to a means-tested flat-rate benefit at the poverty line (Aurich 2007). As a consequence, poverty rates of the unemployed and child poverty have greatly increased.[2]

In cross-national social policy analyses it has been often emphasised that policies favouring social care in West Germany mainly rely on the role of the family for the provision of social care (Esping-Andersen 1999) and that the German welfare state therefore is to be classified as a 'strong male-breadwinner regime' (Lewis 1998). This was clearly true until the 1970s. However, in the field of family policies, since the 1980s substantial change has taken place. The picture is much more complex now. Social rights in relation to care have been greatly extended, including the social right to receive care and the right of parents to give care (according to the definition of Knijn and Kremer 1997). Even though public support of childcare services and family childcare has been extended, the proportion of social expenditure on childcare and eldercare to GDP (3 per cent) is still smaller than in Nordic countries such as Denmark (5.8 per cent) and Finland (4 per cent). What is also different in the Nordic countries is that state finances for childcare are used more for financing family care than for childcare services (see Table 1.2, Appendix 1).

These changes in family policies reflect the change of the dominant cultural family model that has taken place in the West-German population: from the *housewife model of the male-breadwinner family* towards a *male-breadwinner/female part-time carer model* (for the concept of the classification of family models see Pfau-Effinger 2004 and Chapter 2 in this volume). In the *housewife model*, housework and care were seen as the specific task of the housewife who did not participate in wage work. *The male-breadwinner/female part-time carer model* by contrast is based on the value of equal participation of women and men in wage work. However, if there are dependent children in the household, it is expected that the mother should take the main responsibility for childcare, take parental leave, and afterwards be employed part-time during 'active motherhood', sharing the task of caring with other institutions outside the family, such as mainly publicly funded organisations in the nonprofit sector. This presupposes the financial dependency of mainly women who care at home for others—mostly on husbands, who, after the principle of family subsidiarity, are seen as responsible for family maintenance (Pfau-Effinger 2004).

The arrangement of work and welfare was based on rather different principles in the former GDR. The main aim was to achieve social equality and gender equality based on the full inclusion of women in employment already in the 1950s and 1960s, which in West Germany was the golden age of the housewife marriage (Dölling 1993). In the GDR, the freedom of citizens to organise in civil society vis-à-vis the state had been all but destroyed. Then after reunification, during the transformation of the postsocialist society of East Germany, central elements of the West-German social structures and welfare state were implemented (Offe et al. 1996). They were often not adapted in their original West-German form and were considerably modified. The role of the state vis-à-vis the family and civil society is therefore still stronger in East Germany compared with West Germany. Even though social inequality has increased in the East—visible mainly in high unemployment rates—it is still less pronounced than in West Germany. The degree of gender equality is also higher, for the tradition of women's inclusion in full-time employment has survived. This reflects the cultural ideas about the 'best' family form: It is still based on a 'dual breadwinner/state care-provider model', as well as on the public or publicly financed provision of childcare, which is still more comprehensive in East than in West Germany (Pfau-Effinger and Geissler 2002).

The German welfare state started taking increased responsibility for the care of elderly people later—with the government-introduced Long-term Care Insurance Law of 1996 (Social Security Code XI [SGB XI])—than for childcare. This law established the social right of elderly people to get care if in need and new social rights, including pay, for care-giving relatives or family members who assume responsibility of elderly people.

In general, family and civil society are traditionally seen as important counterparts to the state in Germany, and the 'autonomy' of these spheres vis-à-vis the state has been an important value. Complementarily, the general confidence of the German population in political institutions is relatively low, and only at an average level compared with the other FIWE countries: Only 13 per cent say they have confidence in the parliament, whereas that proportion is 20 per cent in Denmark and 22 per cent in Spain. The confidence of the population in parliaments is only lower in Great Britain and Poland (both 6 per cent; see Table 3.1, Appendix).

The idea of the private sphere being autonomous of state control is also reflected in the way in which 'informal employment' (or 'undeclared work') is institutionally framed.[3] On the one hand, the prohibition of undeclared work in sectors such as construction or transport is strictly enforced because it is thought to seriously undermine wage regulation. Undeclared work within the private household, on the other hand, because mainly in the field of 'female' activities such as housework and care-giving, is combatted much less and, though formally prohibited, goes practically unpunished.

German civil society plays a large role in the provision of welfare as well. Such provision is mainly the traditional social care services organised primarily by churches and big welfare associations. These main pillars of social service provision in Germany assume tasks in the public interest which are contracted and mainly financed by the state. However, in the 1980s and 1990s, new, small grassroots organisations in civil society gained importance as providers of social care services. In this context voluntary work—besides formal employment in the nonprofit sector—has always also been part of the provision of social services. Accordingly, voluntary work has traditionally been encouraged and strengthened by the welfare state in West Germany. In East Germany, by contrast, there were nearly no civil organisations apart from the state and the central party. Civic activities were mostly included in this official system. As far as voluntary work existed, it had a very different character in comparison to voluntary work in West Germany, for it was seen as a duty of the citizen towards the state and community (Evers 2005).

5.2. DEVELOPMENT OF FORMAL EMPLOYMENT

With respect to the labour-force participation rate (75 per cent) and the employment to population ratio (67.2 per cent), Germany takes a medium position among the countries in the study, even though since the early 1990s there has been a considerable increase in the labour-force participation rate (since 1994 by 4.5 per cent point) and also some increase in the employment to population ratio (since 1994 by 2.7 per cent point; see Tables 4.1 and 4.2, Appendix 3). That these rates are not higher is often explained by the fact that the share of employment in social services is still below the European average, which contributes substantially to the overall 'service gap' in the German economy (OECD 2002).

To understand the particular structures of formal employment in Germany, however, the differences between the labour markets in the West and East of Germany should be considered. The labour-force participation rate in East Germany (79.2 per cent) is considerably higher than that of West Germany (71.1 per cent). This is mainly due to the fact—a carry-over from the former GDR—that women participate to a substantially higher degree (67.2 per cent) in formal employment in the East than women in the West (56 per cent). The fact that the employment to population ratio of women is higher in East Germany (67.7 per cent) than in West Germany (60 per cent) also contributes to explaining why the overall employment to population ratio is higher in East Germany (70.1 per cent in the East versus 66.2 per cent in the West) (Statistisches Bundesamt 2005a, based on Mikrozensus 2004).

The part-time employment rate of women (the proportion of women in part-time employment to all employed women) in Germany (39.2 per cent) is higher than that of all other countries in the study (Table 4.4, Appendix). This can mainly be explained by the particular working time pattern of mothers in West Germany, who are mostly part-time employed if they participate in the labour force: According to the Microzensus data from 2004, 40 per cent of mothers with children in their household are part-time employed in West Germany, whereas the share is 22.7 per cent in East Germany (Statistisches Bundesamt 2005b). The share of mothers in full-time employment in West Germany is only 16.6 per cent, compared with 44.6 per cent in the East.

Mass unemployment already existed in the 1980s in West Germany, where the unemployment rate was 8 per cent at the beginning of the 1980s (OECD 1997, 163). It had decreased considerably by the end of the 1980s to 4.8 per cent because of the temporary boom after the fall of the Berlin

Wall (OECD 2002, 303). After the unification however, the labour market entered a crisis that mainly affected East Germany: the general German unemployment rate rose to 8.3 per cent in 1994 and reached 10.4 per cent by 2006. The German women's unemployment rate of 10.3 per cent hardly deviates from the general rate. The unemployment rate of East Germany alone is particularly high—14.2 percent, compared with 7.8 per cent for West Germany alone (Statistisches Bundesamt 2007).

5.3. MAIN FEATURES OF INFORMAL WORK

Informal work in general plays a relatively great role in Germany in comparison to other north-west European countries. There are considerable differences between the West and East of Germany, though. The share of informal family childcare is substantially higher in West Germany. Also, in the field of long-term care for elderly people, informal and semiformal family care plays a prominent role. In this field, differences between West and East Germany are relatively marginal. Germany in general could be classified as a 'home-care' society, preferring care given exclusively by family members, even though the options for external care performed by agencies have been substantially improved through the Long-term Care Insurance Law of 1996 (Social Security Code XI [SGB XI]).

Concerning the amount of informal employment in Germany, it is at a medium level compared with the other countries integrated in the study on 'Formal and Informal Work in Europe' (FIWE). It is markedly segregated between two types of informal employment which differ substantially in their main features, and which also overlap with the clear gender segregation of the field. Also, with respect to the share of the population participating in voluntary work, Germany is at a medium level compared with the other FIWE countries.

5.3.1. Policies, Structures, and Explanation with Respect to Family-Based Childcare

5.3.1.1. Welfare-state Policies and Institutional Framework

In family policies on childcare there was an extension of social rights related to care since the 1990s. Children three to six have an individual right to a place in a kindergarten. This group was extended in some Federal Republic states to include two-year-olds, and the 'Great Coalition' (the Christian Social Union and Social Democratic parties) government approved a substantial overall increase of public childcare for this age group in 2007 (Pfau-Effinger 2008). In 2007 the government also introduced a modified parental leave scheme (Elterngeld). The means-tested, flat-rate benefit scheme for childcaring parents of monthly payments of €300 for two years was replaced by an income substitute of 63 per cent of the previous income and a means-tested, flat rate of €300 for low-income earners for one year (see also Pfau-Effinger 2008). Women who are well established professionally in the employment system profit from this in that they can be financially autonomous care-givers and do not have to rely on the income of a male breadwinner, in contrast to low-income women.

5.3.1.2. Amount and Structures of Informal Childcare

General Structures

Concerning the proportion of children under six years cared for outside the family household by any kind of formal organisation, Germany ranks in the middle field among the countries in the study. The share of children under age three years enroled in public childcare is particularly low (9 per cent)—lower than in most of the other study countries except Poland. And even though there is a right to publicly financed childcare for all children age three to six, the actual portion of children of this age group is considerably below 100 percent: The share of children age four in publicly financed childcare is 84.3 percent, and for those age five, 86 per cent (Table 5.1, Appendix).

There are however substantial differences between the East and West of Germany. According to the Socio-Economic Panel (SOEP) of 2005, in West Germany 94.9 per cent of children under three years are exclusively cared for at home by their own parents. This is different for children age three to six years: Three-quarters of the children in these age groups are cared for in kindergartens (75.3 per cent), and 4.1 per cent by child-minders. For a majority of these children (69.7 per cent) the care is provided part-time and limited to morning hours (see Table 5.1).

The use of public childcare is much more common in East Germany. 26.4 per cent of children under three-years-old are cared for in kindergartens. The number of those cared for by child-minders is 2.6 per cent. More than one third of these children are in care full-time (37 per cent). In West Germany, in this age group only 15.2 per cent of the children are cared for full-time. Of children from three to six years in East Germany, even 90.2 per cent are using public childcare, and nearly two-thirds are in full-time care (59.9 per cent) A higher proportion of East-German schoolchildren receive external care provision than West German schoolchildren (18.8 per cent in the East versus 3.3 per cent in the West; see Table 5.1).

The Relationship of Formal Employment to Informal Childcare

In West as well as East Germany, the majority of mothers with children under three (77 per cent) do not participate in formal employment (see Figure 5.1). The majority are on parental leave (47 per cent); a smaller group are not employed (28 per cent). However the share of those who are employed full-time is more than twice as high in East Germany as in the West (12 versus 5 per cent). The differences are much greater among mothers of children

Table 5.1.   Organisation of Childcare in Germany, 2005

| | West Germany | | | East Germany | | |
	Under 3	3–6	School-age 6–12	Under 3	3–6	School-age 6–12
Care in institutions						
Kindergarten/after-school care	1.8	75.3	3.3	26.4	90.2	18.8
Day-care with child-minder	2.5	4.1	1.0	2.6	2.3	2.7
School	0	0	100	0	0	100
None of these	94.9	22.2	0	72.0	7.5	0
Institutions: care hours						
Morning	72.4	69.7	90.0	47.9	32.9	63.0
Afternoon	12.4	3.3	0.1	0	0	0.4
Whole day	15.2	26.0	9.4	37.0	59.9	31.5

Source: Socio-Economic Panel (SOEP) 2005, FIWE calculation by P. Borsdorf.

between three and six years. Here, the share of those who are employed is considerably larger in the East (64 per cent) than in the West (53 per cent). Also, the share of those who are not employed because they are seeking a job, or officially unemployed, is much higher among East-German mothers (23 versus 8 per cent). And mothers in West Germany, compared with East-German mothers, work much more in part-time jobs (43 versus 29 per cent). The share of those who are not employed (but do not define themselves as 'unemployed' either) in West Germany is 39 per cent among mothers of preschool children of three to six years, whereas it is only 12 per cent in East Germany. However in East Germany the share is substantially higher in this group who are officially unemployed (23 versus 9 per cent in the West). The differences between West and East Germany in relation to mothers of schoolchildren are similar to those found for mothers of preschool children.

The relatively large share of mothers in West Germany who take the full period of parental leave and/or take up part-time employment in order to care for their children cannot be explained mainly by the existence of gaps in the public provision of childcare. According to the European Social Survey of 2006, 75 per cent of German women say that the amount of public childcare provision they use is about right. Those who are not satisfied most often think—at least in West Germany—that the hours are too short and inflexible, according to a representative survey by the German Agency for Labour (Bundesagentur für Arbeit 2002; Esch/Stöber-Blossey 2002; Beckman/Engelbrech 2002). Most parents would prefer kindergarten hours somewhere between part-time and full-time, but do not want full-time provision

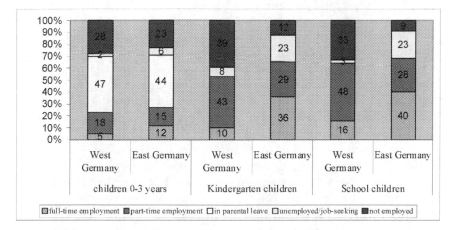

Figure 5.1. Labour-force participation of women with children for West and East Germany in 2000. Source: IAB-Project 3–523, 2000 after Beckmann/Engelbrech 2002.

of public childcare. As far as findings exist from qualitative interviews in which women in West Germany are asked why they want to work part-time, they show that the main reason is that they want time with their children. They also want to limit their children's external childcare, for many think it better for the children to spend their afternoons at home (for a summary see Pfau-Effinger 2004).

5.3.1.3. Explanation of the Main Features of Family-based Childcare in Germany—High Proportion in the West, Low in the East

Characteristic of informal care work in West Germany is that it is to a substantial degree provided by parents within the private household. This can to a substantial part be explained by the family policies. The public provision of care for children under three is relatively scarce, and it is therefore very difficult for women with children under three to be employed. But it is possible for parents to take parental leave for three years, though until 2007 only two years were paid (from then on only one year is paid for the main care-provider). Also, parents have a legal right to temporarily work part-time at their job. The welfare state has thus established some options and restrictions that can reinforce the employment pattern of mothers based on the cultural family model of the male-breadwinner/female part-time care-provider. However there are also disincentives to such behaviour, in that women in part-time work are often excluded from career advancement, and their income levels are below the poverty line. Also, those who conform to this pattern have a high risk of poverty in old age (Meyer and Pfau-Effinger 2006).

That a relatively large proportion of childcare is provided by mothers within the family household cannot be explained by welfare-state policies alone. The specific cultural context in Germany also contributes to the explanation. A majority of women in West Germany share the cultural values of the dominant male breadwinner/female part-time care-provider family model, according to which a 'good childhood' is based on strong elements of 'private childhood'. The high rate of parental leave-taking for the full three years, as well as the large portion of mothers working part-time in West Germany—in spite of the risk of poverty connected with it—also reflects the orientation to this cultural model. It should also be considered that the majority of mothers are satisfied with the amount of external childcare provision or at least do not want their children to be looked after externally full-time.

However a substantial portion of women who are mothers in West Germany would prefer to work part-time instead of not being employed. This is particularly also true for women with a relatively low level of qualification and fewer chances of employment (Bosch 2002). The supply of part-time jobs is, however, also too small for the demand. Even though the 'Red–Green' government introduced the right of childcaring parents to work part-time, this right only extends to those employed by medium and large firms and only for a child's first three years. It therefore does not apply to women who work in small firms, which is the majority of employed women in Germany or to those women who are not employed longer than three years (ibid.).

In the same institutional context of the German welfare state, the majority of mothers in East Germany choose a substantially different employment behaviour based on shorter periods of parental leave and full-time employment afterwards. This shows that the family policies leave options for a broad variety of patterns in which mothers act in relation to the employment system. The main reason this employment behaviour in the East is so different from that in the West is that, at the cultural level, a different family model dominates in the East—'the dual breadwinner/state care-provider model' (Pfau-Effinger and Geissler 2002). Full-time public childcare that starts in early childhood is seen as the best solution for bringing up children. Table 7.1 (Appendix) reflects these differences and shows that in East Germany the general attitude in the population is far more in favour of wage work for mothers than it is in the West. In East Germany the portion of those who think that women as well as men should contribute to the household income is substantially higher (91.2 per cent versus 66.1 per cent); the share of those who think that the man's job is work and woman's the household is smaller (14.6 per cent versus 23.2 per cent). East Germans in a clearly lower proportion think that a preschool child suffers if its mother is employed (32.7 per cent versus 55.8 per cent), and the share of those who think that the family life will suffer in this case is also much smaller (28.2 per cent versus 47.8 per cent). Accordingly, the portion of the population that thinks mothers of children under school age should stay at home is far smaller in East Germany (14.8 per cent versus 52 per cent), and the East also supports in a much higher proportion the full-time work of mothers (34 per cent versus 3.2 per cent). These data show that cultural differences in the work-family arrangement of East and West Germany largely explain the differences in the proportion of informal childcare in both parts of Germany (Pfau-Effinger 2004). The differences in the cultural traditions of childcare in East Germany also cause childcare policies at the local and federal state level to be different, in that there is more public care-provision and, again different from West Germany, it is most often full-time. This also was the result of strong pressure from parent interest groups on the policies of the federal states in East Germany after reunification: These groups wanted to maintain the fairly generous care-provision of the GDR period (Pfau-Effinger and Geissler 2002).

5.3.2. Amount, Patterns, and Explanations of Family-Based Eldercare

5.3.2.1. Welfare-state Policies and Institutional Framework

The German insurance for eldercare has been a compulsory part of the German social insurance system since 1996 and is part of the Social Security Code XI (SGB XI). It is financed by universal insurance contributions from ancillary wage costs, with both employer and employee paying 0.85 per cent of the employee's gross wage. The right to financing care from this insurance is universal: All citizens are included. The benefits of care insurance vary according to categorisation into care-need levels by the medical assessment department of the health insurance companies.

The different assessment levels are defined as follows:

- Level I—considerable need of care (care for 90 minutes a day, of which at least 45 minutes is personal care);
- Level II—substantial need of care (120 minutes per day);
- Level III—most substantial need of care (minimum of 5 hours of care per day, of which at least 4 hours are personal care).

Those in need of long-term care can opt for care-provision from a commercial external provider of long-term care (benefits in kind), or they are cared for by their own relatives, partners, or friends (benefits in cash). The latter option was established by the care insurance law as a semiformal form of care given by relatives or friends, which is paid in relation to the degree of fragility of the elderly person at the rather low rate of about one euro per hour (Pfau-Effinger 2005b).

The specific benefit amounts paid depend both on the medical assessment level and the form of care the recipient has chosen (cash benefits and care provided by the family, home-based nursing services, or residential care):

- Care benefits (care provided by family members) Level I: €205, Level II: €410, Level III: €665;
- Nursing services (home based): Level I: €384, Level II: €921, Level III: €1432;
- Residential care: Level I: €1023, Level II: €1279, Level III: €1432.

5.3.2.2. The Particular Extent and Structures of Informal Eldercare

Care provided exclusively by family members is still the dominant form of long-term care in Germany. Its proportion has only marginally decreased since the 1990s, from 67 per cent in 1991 to 64 per cent in 2002 (TNS Infratest, BMFS 2002–end of the time series).

According to data for Germany for the year 2002, 2.04 million people needed long-term care. Of these about 70 per cent were cared for in private households, and the other 30 per cent, in residential settings.[5] Here the differences between East and West Germany are smaller than those in relation to childcare. However, the share of people in need of care who are in residential care is greater in East Germany; it is 27 per cent in the West and 37 per cent in the East (Schneekloth and Müller 2000).

Among those who are cared for in the private household, the majority (72 per cent), are cared for exclusively by family members, or—in a relatively small minority—by neighbours or friends. The proportion has only relatively marginally decreased from 80 per cent in the year 1996 to 72 per cent in the year 2006 (see Figure 5.2).

The other 28 per cent are cared for in addition, or exclusively, by employees of in-house care agencies organised by the nonprofit sector or by for-profit providers. It is surprising that there has been so little change in this and that the share of those who opt for professional care from agencies introduced by the Long-term Care Insurance Law of 1996 is still relatively small. In general, the share of people of working age who are caring for the ill, disabled, or elderly in their own private households is also greater in Germany than in the other West-European countries in the study (Germany 15 per cent, UK and Spain 11 per cent, Denmark 5 per cent); it is higher only in Poland (18 per cent; see Table 6.1, Appendix).

Sociodemographics of Care Recipients and Providers

The great majority of long-term carers in the private household are female. According to a representative survey by Schneekloth and Müller (2000), the proportion of women among principal carers in private households is 83 per cent. These are mostly wives and daughters of the people in need of care. Particularly interesting is that a majority of these long-term carers of relatives or friends are themselves already relatively old: According to Schneekloth (2006), about two-thirds of in-family care-providers are older than 55 and about one-third are older than 65.

Interrelation Between Informal Care and Gainful Employment

Those who provide semiformal care within the framework of the Long-Term Care Insurance Law in the private household do not in most cases participate in the employment system (77 per cent, see Schneekloth and

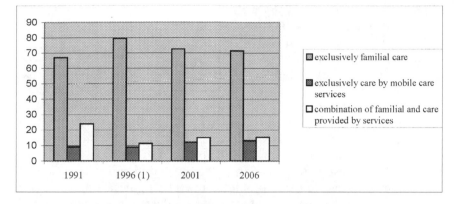

Figure 5.2. Structure of home-based eldercare in Germany, 1991–2006 (in percent). Source: Schneekloth, 2005; Deutscher Bundestag, 2008; Pfau-Effinger et al., 2008.

Müller 2000). Among the 33 per centpecent who are employed, only 10 per cent have full-time jobs, 5 per cent combine the care with 'marginal' employment with considerably reduced job hours, and 7 per cent have part-time employment of at least half of the normal working time (Schneekloth and Müller 2000). This can be largely explained by the relatively large proportion of older people among the care-providers.

5.3.2.3. Explanations for the Relatively Large Share of Informal Eldercare in Germany

The German Nursing Care Insurance Law of 1996 (Social Security Code XI [SGB XI])gives elderly people and their relatives the choice of long-term care performed only by family members in the private household or external, professional long-term care services. The law created a new, semiformal care form based on some pay and integration into the social security system for family care-providers, and thus an incentive for family members—mainly spouses and daughters or sons—to care for their frail elderly relatives. It also opens the option of care given by care services. This option has not been chosen as much as was expected, and long-term care in private households still predominates.

This can be largely explained by the interaction of the incentives for family members to give care and the fact that, in Germany, family care of elderly people is highly esteemed. As Table 7.2 (Appendix) shows, approval of family-based solutions (such as children having their parent live in their home or moving into, or at least closer to, their parent's home) is only higher in Spain (76.4 per cent) than in both parts of Germany (West, 57.4 per cent East, 51.2 per cent); in the other countries studied it is lower. By contrast, a solution whereby the elderly person moves into a care residence or receives paid care through an agency is much more highly valued in Denmark (75.4 per cent) and Finland (67.2 per cent) than in the West and East of Germany (31.5 per cent and 37 per cent).

Cultural values surrounding the quality of life in old age, what constitutes a good quality of long-term care, and moral obligations felt particularly by spouses are crucial to explaining the specific structure and the important role of direct care assumed by relatives, at least in West Germany. These cultural traditions are based on the idea that the best long-term care is guaranteed by close relatives who 'care with their heart' and not mainly because they are paid for it (Pfau-Effinger, Eichler and Och 2007). Correspondingly, mainly daughters and spouses are seen as the persons responsible for and able to provide the best long-term care. Accordingly the great majority of family care-givers say that they provide care voluntarily (98 per cent in the East versus 92 per cent in the West, see Rothgang 1997). This tendency is reinforced by the fact that spouses of elderly people are often pensioners and stay mostly at home anyway (Eichler and Pfau-Effinger 2007).

Germany in general can be classified as a 'home-care' society which deeply values the personal loving care of a relative and considers it the optimal form of old-age care. Still, in East Germany the portion of elderly people in residential care is substantially larger than in the West. Two different factors might contribute to an explanation. For one thing, the average supply of flats was considerably smaller in East Germany than West Germany at the start of the new millennium. It is inconvenient for many adult children of elderly people to have them, or other relatives, live with them in their flats. For another, there are differences in attitudes towards the care of elderly people. From interviews of carers in East and West Germany, the author found that the care of relatives is seen less as a family responsibility in East Germany than in West Germany (Eichler and Pfau-Effinger 2007).

5.3.3. Amount, Patterns, and Explanation with Respect to Informal Employment

5.3.3.1. Informal Employment—Policies and Institutional Framework

Undeclared work became a particular issue in Germany mainly with the beginning of the postsocialist transformation of Central and Eastern European countries (CEE), as an increased flow of often illegal, temporary, or commuting immigrants into Germany took place. This process substantially contributed to extending the supply of workers taking undeclared work for low pay.

The Red–Green government then started strengthening policies against undeclared work in sectors like construction, transport, and restaurants. A new type of centralised authority was established, in which the public administration, police, customs, and National Labour Office (Bundesagentur fuer

Arbeit) began working together. Also, as an incentive for employers to transform undeclared work into formal employment, the instrument of the so-called 'mini jobs' was introduced by the Red–Green government in 2003. Here, employers were to pay a flat-rate tax and social security of 31 per cent for employees not earning more than €400 per month, and the employees did not have to pay contributions. In order to decrease particularly the share of nonregistered employees in private households, this rate was even reduced to 15 per cent for private households acting as employers of workers in mini-jobs. It should be mentioned however that this is a slightly modified version of the so-called 'insurance-free jobs' that had existed since the 1960s (Büchtemann 1989).

5.3.3.2. Main Features of Informal Employment—What is Specific?

The proportion of informal employment in Germany is larger than in other West-European countries; however, estimates are substantially higher for Southern European countries including Spain, and for Eastern Europe in general (Table 8.1, Appendix).

At the same time, estimates of the amount of informal employment in Germany vary substantially—between 4.1 per cent according to questionnaire-based survey data and 16 per cent on the basis of indirect methods of estimation. The figure proposed by Schneider (1997, 34) and Schneider and Enste (2000) is based on an indirect estimation of the size of the 'shadow economy' on the basis of currency flows. According to this, the share of revenue from informal employment in the GDP has increased from 2.7 per cent in 1970 to 10.3 per cent in 1980 and to 15.0 per cent in 1997.[6] On the basis of the same type of estimation Cyprian (2003)[7] came to the conclusion that by 2002, the amount of earnings from informal employment had increased to 16.3 per cent of GDP.[8] Furthermore in estimates made by the IAB (Institut für Arbeitsmarktforschung der Bundesanstalt für Arbeit), informal employment increased by 38 per cent between 1990 and 2002 (Cyprian 2003). However information on the actual share of informal employment earnings compared to that from other types of activities within the 'shadow economy' (such as, according to Schneider and Enste (2000), nonmonetary transactions of goods and services and tax evasion on property or capital gains) is missing. Therefore the estimates of these authors on the extent and development of informal employment are not very reliable.

Pedersen (2003), using survey data, came to rather different conclusions: Using a questionnaire survey in 2001 he found that 10.4 per cent of those interviewed in Germany had carried out so-called 'black work'. This corresponds to a 4.1 per cent share of GDP, which is much lower than Schneider's estimate, but slightly higher than in the other countries in the same survey. It should be stressed though that migrants were not interviewed, and private households were highly underrepresented in the data.

In Germany, there are two main forms of informal employment:

- undeclared work, through which mainly unemployed persons with low unemployment benefits, and immigrants with restrictions on entering formal employment, try to escape poverty; also called the 'poverty-escape type' (Pfau-Effinger, forthcoming);
- undeclared work performed mainly by male professionals and craftsmen in addition to their jobs in formal employment in order to increase the affluence of their households, but not as their main source of employment income, also called the 'moonlighting type' (Pfau-Effinger, forthcoming).

Here we outline the ways in which each type is differently connected with the economic and social structures of society.

The Particular Size, Extent, and Structures of Informal Employment

The principal economic sectors for the poverty-escape type of informal employment are relatively unregulated and are characterised by low-skilled jobs, low productivity, and relatively high fluctuation in demand; they are rather decentralised, such as the construction, transport, and restaurant sectors (Baumeister et al. 1990; Portes and Castells 1999); and they are composed of smaller firms rather than large ones (Portes et. al. 1989; Blair and Endres 1994). Also, private households are a main group of users of this type of informal employment, primarily for domestic work.

It seems that in Germany the proportion of informal employment corresponding to the 'poverty-escape' type is particularly high. This is supported by the comparative representative survey of the Rockwool Foundation for Denmark, Germany, and the United Kingdom. In these findings the share of informal employees for whom informal employment is the only source of employment is considerably higher in Germany than in the other countries. Also, the average amount of time per week that workers spend in informal employment is considerably higher (8 hours, 14 minutes in Germany versus 5 hours, 10 minutes in Denmark and only 3 hours, 48 minutes in Great Britain (Pedersen 2003, 105). Moreover, the share of those who work in informal employment is particularly high among the unemployed in Germany at 20.7 per cent compared with 9.9 per cent in Denmark and 9.2 per cent in the United Kingdom. (Table 8.1, Appendix).[9] In addition, participation in informal employment is more common in the lowest income group in Germany when compared with the other two countries (Pedersen 2003, 83). The income from informal employment in Germany is nevertheless the lowest among the three countries. In Germany hourly wages of informal employees are €10.3, substantially lower than that in Great Britain (€14.4) and Denmark (€15.7) (see Pedersen 2003, 85).

It seems that the sector of private households is the largest sphere of informal employment of the 'poverty-escape' type. According to data from the 'Socio-Economic Panel', at least 11 per cent—about 3.5 million (Schupp 2002)—of all households in Germany employed one domestic worker in 1999, but the number of households declaring the employment of domestic workers was only 38,000 in 2000. From this gap it can be concluded that the great majority of these work relationships (about 3.46 million) were informal, that is, unregistered employment (Schupp 2002). Also, according to the data of the 'Socio-Economic Panel', for a majority (88 per cent) of informally employed domestic workers, informal employment was their only job (Schupp 2002). And according to more recent analyses by Renooy (2007), the share of informal employment in private households has not decreased in spite of government measures aimed at reducing it.

Typical employers are upper middle-class couples: Both spouses work and therefore they employ a working-class woman—unemployed or a housewife or a migrant—to perform household tasks that are culturally constructed as 'female' (Geissler 2002). Undeclared household work is often precarious, for it is based on low pay, and the workers do not have any rights under labour law and social security. They also have rather little negotiating power.

The poverty-escape type also includes many immigrants without a work permit, or unemployed on a low level of unemployment benefits, and/or rigid restrictions on earning additional income in formal employment, who want to earn additional money—though illegally—in order to avoid poverty. These groups can access only employment that is undeclared. Therefore it can be assumed that the 'mini-job' legislation as a substitute for 'social insurance-free jobs' was not a very efficient method of transforming undeclared work into formal employment.

The private household is not the only sector where migrants are informally employed. The construction and restaurant sectors are also well known for informal employment of migrants. However it seems that the private household sector is the largest employer of migrants, mainly women (Geissler 2002; Hillmann 2005; Lutz 2002). Even if domestic work requires little skill, this does not necessarily mean that the workers themselves are low skilled. In particular, migrant women from Eastern Europe are often well educated, in many cases even holding university degrees (Lutz 2002).

The moonlighting type is a strategy of professional employees, mainly craftsmen and self-employed professionals in technical areas, for a kind of additional income-generating activity besides formal employment, mainly in the fields of construction, repair, and services. This is also the conclusion of an empirical study conducted in a region in the north-west of Germany in the late 1980s. Private households are their main informal employers (Siebel et al. 1988). The relatively great importance of 'moonlighting' in this direct survey corresponds to the large share of informal employment in the indirect data-based estimates for the fields of construction, renovation, and repair found by Schneider and Enste (2000) in 1997 and 1998. In their findings 44 per cent of informal employment is in this sector. It is mainly a 'second shift' performed by the workers in addition to their 'first' job in formal employment.

Undeclared 'moonlighting' is also strongly bound to the long tradition of highly professionalised craftsmanship in the arrangement of work and welfare in Germany. Moonlighters are mainly male citizens of German origin. Their contracts with the users (employers) are usually of undeclared self-employment, in contrast to their main job, which is most often regular dependent employment. This contractual status of self-employment usually means relatively great autonomy in the relationship with the 'user' of the work and therefore in many cases also relatively great negotiating power (Siebel et al. 1988).

Analysis shows a clear segmentation between moonlighting and poverty-escape informal work sectors. Professional, qualified, self-employed moonlighters have relatively good contractual conditions. Those in the poverty-escape sector have low-skilled, badly paid, and unprotected forms of informal employment, and the income is the main source of a living. This segmentation overlaps with the gender and ethnic segregation of the division of labour.

5.3.3.3. Explanation of the Specific Features of Informal Employment

It seems that the general distrust of public institutions typical in Germany is a main factor contributing to a relatively high tolerance in the population towards informal employment and to explaining the relatively high amount of undeclared work in Germany in general.

Several more factors contribute to the explanation for the prevalence of the two main types of undeclared work in Germany We begin with those relating to the relatively high prevalence of the 'poverty-escape' type. They include:

Strong barriers towards the formal employment of migrants. For immigrants from countries outside the European Union, and from the new Central European member-states, there are considerable restrictions to becoming German citizens and accordingly, legal barriers to participation in formal employment. As a consequence there is a relatively high proportion of 'tolerated' immigrants and of illegal immigrants, neither of which groups has the right to take up formal employment. Since German reunification moreover, new forms of migration from Central and Eastern European countries have developed, such as temporary stays of persons on tourist visas, and among these, the proportion seeking undeclared work is relatively high (Lutz 2002).

Enduring mass unemployment with relatively low-level unemployment benefits. As mentioned in 5.3.3.2 there was already mass unemployment in the 1980s in West Germany, and it increased in the 1990s in both parts of Germany (Table 4.3, Appendix 3). Unemployment benefits are also at the poverty-line level for married women and for long-term unemployed. According to a current survey on the financial situation of the unemployed, 40 per cent of the unemployed were poor in 2002 (Schupp 2002),[10] and this share has increased substantially with the introduction of the 'Hartz IV' law in 2005. These unemployed groups form another basis for the recruitment of undeclared workers by firms and private households.

Insufficient provision of childcare by the welfare state. The discrepancy between public childcare provision on one hand—often limited to half-day provision—and the need of the families who often would prefer two-thirds of a day, means substantial dilemmas for mothers, as it is often difficult to combine public childcare and part-time formal employment (Pfau-Effinger 2001, 2005b; Pfau-Effinger and Geissler 2002). Employing cleaning ladies and child-minders is used to bridge this inadequacy. Taking up employment as a cleaning lady/child-minder is one type of unde-clared, poverty-escape work.

The factors that contribute to explaining the relatively strong development of the 'moonlighting type' of undeclared work are, in part, different. They include:

The role of high social insurance contributions and taxes due on an additional, second (formal) employment. For workers with a second job in addition to their regular employment, it would be possible to make a contract for a 'mini-job', if the pay were not more than €400 per month. However, such a second job could substantially increase their taxes because the German tax system is based on progressive taxation. Also, the employer has to pay 30.1 per cent social security contributions for somebody who is employed in a mini-job (www.minijob-zentrale.de). In case of a decision to take a second job, this can be an incentive to prefer informal employment.

The strong tradition of professional craftsmanship. The escape to moonlighting by craftsmen in this context may also be explained by the strong regulation in the field of crafts work which prohibits self-employment by craftsmen not holding the 'Handwerksmeister' (master craftsman) qualification, which is awarded after rather demanding additional education following the standard three years of professional education (Schneider 1997; Siebel et al. 1988).

5.3.4. Extent, Patterns, and Explanations with Respect to Voluntary Work

5.3.4.1. Policies and Legal Framework

The role of voluntary work in the German welfare state changed in the 1990s, with the fiscal crisis mainly caused by German reunification. On one hand, the new ideal of the state administration, inspired by the concept of 'New Public Management', led to a strengthening of principles of control, efficiency, and quality and a weakening of the practice of using the work of volunteers (Evers 2005). At the same time, a new discourse based on communitarian thinking emerged among social scientists and political elites, where the use of voluntary work was seen as a new option for solving problems of employment and social services provision in times of scarce finances. The need to support voluntary work was high on the agenda (Beck 2000; for a discussion see Effinger and Pfau-Effinger 1999).

5.3.4.2. What is Specific in Voluntary Work?

About one-third of the German population participate in voluntary work (Dathe and Kistler 2002). In West Germany, the share of the population doing voluntary work has substantially increased since the middle of the 1980s, from 22.6 to 32.5 per cent; it is about one-third now. In the former GDR and just after unification the share of those providing voluntary work was substantially smaller (1994: 18 versus 25 per cent). During the process of transformation in the postsocialist era it has grown continuously and was 26.7 per cent in 2005, which is however still considerably less than in West Germany (Socio-Economic Panel; FIWE project calculations by P. Borsdorf).

Traditionally, voluntary work in West Germany is organised within the big welfare organisations of the nonprofit sector. Since the 1980s new grassroots, self-organised forms of voluntary work in civil society have been established, mainly in the cultural and ecological sectors (Mutz 2002, 23). The proportion of this type of voluntary work is about 13 per cent (Bundesministerium 2000), and it is most common in sports, charity work including social affairs, health, schools/kindergartens, church activities, leisure, and culture (Enquete-Kommission Bürgerschaftliches Engagement, 2002, 95).

The Relationship of Voluntary Work to Formal Employment

Specific to voluntary work in Germany is that only about one-third of the voluntary workers are gainfully employed (West Germany 32.6 per cent, East Germany 32.6 per cent). In West Germany the share of both nonemployed or officially unemployed persons is much higher (nonemployed 28.6 per cent, unemployed 24.9 per cent); in East Germany the share of both groups is considerably lower (non-employed 21 per cent, unemployed 20.4 per cent) (Socio-Economic Panel 2005 and FIWE project calculations by P. Borsdorf).

In general, voluntary engagement increases with the level of education (Priller 1996, 290 for the former GDR; Bundesministerium für Familie, Senioren, Frauen und Jugend 2002, 47 for the whole of Germany). The engagement level of men as volunteers is slightly higher than that of women. The structures of voluntary work are gendered: Men are usually active in voluntary work besides having full-time employment and mainly engage in politically or professionally related voluntary work, often in leadership roles, which can also contribute to improving their professional reputation and career chances. Women who volunteer are much more often not employed or part-time employed, and their activity is most often in charity work and social services (Dathe and Kistler 2002, calculations by SOEP, Socio-Economic Panel). According to Reichert (2000, 42) women do more groundwork, whereas men are more often active in leading positions.

5.3.4.3. Explanations for the Specific Structures of Voluntary Work in the Context of the Work-welfare Arrangement in Germany

Voluntary work in West Germany is firmly rooted in the strong civil society and principally helps with the provision of social services through the churches and big welfare associations. It is also related to the tradition of the male-breadwinner model of the family, in which older housewives, in particular, participate in voluntary work. This also corresponds to the traditional cultural construction of gender differences and gender hierarchies in the male-breadwinner family model, in which it is men who should have a career, and women are the gender responsible for altruism and care-giving. Therefore the share of people providing voluntary work in West Germany was substantially larger than in East Germany after reunification, where substantial parts of the civil society and its cultural importance were uprooted during the GDR era. Also, the tradition of the male breadwinner family model no longer exists in East Germany.

5.4. CONCLUSION: THE RELATIVELY PROMINENT ROLE OF INFORMAL WORK IN THE CONSERVATIVE WORK-WELFARE ARRANGEMENT OF GERMANY

As we have outlined, informal work in general plays a relatively great role in Germany in comparison to other north-west European countries. The share of informal childcare work is medium among the study countries, but greater than in the Nordic study countries. There are considerable differences between West and East Germany: The share of family-based childcare is substantially higher in West Germany. In the field of long-term care for elderly people, informal and semiformal family care is the predominant form of care-provision in both parts of Germany, even after the option for external care by agencies was substantially extended with the Long-Term Care Insurance Law of 1996. Still, residential care of elderly people is more common in East Germany than in West Germany.

Informal employment in Germany is strongly differentiated: There is a precarious, low-income type of dependent employment at a low-skill level, which specific social groups of unemployed or immigrant women and men take in order to avoid poverty, and another type, most often based on self-employment and mainly performed by male professionals or craftsmen for extra income beyond that from formal, full-time employment. In both cases, firms as well as private households use the labour to avoid paying taxes and social security contributions. This basic differentiation overlaps with the strong gender segregation of the work involved. A relatively strong gender segregation is also seen in voluntary work, where men are more active in leading positions in politically and professionally oriented voluntary work in stages of life when they are full-time employed, and women are more often active when they are housewives, part-time employed, or retired and often perform groundwork in the social-service sector.

The differences in the proportions and structures of informal work in West and East Germany can mainly be explained by differences in the institutional and cultural traditions which together form the specific arrangement of work and welfare in both parts of the society. The traditions related to the dominant cultural model and structures of the family, and the way these are framed by welfare-state policies, especially contribute to explaining the relatively great role and the particular structures of informal work in West Germany. The relatively large share of informal childcare in West Germany can to a fair extent be explained by the ways in which the dominant cultural model of the family and the institutional context interact. A male-breadwinner/female part-time care-provider model of the family is dominant. In this model, children need the care of their mothers or parents at least in part in their own home when they are very young and in general in the afternoon. A majority of mothers are oriented in their employment behaviour towards this model and organise their labour-force participation on the basis of long parental leaves and part-time employment. The parental leave system, the school system, and the public childcare system are organised around this model, even though up to today, the opening-hour structures of public childcare in part do not well match the needs of part-time working mothers.

There are considerable differences in the ways families manage childcare in East Germany, even though the institutional framework of welfare-state policies is the same as West Germany's. The majority of the population in East Germany continues to be oriented towards the 'old'—but today still predominant—cultural family model of GDR times, which is a dual-breadwinner/state care-provider model. Women act in accordance with this model in that they choose relatively short parental leaves and full-time employment afterwards, even when it is not always possible to realise this orientation in times of high unemployment in East Germany. Additionally, the institutional framework of school hours and public childcare is organised on the full-time principle. This is also a main reason that the share of undeclared household work in private households is much smaller in East than in West Germany. In general, therefore, we can also speak of 'two different Germanies' in relation to the extent and role of informal childcare.

This also partly explains why the level of undeclared work, particularly in private middle-class households, is relatively high in West Germany and not in the East. The increase in undeclared work performed by immigrants has in part contributed to modifications in the private care arrangements in family households. It is in some parts used to bridge the daily intervals between the job hours of the parents and childcare institution or school hours of the children.[11] Accordingly, the undeclared work of immigrants has increasingly become a crucial element in realising the new middle-class lifestyle mainly in West Germany—a lifestyle based on a male-breadwinner/part-time female care-provider family model (Hillmann 2005; Pfau-Effinger, forthcoming).

The dominance of the cultural model of the male-breadwinner/female part-time carer family also helps explain how the majority of elderly people in need of care in West Germany can be cared for exclusively by family members. Another explanation is that family care-givers can receive some pay if they care for their elderly relatives. Financial incentives alone, however, do not explain the prominent role of the family, for the pay that relatives can receive is clearly lower than income from employment, and the law also gives private households access to funding for care from outside agencies.

The differences between East and West Germany are smaller in the field of long-term care for the elderly than those regarding childcare. In eldercare Germany can generally be called a 'home-care' society, in which priority care is that provided only by family members in the private household, even after options for external care by care agencies were greatly improved by a Long-Term Care Insurance Law in 1996. That the share of family care is large in East and West Germany, and the differences relatively small between both parts of Germany, can be explained by the fact that in GDR times, the state did not take over substantial eldercare tasks, as it did for childcare, but left the matter mainly to families, and so the traditionally strong orientation in the German population towards family care did not change much during those times. However the share of elderly people cared for in residential care settings is greater in East Germany. This can be explained by the fact that average-size flats are smaller in East Germany, so that offspring of elderly people are less likely to choose the option of live-in parents. Another reason is that the value of family care is less well anchored in the East German population, even though the differences between West and East Germany in relation to eldercare seem less significant compared to those concerning childcare.

Along with the family, civil society traditionally plays a relatively great role vis-à-vis the state in West Germany, in contrast to East Germany, where the civil society was severely weakened in the GDR. This is another reason that the share of the population doing voluntary work is relatively great in West Germany and greater than that in the East. Voluntary workers contribute to the provision of social services through the big welfare associations in West Germany, who also employ professionals. The gender hierarchies and roles characteristic of formal employment, based on the cultural model of the male-breadwinner/female part-time carer, are also reflected in the gender segregation of voluntary work.

Another main feature of the arrangement of work and welfare in Germany is that it is based on a 'conservative' welfare regime (Esping-Andersen 1990, 1999). This means that integration into formal employment is not only the main basis for an income, but also the main basis of social security. The consequence is that those social groups who do not work continuously in full-time employment have a particular risk of poverty when they are getting unemployment benefits or pensions because the benefits are low. This is one factor—together with strong legal restrictions against employment of immigrants and other specific factors—explaining why the share of undeclared work in Germany, particularly the 'poverty-escape' type of undeclared work, is relatively great. The fairly high contributions to the social insurance system that employers have to pay, on the other hand, help explain why the 'moonlighting' type of informal employment is also rather widespread.

Another reason why undeclared work, particularly in private households, is relatively prevalent in Germany is that the family is seen as a kind of autonomous sphere which should not be controlled by the state. Another factor might be that the general confidence of the population in political institutions is, as mentioned, relatively weak, at least when compared to that of the populations of the Nordic study countries. However it is significant that undeclared work in Germany is only at an average level in comparison with the other study countries and that it is not particularly attractive to wide sections of employers and employees—in contrast to other countries, such as Poland or Spain.

NOTES

1. 'Informal work' is defined here as 'the production of goods and services which take[s] place outside formal employment, that is, in the black or grey parts of the economy, in civil society or in the family. It can be paid or unpaid (Pfau-Effinger et al. 2003, 9). The 'formality' or 'informality' of an activity is seen

here as a social construction: it can be organised in formal or informal ways in different societies (Portes, 1994; Williams and Windebank 1998, 4).
2. The share of social expenditure out of GDP is the second highest compared with the other study countries (Table 5.1, Appendix). This does not indicate a particularly high level of decommodification or of social services, but is mainly due to a particularly great share of expenses related to health services (xxx).
3. The terms *Informal employment* and *undeclared work* are used here for the same social phenomenon. Undeclared work is defined, following Renooy et al. (2004), as 'productive activities that are lawful as regards to their nature, but are not declared to the public authorities.'
4. The basis for the calculation is the population age 15–64.
5. Statistisches Bundesamt (2003), Pflegestatistik 2001, 8
6. Ibid., 34
7. Ibid., 34
8. Cyprian, R. (2003): 'Im Mini aus der Schwarzarbeit', IAB Materialien Nr. 1/2003, 7–8, www.iab.de. The article is based on estimations by Schneider 2002.
9. However, it should be noted that the figures for Denmark and the UK are based on less than twenty observations and therefore only to a rather limited degree reliable (Pedersen 2003, 66).
10. Poverty is defined in the study as an income below 60 per cent in relation to the average income of the respective age group (Schupp 2002).
11. The shift in family policies since 2007 has greatly increased the incentives for mothers, as well as the number of options, to shorten the duration of family leaves to two years. The future will show whether this leads to an average abbreviation of parental leaves in West Germany, too.

REFERENCES

Aurich, P. (2007) *Changes in Social Security and Labour Market Policy: The Case of Activation in Germany*, 5th Annual ESPAnet-Conference, September 20–22, 2007, Vienna.

Baumeister, H., Bollinger, D., Cornetz, W., and Pfau-Effinger, B. (1990) *Atypische Beschäftigung–die typische Beschäftigung der Zukunft?*, Bremen: Universität Bremen.

Beck, U. (2000) 'Die Seele der Demokratie: bezahlte Bürgerarbeit', in U. Beck (ed.) *Die Zukunft von Arbeit und Demokratie*, Frankfurt/M.: Suhrkamp.

Beckmann, P., and Engelbrech, G. (2002) 'Vereinbarkeit von Familie und Beruf: Kinderbetreuung und Beschäftigungsmöglichkeiten von Frauen mit Kindern', in G. Engelbrech (ed.) *Arbeitsmarktchancen für Frauen*, Beitr, AM 259, Nürnberg: Bundesanstalt für Arbeit: 263–282.

Beckmann, P., and Kurtz, B. (2001) 'Erwerbsbeteiligung von Frauen. Die Betreuung der Kinder ist der Schlüssel', *IAB Kurzbericht, Aktuelle Analysen aus dem Institut für Arbeitsmarkt- und Berufsforschung der Bundesanstalt für Arbeit*, 10.

Blair, J.P., and Endres, C.P. (1994) 'Hidden economic cevelopment assets', *Economic Development Quarterly* 8(3):286–291.

Bosch, G. (2002) *Die Zukunft von Dienstleistungen: ihre Auswirkung auf Arbeit, Umwelt und Lebensqualität*, Frankfurt/Main: Campus-Verl.

Büchtemann, Ch. (1989) *Befristete Arbeitsverträge nach dem Beschäftigungsförderungsgesetz (BeschFG 1985)*, Bonn: Bundesminister für Arbeit u. Sozialordnung.

Bundesministerium für Familie, Senioren, Frauen und Jugend (BMFSFJ) (eds) (2002) Ergebnisse der Repräsentativerhebung 1999 zu Ehrenamt, Freiwilligenarbeit und bürgerschaftliches Engagement—Band 1: Freiwilliges Engagement in Deutschland: Gesamtbericht von Bernhart von Rosenbladt, Stuttgart, Berlin, Köln.

Cyprian, R. (2003) 'Im Mini aus der Schwarzarbeit', *IAB Materialien* 1:7–8, http://www.iab.de.

Dathe, D., and Kistler, E. (2002) 'Entwicklung und Strukturwandel bürgerschaftlichen Engagements', *Teil A des Gutachtens für die Enquete-Kommission Zukunft des bürgerschaftlichen Engagements zum Thema "Struktur und Motivationswandel bürgerschaftlichen Engagements bei Erwerbstätigen und Arbeitslosen unter besonderer Berücksichtigung der gender-Perspektive"* KDrs:14(180): Berlin.

Deutscher Bundestag (2008) Vierter Bericht über die Entwicklung der Pflegeversicherung. Drucksache 16/7772, Berlin.

Dölling, I. (1993) 'Gespaltenes Bewußtsein—Frauen und Männerbilder in der DDR', in G. Helwig and H.M. Nickel (eds) *Frauen in Deutschland: 1945–1992*, Berlin: Akademie Verlag, 23–52.

Effinger, H., and Pfau-Effinger, B. (1999) 'Freiwilliges Engagement im Sozialwesen–Ausweg aus der Krise der Erwerbsgesellschaft und des Wohlfahrtsstaates?', in E. Kistler, H.-H. Noll, and E. Priller (eds) (2002) *Perspektiven gesellschaftlichen Zusammenhalts, Empirische Befunde, Praxiserfahrungen, Messkonzepte*, edition sigma, Berlin: Enquete-Kommission Bürgerschaftliches Engagement, 6.

Eichler, M., and Pfau-Effinger, B. (2007) 'Informelle Arbeit im Alter. Zur Pflegetätigkeit von Frauen in der nachberuflichen Phase', in M. Erlinghagen and K. Hank (eds) *Produktives Altern und informelle Arbeit in modernen Gesellschaften*, Wiesbaden: VS-Verlag.

Enquete Kommission Bürgerschaftliches Engagement (2002): Bürgerschaftliches Engagement in Deutschland, vol. 6, Berlin Esch, K., and Stöber-Blossey, S. (2002) 'Kinderbetreuung: Ganztags für alle?—Differenzierte Arbeitszeiten erfordern flexible Angebote', *IAT-Report* 09, Gelsenkirchen: Institut für Arbeit und Technik.

Esping-Andersen, G. (1990) *The Three Worlds of Welfare Capitalism*, Cambridge: Polity Press.

——. (1999) *Social Foundations of Postindustrial Economies*, Oxford: Oxford University Press.

Evers, A. (2005) 'Mixed welfare systems and hybrid organizations: Changes in the governance and provision of social services', in *International Journal of Public Administration* 28(9&10):736–748.

Geissler, B. (2002) Die Dienstleistungslücke im Haushalt. Der neue Bedarf nach Dienstleistungen und die Handlungslogik der privaten Arbeit', in C. Gather, B. Geissler, and M.S. Rerrich (eds) *Weltmarkt Privathaushalt. Bezahlte Haushaltsarbeit im globalen Wandel*, Münster: Westfälisches Dampfboot.

Grünert, H., and Lutz, B. (2001) 'Beschäftigung und Arbeitsmarkt', in H. Bertram and R. Kollmorgen (eds) *Die Transformation Ostdeutschlands. Bericht zum sozialen und politischen Wandel in den neuen Bundesländern*, Opladen: Leske + Budrich:133–162.

Hillmann, F. (2005) 'Migrant's care work in private households, or the strength of bilocal and transnational ties as a last(ing) resource in global migration', in B. Pfau-Effinger and B. Geissler (eds) *Care Arrangements in Europe—Variations and Change*, Bristol: Policy Press.

Jensen, P.H., and Pfau-Effinger, B. (2005) 'Towards active citizenship', in G. Andersen, A.M. Guillemard, P. Jensen, and B. Pfau-Effinger (eds) *The New Face of Welfare. Welfare States, Marginalisation and Citizenship*, Bristol: Policy Press.

Kaufmann, F.-X. (2004) Varianten des Wohlfahrtsstaats: der deutsche Sozialstaat im internationalen Vergleich, Frankfurt am Main: Suhrkamp.

Knijn, T., and Kremer, M. (1997) 'Gender and the Caring dimension of welfare states: Towards inclusive citizenship', *Social Politics* 3:328–361.

Lessenich, S. (2005) *Den Sozialstaat neu denken*, Hamburg: VSA-Verl.

Lewis, J. (ed.) (1998) *Gender, Social Care and Welfare State Restructuring in Europe*, Aldershot: Ashgate.

Lutz, H. (2002) 'Transnationalität im Haushalt', in C. Gather, B. Geißler, and M.S. Rerrich (eds) "Weltmarkt Privathaushalt—bezahlte Haushaltsarbeit im globalen Wandel"; *Forum Frauenfors chung—Schriftenreihe der Sektion Frauenforschung in der Deutschen Gesellschaft für Soziologie* 15, Münster: Verlag Westfälisches Dampfboot.

Meyer, T., and Pfau-Effinger, B. (2006) 'The gender dimension of the restructuring of pension systems—a comparison of Britain and Germany', *International Journal of Ageing and Later Life*, 4.

Mutz, G. (2002) 'Pluralisierung und Entgrenzung in der Erwerbsarbeit, im Bürgerengagement und in der Eigenarbeit', *Arbeit* 14:21–32.

Organisation for Economic Co-operation and Development (OECD) (ed.) (2002) *Employment Outlook*, Paris.

———(ed.) (1997) *Employment Outlook*, Paris.

Offe C. et al. (1996) *Politische Theorien in der Ära der Transformation*, Opladen: Westdt. Verlag.

Pedersen, S. (2003) 'The shadow economy in Germany, Great Britain and Scandinavia. A measurement based on questionnaire surveys', *Rockwool Foundation Study* 10, Copenhagen: The Rockwool Foundation Research Unit.

Pfau-Effinger, B. (2001) 'Wandel wohlfahrtsstaatlicher Geschlechterpolitiken im soziokulturellen Kontext', *Kölner Zeitschrift für Soziologie und Sozialpsychologie* 41, Special Volume 41, 488–511.

———. (2004a) 'Development of culture, welfare states and women's employment', Aldershot: Ashgate.

———. (2004b) 'Umbau der skandinavischen Volksheime?', in *Geographische Rundschau*, 35 2.

———. (2005a) 'Culture and welfare state policies: Reflections on a complex interrelation', *Journal of Social Policy* 34 1:3–20.

———. (2005b) 'Welfare state policies and care arrangements', *European Societies* 7 (2):321–347.

———. (2009) 'The theoretical approach of the 'arrangement of work and welfare', in B. Pfau-Effinger, L. Flaquer, and P. Jensen (eds) *Formal and Informal Work. The Hidden Work Regime*, New York: Routledge.

———. (forthcoming) Varieties of Undeclared Work in Europe. *British Journal of Inudustrial Relations*.

Pfau-Effinger, B., Eichler, M., and Och, R. (2007) 'Ökonomisierung, Pflegepolitik und Strukturen der Pflege älterer Menschen', in A. Evers and R. Heinze (eds) *Sozialpolitik: Ökonomisierung und Entgrenzung*, Wiesbaden: VS-Verlag.

Pfau-Effinger, B., and Geissler, B. (2002) 'Cultural change and family policies in East and West Germany', in A. Carling, S.S. Duncan, and R. Edwards (eds) *Analysing Families: Morality and Rationality in Policy and Practice*, London, New York: Routledge.

Pfau-Effinger, B., Lemnitzer, J., Sakač Magdalenić, S., and Stitz, U. (2003) *Formal and informal work: Statistical mapping. The report on Germany*, University of Hamburg, Hamburg.

Portes, A. (1994) 'The informal economy and its paradoxes', in N.J. Smelser and R. Swedberg (eds) *The Handbook of Economic Sociology*, Princeton, New York: Princeton University Press.

Portes, A., Castells, M., and Benton, L.A. (1989) *The Informal Economy: Studies in Advanced and less developed countries*. Baltimore, MD: John Hopkins University Press.

Priller, E. (1996) 'Veränderungen in der politischen und sozialen Beteiligung in Ostdeutschland', in W. Zapf and R. Habich (eds) *Wohlfahrtsentwicklung im vereinten Deutschland. Sozialstruktur, sozialer Wandel und Lebensqualität*, Berlin: 283–305, Ed. Sigma.

Reichert, S. (2000) *Transformationsprozesse: der Umbau der LVZ*, Münster: Lit.

Renooy, P. (2007) 'Undeclared work: A new source of employment?', *International Journal of Sociology and Social Policy* 27(5/6): 250–256.

Renooy, P., Ivarsson, S., Wusten-Gritsai, O. van der, Meijer, E. (2004): 'Undeclared work in an enlarged union. An analysis of undeclared work: An in-depth study of specific items', *European Commission*, http://europa.eu.int/comm/employment_social/employment_analysis/work/undecl_work_final_en.pdf.

Rothgang, H. (1997) *Ziele und Wirkungen der Pflegeversicherung: eine ökonomische Analyse*, Frankfurt/Main: Campus.

Schneekloth, U. (2006) *Selbständigkeit und Hilfebedarf bei älteren Menschen in Privathaushalten: Pflegearrangements, Demenz, Versorgungsangebote*, Stuttgart: Kohlhammer.

Schneekloth, U. (2005): Leben mit Hilfe und Pflege zu Hause. Möglichkeiten und Grenzen. Vortrag zur Abschlusstagung des Forschungsverbundes am 16. Juni, Berlin

Schneekloth, U., and Müller, U. (2000) *Wirkungen der Pflegeversicherung. Forschungsprojekt im Auftrag des Bundesministeriums für Gesundheit*, Baden-Baden: Nomos.

Schneider, F. (1997) *Empirical Results for the Size of Shadow Economy of Western European Countries Over Time* Linz, Working Paper No. 9710, Institut für Volkswirtschaftslehre, Johannes Kepler Universität Linz.

Schneider, F., and Enste, D. (2000) *"Schattenwirtschaft und Schwarzarbeit: Umfang, Ursachen, Wirkungen und wirtschaftliche Empfehlungen"*, München, Wien: Oldenbourg Wissenschaftsverlag (Forum Wirtschaft und Soziales).

Schupp, J. (2002) 'Quantitative Verbreitung von Erwerbstätigkeit in privaten Haushalten Deutschlands', in C. Gather, B. Geissler, and M.S. Rerrich (eds) *Weltmarkt Privathaushalt. Bezahlte Haushaltsarbeit im globalen Wandel*, Münster: Westfälisches Dampfboot: 50–71.

Siebel, W., Jessen, J., Siebel-Rebell, Ch., Walther, U.J., and Weyrather, I. (1988) *Arbeit nach der Arbeit. Schattenwirtschaft, Wertewandel und Industriearbeit*, Opladen: Westdeutscher Verlag.

Social Security Code XI (SGB XI)

Socio-Economic Panel Study (SOEP), (2005): Data from 'Deutsches Institut für Wirtschaftsforschung, Berlin.

Statistisches Bundesamt (2003) *Pflegestatistik 2001. Pflege im Rahmen der Pflegeversicherung, Deutschlandergebnisse*, Bonn: Statistisches Bundesamt

———. (2005a) *Ergebnisse des Mikrozensus 2004: Bevölkerung und Erwerbstätigkeit—Haushalte und Familien*, Wiesbaden: Statistisches Bundesamt.

———. (2005b) *Rund zwei Fünftel der Mütter arbeiten Teilzeit*, Wiesbaden: Statistisches Bundesamt: Pressemitteilung vom 3, Mai.

———. (2007) *Erwerbsstatistik*, Wiesbaden: Statistisches Bundesamt.

TNS Infratest, BMFS (2002)

Williams, C.C., and Windebank, J. (1998) *Informal Employment in the Advanced Economies. Implications for Work and Welfare*, London, New York: Routledge.

Internet sources:

http://www.iab.de
http://www.minijob-zentrale.de

6   Formal and Informal Work in a Liberal Regime
The Case of Britain

Traute Meyer and Graham Baxendale[1]

INTRODUCTION

In comparative studies the United Kingdom is frequently cited as an example of a liberal regime. Its welfare state is based on minimal benefits, often means-tested against income loss, and child and eldercare have traditionally been seen as a predominantly private concern. Thus, the market is more important for the protection of people from poverty than perhaps in any of the other countries included in this book. Since the 1970s employment rates in the United Kingdom have been comparatively high, and since the 1990s they were second highest in the countries included in this study after Denmark (see Table 4.2 Appendix). Private pension provision has always played an important role in the United Kingdom (Bridgen and Meyer 2005), and the demand for private care services has been growing steadily, too (Kendall 2003, 31). In liberal capitalism more is expected of the market, but employment and businesses are less regulated than in more coordinated countries such as Germany or Denmark (Hall and Soskice 2001); thus income differentials are larger (Glyn 2001), with very low wages at the bottom of the scale, and private pensions and care services only available to the more affluent. As a result, for a long time, the United Kingdom has been battling against high poverty rates, which hit families with children and the elderly in particular (Bridgen and Meyer 2007; Gregg and Wadsworth 2001; Papadopoulos and Tsakloglou 2002 for a comparative perspective).

The extent and dynamics of informal work are of course affected by the high level of commodification that market dominance brings. On the one hand the importance of labour-market generated income for protection has the strong potential to crowd out informal work and to some extent this is the case in the United Kingdom. However, because affordable care services are lacking, the informal sector also plays an important role in the arrangement of work and welfare in Britain; this is expressed by very high rates of women working part-time and economic inactivity of single parents (e.g., Clasen 2003; Paull, Taylor, and Duncan 2002).

Our aim in this chapter is to analyse the patterns and dynamics of informal work in the United Kingdom. Because the extent to which informal employment, unpaid care work, and voluntary work develop are affected by the structure and dynamics of formal employment, we will first give an overview of its dynamics and significance for citizens since the 1980s, a time when the welfare state became more liberal after a social democratic phase. This is followed by a more detailed study of informal work and its determinants in the second part.

6.1. THE ARRANGEMENT OF WORK AND WELFARE

In 1979, when the Conservative Party led by Margaret Thatcher came to power, significant changes in the arrangement of work and welfare, that is, the welfare state, the employment structure, and informal work were already underway.

Until the early 1970s the (post-war) consensus had characterised British politics. Its foundations were a commitment by all parties to a mixed economy, partly in public ownership and partly managed by Keynesian economic policies with the aim of full employment. The Beveridgean welfare state supported a universal health service and social rights against income loss for all citizens to eradicate poverty (e.g., Kavanagh 1990), but it also enforced gendered inequality through poor service provision and legislation, preventing many married women from generating independent social rights (Clarke and Newman 1997; Lewis 1992). Socioeconomically the arrangement was accompanied by high, fairly stable male and low female employment, and the dominance of the male-breadwinner model.

During the 1970s this arrangement had started to disintegrate. The oil price shock in 1973 triggered a deepening economic and political crisis in Britain (e.g., Hay 1996, 259). However, the 1970s were also a time of social reform, of the women's movement, and of gendered employment change, all of which weakened the male-breadwinner model (e.g., Clarke and Newman 1997). Thus the foundations of the (post-war) consensus had already lost its solidity by 1979 (Hall 1993; Hewitt 1992, 64–67).[2] Throughout the 1980s they were radically questioned by the New Right. Margaret Thatcher proposed that to revitalize economy and society cuts in welfare spending, an end to public ownership, and a turn towards demand-side economic policies were needed (Taylor-Gooby 2001).[3] An extensive debate has taken place since concerning how successful the Conservatives have been regarding these ends (Clasen 2003); however, if we focus on policies most relevant to formal and informal work, it is clear that the quality of citizens' protection against income loss declined (Nickell 2001b), reenforcing their dependency on the market and increasing the poverty risks of those not in paid work. Macro economic policies exacerbated the pace of deindustrialisation and led to an increase in male inactivity rates (see section 6.2). From the perspective of gender relations some of the reformist social policies that had improved women's entitlements to benefits during the 1970s were cut again in the 1980s, making women more dependent on the market or a partner, and the lack of support for care responsibilities largely remained until 1997 (Marchbank 2000).

Taking into account these reforms of the 1980s, Esping-Andersen (1990) identified the British welfare state as the only one in Europe that came close to the liberal ideal type (see also Clasen 2003, 580).

When the Labour Party formed the government in 1997 they, too, pledged to strengthen the market principle and to increase employment participation, albeit with a stronger focus on social inclusion and on enabling active citizenship. Influenced by the politics of the Third Way, government promised protection against poverty and new opportunities for those unable to be employed, many of them children (Clasen 2003, 574; Lister 2003, 429; Hills and Waldfogel 2004; Rake 2001, 209, 223).

6.2. DEVELOPMENT OF FORMAL EMPLOYMENT AND ECONOMIC CHANGE

The political changes outlined affected the transformation of the arrangement of welfare and work in Britain, but they were of course not the only drivers. Most importantly the economy and employment structure changed fundamentally during the 1980s. As in all western societies, employment shifted from manufacturing towards services, driven by increased productivity, the internationalisation of trade, and more demand for education and consumer-related services. In Britain this deindustrialisation was more extreme than elsewhere in Europe, because macroeconomic policies adopted by the Conservative governments during the 1980s helped to accelerate the decline in manufacturing (Nickell 2001a, 623; Rowthorn 2000, 141–148, 154–163). To cast light on the changing relationship between formal and informal work we will examine the implications of these trends from the perspective of gender and households.

Gender Disparities

The changes meant a decline in men's labour-force participation rates and an increase in women's (Table 4.2, Appendix). Mothers spent less time outside the labour force after childbirth; the percentage of employed women with dependent children under five rose from 36 per cent in 1988 to 56 percent in 2005 (Government Statistics Services 1999, 119; ONS 2005, 2007). Of the countries studied in this book, female employment rates are highest in Britain, Denmark, and Finland, and because of rising female and declining male employment the British traditional male-breadwinner model has become weaker (Tables 4.1, 4.2, Appendix), but only to a limited extent:

Table 6.1. Female Part-Time as Percentage of Female Employment

	1984	1986	1988	1990	1992	1994	1996	1998	2000	2002	2004	2006	Average 84–06	Change 1984–2006
Denmark	36.7	32.9	31.4	29.6	29.0	26.2	24.3	25.5	23.5	22.6	24.0	25.6	27.6	-11.1
Germany	25.8	25.9	26.4	29.8	26.1	28.0	29.9	32.4	33.9	35.3	37.0	39.2	30.8	13.4
Finland	12.6	11.6	10.5	10.6	10.6	11.5	11.3	13.0	13.9	14.8	14.9	14.9	12.5	2.3
Spain			12.1	11.5	12.8	14.4	16.2	16.6	16.5	16.4	17.6	21.4	15.6	9.3
UK	41.2	41.6	40.8	39.5	40.6	41.2	41.4	41.2	40.8	39.9	40.3	38.8	40.6	-2.4
Poland								16.6	17.9	16.7	17.5	16.3	17.0	-0.3
Average	29.1	28.0	24.2	24.2	23.8	24.3	25.2	24.2	24.4	24.3	25.2	26.0	25.2	1.8

Source: OECD 2002; 2007.

Work hours of British men and women have been far more unequal than in any of the countries studied here. Between 1984 and 2006, an average of 41 percent of all employed women worked part-time, that is, fewer than 30 hours a week; this is a much higher percentage than in all other countries (Table 6.1; Table 4.4 in Appendix). In addition, British men working full-time in the United Kingdom averaged over 43 weekly hours between 1984 and 2007—longer hours than in the other five countries except for Germany; while British women working part-time had the shortest average working hours in our sample. Thus, the gender gap between average hours worked of full-time men and part-time women between 1984 and 2007 is 26 hours, while the average gap between full-time men and women is five hours; these differences are greater than anywhere else (Table 6.2).

If we disaggregate these general trends further it emerges that men without or with low qualifications were hardest hit by deindustrialisation. During the 1980s a generation of workers in manufacturing and coal mining were made redundant, many of whom did not find jobs again. The picture does not change during the 1990s and beyond; men with low qualifications had bad job prospects, and of those without qualifications in 2000 almost one-third was economically inactive (Nickell 2001b, 732). Given the marked increase in the demand for qualified employees that deindustrialisation brought and the need for service jobs deemed to be more suitable for women, unqualified men simply have had bad employment prospects since the 1980s (Nickell 2001b). Adult British males have therefore been divided by the economic changes of the last decades. The majority are working full-time at long hours, but an increased minority with low qualifications is poor and economically inactive.

By the same token, the majority of women are now employed, and the expansion of the service sector increased the share of qualified jobs for them. At the same time, their working hours are comparatively short.

Disparities Between Households

Our more detailed look at men and women already suggests that on the level of the household the changes in the employment structure were no zero-sum game with regard to gender, in the sense that men lost jobs and women gained them (Rowthorn 2000, 154). Instead a new pattern of distribution of paid work developed. Until the seventies, when the strong male-breadwinner model was dominant, employment was spread more evenly across households, mainly because their male heads were employed. Since deindustrialisation and the increase of women in employment, the adult population before retirement either live in households where all adults work, true for the majority, or none work.

Between 1975 and 2001 the number of households with no adults in paid work more than doubled, from 6.5 percent of all[4] in 1975 to 16.6 percent in 2001, and the majority of these citizens were not looking for work. Most of

Table 6.2. Average Weekly Working Hours

	1984	1986	1988	1990	1992	1994	1996	1998	2000	2002	2004	2006	2007	Average 84–07
Full-time male employees														
Denmark	41	41.4	40.7	40.8	40.3	40.8	39.4	39	39.4	40.3	39.5	40.9	40.6	40.3
Germany	43.3	43.7	43.3	43.1	42.9	43	43.4	43.5	43.7	43.4	43.2	43.1	43.2	43.3
Finland							42	41.7	40.6	40.5	40.3	40.9	40.7	41.0
Spain			40.6	40.5	40.2	40.9	40.2	40.8	40.9	40.9	41	42.2	42	40.9
UK	42.9	43.8	44.5	44.1	43.5	44.1	44.3	43.9	43.5	43.2	42.9	42.7	42.7	43.5
Average	42.4	43.0	42.3	42.1	41.7	42.2	41.9	41.8	41.6	41.7	41.4	42.0	41.8	42.0
Full-time female employees														
Denmark	36.8	38	37.4	37.4	36.8	37.4	35.4	35.9	35.5	36.4	35.3	37.1	37.1	36.7
Germany	42	42.1	41.7	41.1	40.7	40.7	40.8	40.8	40.8	40.7	40.5	40.3	40.4	41.0
Finland							37.2	37.5	36.7	37	36.8	37.4	37.4	37.1
Spain	37.5		39.4	39	38.9	39.3	38.7	39	38.9	39	38.9	39.5	39.5	39.1
UK		39	38.6	38	38.1	38.7	38.8	38.7	38.5	38.5	38.3	38.6	38.6	38.5
Average	38.8	39.7	39.3	38.9	38.6	39.0	38.2	38.4	38.1	38.3	38.0	38.6	38.6	38.6
Part-time female employees														
Denmark	17.8	21.2	21.3	21.1	20.9	21	20.6	20.9	21.3	20	20.3	20.8	21.6	20.7
Germany	21.7	20.7	21	19.7	20.3	20.3	19.1	18.7	18.5	18.2	18.2	18.2	18.3	19.5
Finland							20	21.3	20.6	20.4	20.6	20.7	20.7	20.6

Spain	16.5		17.5	17.2	17.5	17.2	16.8	16.9	17.3	17.7	18	18.8	18.9	17.6
UK	17.1	17.1	17.1	17.1	16.8	17.1	17.4	17.5	17.9	18.3	18.3	18.5	18.5	17.5
Average	18.7	19.7	19.2	18.8	18.9	18.9	18.8	19.1	19.1	18.9	19.1	19.4	19.6	19.1
Number of hours full-time men work longer than full-time women														
Denmark	4.2	3.4	3.3	3.4	3.5	3.4	4	3.1	3.9	3.9	4.2	3.8	3.5	3.7
Germany	1.3	1.6	1.6	2	2.2	2.3	2.6	2.7	2.9	2.7	2.7	2.8	2.8	2.3
Finland							4.8	4.2	3.9	3.5	3.5	3.5	3.3	3.8
Spain			1.2	1.5	1.3	1.6	1.5	1.8	2	1.9	2.1	2.7	2.5	1.8
UK	5.4	4.8	5.9	6.1	5.4	5.4	5.5	5.2	5	4.7	4.6	4.1	4.1	5.1
Average	3.6	3.3	3.0	3.3	3.1	3.2	3.7	3.4	3.5	3.3	3.4	3.4	3.2	3.3
Number of hours fulltime men work longer than part-time women														
Denmark	23.2	20.2	19.4	19.7	19.4	19.8	18.8	18.1	18.1	20.3	19.2	20.1	19	19.6
Germany	21.6	23	22.3	23.4	22.6	22.7	24.3	24.8	25.2	25.2	25	24.9	24.9	23.8
Finland							22	20.4	20	20.1	19.7	20.2	20	20.3
Spain		23.1	23.1	23.3	22.7	23.7	23.4	23.9	23.6	23.2	23	23.4	23.1	23.3
UK	26.4	26.7	27.4	27	26.7	27	26.9	26.4	25.6	24.9	24.6	24.2	24.2	26.0
Average	23.7	23.3	23.1	23.4	22.9	23.3	23.1	22.7	22.5	22.7	22.3	22.6	22.2	22.9

Source: Eurostat ,Labour Force Survey Results, unpublished data obtained on request.

these households consisted of single men, and the next largest group were single parents (Gregg and Wadsworth 2001, 778–785; ONS 2006, 37–38). In 2007 the employment rate for lone parents was 57 percent, compared with 72 percent for married and cohabiting mothers (ONS 2007, 6).

These trends mean significant groups of the population are excluded from formal employment, and the children who grow up in such households are exposed to poverty and the high risk of permanent exclusion. The 'welfare to work focus' of the Labour governments and their commitment to lifting children out of poverty must be seen against this background. From the perspective of the changing boundaries of formal and informal work, the trends pose the question of what patterns of informal work develop among deprived groups. We discuss this in section 6.3.1.

The majority of adults live in households where all adults work, and the share of such households has increased from 57 per cent of all households in 1975 to 66 per cent in 2001 (Gregg and Wadsworth 2001, 780). Thus, according to Gregg and Wadsworth, the United Kingdom has the highest level of polarisation across OECD countries; that is, for Britain it is truer than for any other country that 'there are more workless households than would be predicted by a random distribution of employment across all working age adults' (2001, 790).

We can therefore say that with regard to the change in employment since the 1970s, the main story of is one of more even distribution within households and greater polarisation between them. Concentrated in the South are households dependent on the wages of two earners. Even though these are still strongly organized on the basis of a full-time worker/part-time worker and carer model (see also Lewis, Campbell, and Huerta 2008, 24), their division of labour has changed, and particularly the women have less time for housework and care responsibilities. Such households therefore generate increasing demand for paid care and support. They are the potential consumers of household related services and informal employment.

On the other hand a substantial share of workless households, with and without children, exist. These are poor and consist mainly of single men and single parents. They are unlikely to generate demand for household related services nor for informal employment. Instead it is much more likely that they are involved in informal work themselves and are financed by state benefits. The following will explore these issues in more detail.

6.3. MAIN FEATURES OF INFORMAL WORK

We have given a range of reasons why one would expect that informal work—paid and unpaid—should be an important part of British society: A liberal welfare state, providing only basic benefits and social services, leaves substantial room for private households and charities to engage. A polarized employment structure increases demand by two-earner households for support with childcare and household maintenance and encourages informal economic activities for those households excluded from the formal employment sphere. Against this background, in the following sections we assess the significance of paid and unpaid forms of care or maintenance work in the household, neighbourly support, and voluntary engagement in charitable institutions. In each section we first give an overview of main social policies in each area, next examine the extent of this type of work, with particular focus on the question of who are the providers and consumers, and finally assess possible driving forces for these developments.

6.3.1. Size, Patterns, and Explanation with Respect to Family-Based Childcare

6.3.1.1 Welfare State Policies and Institutional Framework

Until the late 1990s the welfare state did not support the expansion of childcare places in the public domain (e.g., Lewis 2003). In the 1960s and 1970s governments' dominant view was that the state should only provide care in the case of family breakdown. Even though in the 1970s awareness about the value of women's unpaid work grew and since 1975 the pension system has recognized care work (Meyer and Pfau-Effinger 2006), the belief that mothers should care for their children at home remained throughout the 1980s and into the 1990s (Marchbank 2000, 75–77), until the Conservative government shifted its position slightly by introducing childcare subsidies for low-wage families (Kiernan, Land, and Lewis 1998, 273).

When the Labour government came into power in 1997 positions began to change more substantially. *Welfare to Work* policies sought to get people 'off benefits and into work' by ensuring that earnings were higher than benefits, and new family supporting measures aimed to reduce social exclusion and to educate children (Clasen 2005, 172–178; Hills and Waldfogel 2004; Lewis 2003; Lister 2006; Millar 2000; Williams 2004; Wincott 2006, 291–292). Lewis argues that the pursuit of these aims, rather than of a comprehensive childcare strategy, though improving parents' employment opportunities somewhat, also led to the emergence of a fragmented system of payments and heterogeneous services (Lewis 2003, 235–236).

Despite the focus on activation, the poor, and the low paid, some low tax credits were also available for families with higher incomes.[5] Moreover, all employed mothers became entitled to one year of maternity leave and to Statutory Maternity Pay (SMP) during the first six weeks, worth 90% of individual weekly earnings, and a flat-rate benefit for the following 33 weeks.[6] Paternity leave and pay were also introduced at the same basic flat-rate as SMP but limited to two weeks (DWP 2006). Again, these measures give parents greater flexibility, but apart from the first weeks they do not provide a substantial boost to the income of middle-class earners.

The provision of childcare, even though fragmented, has also improved for all parents. Since 2004 free nursery education has been available to all three-year-olds, albeit on a part-time basis of around two and one-half hours a day only (Clasen 2005, 146). But the government has pledged to extend the hours offered to 15 a week by 2010 and to support schools in extending after-school care to offer all-day childcare to all children between 3 and 14 years by 2010 (Cabinet Office 2007). Since 2005 there has also been tax or social insurance relief for employers who offer childcare (HM Revenue & Customs 2007, 3).

These changes modernise the British breadwinner model because social policies are now based on the notion that every adult can be expected to be economically independent and that the state accepts some responsibility for childcare costs and provision, as well as for preschool education (Annesley 2003, 160; Lister 2006, 319; Pascall 1999, 270; Randall 2000, 197). At the same time, although Labour's intention has been to improve the public childcare situation for all parents (Wincott 2006), the first concerns lay with nonemployed adults, the education of preschool children, and families on benefits.

6.3.1.2 Extent of Childcare in the Home and the Public Sphere

Meanwhile most childcare still takes place informally on an unpaid basis. In 2005 three-quarters of mothers with children under the age of six relied mainly on unpaid (grand)parental childcare in the home (Table 1.1, Appendix). In comparison with the other countries analysed in this study this result is not exceptional; figures are higher in Poland, Spain, and Germany, and even in Finland more than half of all young children are mainly looked after by parents and grandparents at home. However, it is noteworthy that between 1999 and 2004–2005 the significance of nonparental informal childcare by family members, friends, or neighbours, rarely paid, has only gone up by one percentage point to 42 per cent of all English households with children and that the increase was strongest amongst better-off households (Bryson, Kazimirsky, and Southwood 2006, 51–52, 56).

Although informal care remains dominant, paid forms of childcare have also increased significantly. Between 2003 and 2006 the number of registered childcare places in England rose by 20 per cent, to 1.5 million, and this growth was strongest in the area of full-day care (48 per cent) and crèches (42 per cent), the former offering longer hours, the latter fewer (OFSTED 2003, 2006; own calculations).

In line with such expansion, demand for formal childcare, that is, from some paid provider, has increased strongly between 1999 and 2004–2005, from 28 to 41 per cent of all parents (Bryson, Kazimirsky, and Southwood 2006, 51–52, 104). The increase in formal demand mainly took place in the area of nursery or reception classes and after- or preschool clubs (6 per cent increase each between 2001 and 2004), and in line with this it has most strongly increased for children between 3 and 4 years old (Bryson,

Kazimirsky, and Southwood 2006, 53–54). This seems to show that the government's childcare policies have had an effect. And indeed, 56 per cent of very low-income households used formal childcare in 2004–2005, which is an increase of 7 percentage points since 2001. At the same time, higher-income households (above £32,000 p.a.) were also more likely to use formal care, and this demand increased even more strongly, from 41 to 52 per cent during the same time, despite the fact that higher earners paid about three times more for childcare than lower earners did, disregarding subsidies. Higher earners found it easier to meet these costs (Bryson, Kazimirsky, and Southwood 2006, 4, 12, 56, 115, 118).

Against this background a growing tendency towards the formalisation of childcare is obvious; at the same time, most families used these services to complement informal care, which continues to be the main form of provision.

6.3.1.3 Explanations for the Dynamics of Formal and Informal Childcare

Expansion in formal childcare was first driven by social and economic trends: the changed labour-market behaviour of mothers, increased rates of lone-parent households, and changed attitudes of mothers.

New Labour's social policies had an effect, too; the free part-time places available to the three- to four-year-olds as well as support to families with low- or no incomes increased formal childcare use (Bryson, Kazimirsky, and Southwood 2006, 4). However, because these policies offered the most encompassing support to a limited group of households, they are less significant than the socioeconomic changes for an overall change in parents' behaviour.

At the same time, a fundamental reconstruction of the relationship between gender and mothering has not occurred (Marchbank 2000, 37), and the ideal of the male breadwinner still retains considerable cultural and material relevance in British society. 'Proper' work for men is still full-time employment, and this helps to perpetuate the male-breadwinner/female part-time worker and carer model, where women organize childcare in order to make possible their own and other family members' paid work and other activities (McKie, Bowlby, and Gregory 2001, 238–239). Even if a man and woman share equivalent class, pay, and work hours, it is likely that the woman will still do considerably more housework (Bond and Sales 2001, 245).

6.3.2. Size, Patterns, and Explanation with Respect to Family-Based Eldercare

6.3.2.1. Welfare-state Policies and Institutional Framework

Like childcare, eldercare in the United Kingdom has long been mainly provided by the family. The state only stepped in when no such personal provision was available. This notwithstanding, social policies relating to eldercare have changed in important ways since the early 1990s.

The Conservative government's dislike of large welfare-state institutions and its support for individualism motivated a policy shift towards Care in the Community, for which momentum within the Conservative Party but also in society at large had been building since the 1960s. Thus, the New Right's agenda of consumer choice and marketisation resonated with widespread criticisms citizens had of public services (Spandler 2004, 190).

Against this background the government thought that first, the costs of institutionalised care contributed to the fiscal burden of the welfare state, especially because costly improvements to the 'Dickensian' facilities were desperately needed, should they remain. Second, they called the ethics and efficacy of institutionalisation into question and argued that the needs of mental patients and the elderly would be better and more cheaply met by their integration in the community, with support from community-based services (Means and Smith, 1998, 47; Symonds and Kelly, 1998, 39).

These concerns led to the Community Care (Direct Payments) Act 1996 which gave local authorities the permission to make means-tested cash payments to disabled citizens for the first time. This right was later extended to citizens over 65 and younger disabled people, and in 2002 it became obligatory for local authorities to offer direct payments (Scourfield 2005, 470–472; Spandler 2004, 189). Since these changes, elderly people have become potential purchasers of care; if they qualify by passing the means-test they can choose care-workers either from private companies or from their own communal networks. In this regard, the care users' independence and control have been expanded in principle. These changes instated a market for the provision of care based on a purchaser–provider split (Ungerson 2000, 626).

Labour governments have shared this focus on care in the community for the elderly with their Conservative predecessors, and on an ideological level the policy was promoted with reference to enhanced choice and independence (Scourfield 2005, 472; Fernández et al. 2007, 99).

Labour's broader view of ageing was that 'active elderly citizens' should be encouraged, through the partnership between government and the voluntary sector, to participate in society and to engage in activities that allow them to contribute to the economy as producers and consumers. A strong economic motive was also behind this, not dissimilar to that of the Conservative government that preceded it, that is, the expectation that active older citizens, as volunteers and casual workers financed by cash payments, would provide services that would otherwise be more expensive to the public purse (Powell and Edwards 2002; see also Spandler 2004, 193–194).

Labour introduced a new range of services for the elderly aimed at enabling more elderly people to function independently and at bridging the gap between hospital, primary, and community care and improving the cooperation between health and social services (Glendinning 2003; Lewis 2001; Wanless 2006, 72–74). The Community Care (Delayed Discharges) Act 2003 introduced fines for local authorities if patients could not be discharged from hospital because social services failed to provide an assessment and appropriate social care (Office of Public Sector Information 2003). At the same time the eligibility criteria for community care services have been tightened, making it more difficult for people to use them (Spandler 2004, 197).

6.3.2.2. Extent of Elderly Care in the Home and the Public Sphere

The policies described in the previous section have only affected the lives of a relatively small share of carers and cared-for. Informal and unpaid eldercare is still by far the dominant form; the percentage of informal adult carers in the population slightly increased between 1985 and 2000, but in general, between 1990 and 2000, informal care has not changed much (ONS 2002, 3). In 2001, 11 per cent of the population older than five years were involved in the unpaid care of the sick, disabled, or elderly. Of these, 45 per cent were adults between 45 and 65, and most likely to be female; only 20 per cent were older than 65 (ONS 2001, 2002, 12). Intensity of care increases with age. Hours spent caring rise significantly with age for men and women, and men above 70 are more likely to be carers, and to be carrying a heavy load, than women because older women need greater physical support (Arber and Ginn 1993, 33–46; Dahlberg, Demack, and Bambra 2007).

The Community Care policies had some limited influence. Between 1997 and 2006 the number of contact hours for an average household receiving care services doubled, to 10.8 hours; however, since 2000, the number of households receiving such care declined by 13 per cent. In 2006 nonstate institutions provided three quarters of these services (Information Centre 2007, 1–6).

With regard to Direct Payment, take-up was very poor, and it was particularly low amongst older people, who were only 30 per cent of the overall recipients in 2003–2004. Amongst the causes for low take-up were lack of information amongst potential recipients and professionals, unwillingness of professionals to offer it, and resource rationing of Local Authorities (Fernández et al. 2007, 100–103).

Thus, more home care is financed by the state, delivered by independent service providers, and it is increasingly targeted. Overall, public spending on residential care, home-help services, and local authority personal social services has remained fairly constant in relation to GDP between 1980 and 2003[7], suggesting that by endorsing Care in the Community governments indeed contained spending.

What is the Impact of these Changes for Careers?

Unfortunately for the majority of carers, who are economically active, mainly female, or elderly themselves, nothing has changed. They remain in stressful situations without much support (Arksey and Glendinning 2008, 3; Dahlberg, Demack, and Bambra 2007).

At the same time, the provision of cash for care has acknowledged unpaid work. The policy supports a variety of care relationships, including small-scale care networks of neighbours, relatives, and friends; it was thus assessed to be 'consistent with the ethos and discourse of consumerism and empowerment'

(Ungerson 2004, 15; see also Glendinning et al. 2000; Spandler 2004, 199). This 'commodification' of the care market has also led to the development of two segmented markets for women as carers (Ungerson 2000, 628–630). The first mainly relies upon their employment as personal assistants through close social networks or agencies on a casual basis for low pay (Ungerson 1997, 50–51). The second comprises jobs with local authorities and voluntary organisations that are designed to deliver complex care services with trained and skilled staff.

To conclude, the ageing population and decreasing institutional eldercare generated extra need for localized care, and new policies empowered some existing care relationships through cash for care and expanded job opportunities for qualified care staff. But the policies also contributed to a casualisation of employment relationships in the social-service sector; moreover, cost constraints meant that relative spending in this area did not increase, and therefore service availability still remains extremely limited, putting a lot of strain on the majority of informal carers.

6.3.2.3 Explanations for Family-based Eldercare

In Britain eldercare, like childcare, has mainly been provided in private households on an unpaid basis and continues to be done in this way. In this respect Britain is similar to Spain and Poland and very different from Denmark and Finland. The explanation for this pattern is that there is no substantive and affordable support available to informal carers.

However, when we focus our attention on the changes that have taken place since the 1980s, we see that public policy has had some effect. The reduction of places in public institutions and the introduction of direct payments rewarded some selected previously unpaid informal care arrangements, namely those where the cared-for qualify for state assistance and where there is increased demand for local service providers. The extent of paid informal work thus increased. This policy was adopted for conflicting reasons, making it highly contested in the literature (Scourfield 2005; Spandler 2004, 190–191): Governments expected that 'care in the community' would be cheaper than care in large institutions, but institutionalisation was rejected by many (potential) users of care who wanted more autonomy in their homes.

6.3.3. Size, Patterns, and Explanation with Respect to Informal Employment

6.3.3.1 Social Policies and Extent

Like government in most countries, British governments have actively discouraged informal employment because it often brings with it tax evasion and benefit fraud. Social policies therefore do not support informal employment, rather the state has adopted punitive measures, including prosecution or fines, to suppress it.

Because informal employment is illegal it mostly escapes official registration; its extent and development is therefore notoriously difficult to quantify. An official report on the informal economy for the British government assumed it involved 'billions of pounds' (Lord Grabiner QC 2000, 3). If we take the comparative overviews in the introduction to this book as indicators, it seems that the informal employment sector is less developed in Britain than in many other European countries, only 2 per cent of GDP was spent on it in 2000. According to two different studies, its size is about half that in Germany and Denmark and the second lowest in the countries studied in this book (see Table 8.1, Appendix 5).

These attempts at quantification would bear out our initial characterisation of Britain as a commodified liberal market economy, which crowds out informal work. However, we have to bear in mind their tentative nature. Moreover, the figures do not tell us under what circumstances informal employment is used and who is involved in it. In recent years, based on qualitative studies, a more detailed and contextualized understanding of who performs paid informal work and for what motivation has developed among policy-makers and researchers.

In particular, Williams and Windebank have argued that engagement in informal work is driven not just by economic gain, as had often been assumed. Their research in two English cities came to the conclusion that affluent and less-affluent households engaged in informal economic activities in very different ways.

Contrary to our initial assumption that an increase in formal employment may squeeze out informal paid work, Williams and Windebank (2002b) show that households in affluent areas were more likely to engage in paid informal activities as customers and providers than those in less-affluent areas, that this work was much higher paid than that in deprived parts of town, and was much more often provided by people not previously known to the customer. The prime motivation to pay for such work was that it was cheaper than formally hiring a company, and the prime motivation to do it was to make money (2002a, 73–77). In addition, the better-off were also more likely to engage in other, unpaid activities for their own household, such as home decorating or gardening.

In contrast, households in deprived areas engaged more than affluent ones in mutual aid, that is, in unpaid work done for people outside the respondent's household. Such engagement was not an expression of community spirit, but of a shortage of money. People with a lack of resources helped out their relatives, who were likely to live close by, but they expressed reluctance to accept from or give help to anyone else because they had little faith in reciprocity (Williams and Windebank 2002a, 76; 2002b, 241–242). However, when people in these areas did pay for informal work a much stronger motivation than in the affluent areas was to help the provider; by the same token, providers had a strong motive to help customers, thus this work served a community building and redistribution function (Williams and Windebank 2002a, 77–78).

Engagement in informal paid work also differs by gender. Men and women pursue tasks considered to be 'typical' male or female work, and women are lower paid. A significant amount of informal paid work is performed by higher-income, skilled men who are active in the formal labour market and who use their formal skills for informal purposes (Morris 1995; Pahl 1984; Williams and Windebank 1998). In deprived areas, men were also much more likely than women to see informal paid work as economically necessary (Williams and Windebank 2003, 293). This result is corroborated by interviews with informal workers we conducted between 2003 and 2005;[8] with one exception, the women's earnings complemented other forms of household income, and most important to them was the flexibility, which allowed them to combine informal employment with commitments in their own home. In contrast, the male gardeners and handymen saw their informal employment as an occupation and aimed to earn a family wage in this way.

6.3.3.2. Explaining Trends

Informal employment appears to be less extensive in Britain than elsewhere in Europe, which could be the effect of a liberal regime that enhances formal employment and suppresses informal working models.

The Labour government pursued policies that have a strong focus on social inclusion through labour-market activation and that target low-income families and women with children in particular. Aided by the very favourable economic conditions between 1997 and 2007, these activation policies contributed to a decline in unemployment (Table 4.3, Appendix 3). Following this line of thought, informal employment should have declined further.

However, given that informal paid work is impossible to measure accurately, the comparative figures need to be treated with caution. Indeed, if we use Williams' and Windebank's finding that rising income makes informal economic engagement more and not less likely, it is entirely possible that the increase in employment has led to an expansion of informal paid work, rather than its reduction.

6.3.4. Size, Patterns, and Explanation with Respect to Voluntary Work

Policies

Britain has a long tradition of voluntary activity, going beyond the philanthropical heydays of the nineteenth century (Kendall 2003, 1–4), yet only

since the 1970s have governments started to acknowledge voluntary organisations as a distinct sector of the economy (Harris, Rochester, and Halfpenny 2001, 2). Since then recognition has grown (Harris, Rochester, and
Halfpenny 2001, 3; Kendall 2003, 54–56), and hand in hand with official
acceptance went a marketisation of the relationship between voluntary sector and state; the voluntary sector had to compete for public contracts, and
thus their services had to deliver measurable outcomes (Harris, Rochester,
and Halfpenny 2001, 3–4).

But what precisely is the voluntary sector? Its formal part is comprised
of organisations which are 'non-profit distributing, constitutionally independent of the state, self-governing and benefiting from voluntarism' (Kendall 2003, 6). Services can be 'found across all social activities, including
advocacy and self-help, support for the arts, sport and young people and
faith and faith-linked organizations, medical research and support services
for the elderly, infirm and vulnerable, housing and social enterprises' (Kelly
2007, 1,005). Considering the broadness of such definitions it is clear why
the number of voluntary organisations is very difficult to quantify (Cabinet
Office 2006, 10; Kelly 2007, 1,005–1,006).

Formal voluntary-sector institutions use employees as well as volunteers,
that is, individuals engaged in unpaid activities. The latter, which are of
greater interest to us here, can be divided into two types: formal volunteers
engaged in collective forms and the more numerous informal, individual
volunteers not connected to any establishments or organisations (Low et
al. 2007, 10–11).

When the Labour government came to power, the voluntary sector
became an important subject of public policy, and some argue that in the
mid-2000s it occupied a more central position in policy discussions than
at any time since the nineteenth century (Deakin 2001; Kendall 2003, 267;
Mohan et al. 2006). To promote voluntary institutions and volunteering
was in line with the government's belief in active citizenship, and such promotion was also evident in eldercare (Milligan and Fyfe 2005, 430).

In 1998 the government entered into a high-profile compact, which
proposed that the relationship between the formal voluntary sector and
the state should be based on the recognition of the sector's independence.
It announced new principles for funding, centred on longer term sustainability, offered voluntary institutions involvement in policy formulation
(Deakin 2001, 32; Kelly 2007), and established the Office of the Third Sector, thereby unifying state responsibilities under one roof (Cabinet Office
2008). In addition, taxation was changed in favour of private giving to voluntary organisations, giving Britain 'one of the most favourable tax envi-
ronments for the sector anywhere in the world' (Kendall 2003, 46). Formal
employment in the sector grew substantially as a result (Clark 2007, 3).

Critics of government policy have pointed out that increased regulation
and monitoring of performance can be much more easily incorporated by
large organisations; smaller ones could be disadvantaged in the competition

for funding, and informal volunteering networks may be entirely passed over (Harris 2001, 217). Williams (2002, 249) argues that by ignoring informal contributions government polarizes formal and informal voluntary work, and he thus proposes to treat the informal work in which the deprived low-income population engages as the 'fourth sector' (2002, 259).

Extent of Voluntary Sector

The extent of unpaid volunteering is difficult to measure. For a long time surveys focussed on formal volunteers and thus underestimated activities such as neighbourly support, obscuring in particular the activities of marginalized citizens (Williams and Windebank 2002a; Williams 2002).

Information has become more comprehensive since 2000, when government-funded representative studies of formal and informal volunteering in England were published. Defining volunteering as individual unpaid help to a nonrelative, they found that in 2005 half of all interviewees had been active volunteers at least once a month in the previous year and that informal was much more common than formal engagement (Department for Communities and Local Government 2006, 3).

Who were these volunteers, and what types of activities did they engage in? If we turn to the informal volunteers first, the main story is that a minimum of one-third of all age groups volunteered at least once a month, they came from all social backgrounds, were male and female, and no big difference existed between the degree of informal volunteering in the least and the most deprived areas of England. Informal volunteers helped others with everyday life tasks, they gave advice (52 per cent), escorted people, looked after pets or belongings, and ran little errands (between 34 and 38 per cent) (Department for Communities and Local Government 2006, 5). Looking at differences, engagement was strongest amongst the young and declined with age; half of all 16 to 19 year olds were informal volunteers, but only 29 per cent of all older than 74 were; the more excluded members of society were less active (27 per cent of long-term unemployed and inactive) than more established groups (from 30–45 per cent for everyone else, with students on top), and women (41 per cent) were more likely to engage than men (32 per cent) (Department for Communities and Local Government 2006, 54, 58).

Moving to formal volunteers, we find slightly lower engagement overall, but a fairly similar level across all age groups. In 2005, one-third of the English adult population was engaged at least once a month, running activities, events, or raising money (around 53 per cent), serving on committees, acting as drivers, or giving advice (around 30 per cent). About one-third of these activities were related to educational institutions and less than a quarter to religious, sport-, and health-related organisations (Low, et al. 2007, 25). Only respondents aged between 20 and 34 (about 25 per cent) and those older than 74 were less active (21 per cent) (Department for

Communities and Local Government 2006, 7, 54). In contrast to informal volunteering, in the formal sphere social differences were much more pronounced; citizens without (22 per cent) or with low (16 per cent) qualifications were much less engaged than the well-qualified (around 37 per cent), and those from the most deprived areas were far less likely (19 per cent) to engage than those from the least deprived areas (38 per cent) (Department for Communities and Local Government 2006, 58, 53; see also Mohan et al. 2006, 268, 279–280).

The increased investment and capacity building measures of the Labour government have led to an increase in the number of formal volunteers[9] and have also lifted their morale: In 2007, only 8 per cent thought that their organisation wasn't going anywhere, a decline by half since 1997. By the same token, in 2007 only 3 per cent of voluntary workers could not cope with the work they were asked to do, a dramatic decrease from 30 per cent ten years earlier (Low et al. 2007, 55; Smith 1998). This policy shift is not without costs; the increased emphasis on performance measurability and standardization in order to obtain funding has led to concerns that the traditional virtues of the sector, such as independence and responsiveness to needs, have been damaged and that the sector it has become more standardised (Barman 2007, 103; Kelly 2007). This may be why, in 2007, 28 per cent of formal voluntary workers found the sector too bureaucratic and 17 per cent thought it was becoming 'like paid work' (Low et al. 2007, 56).

Institutional Factors Explaining Voluntary Work

The role of voluntary work in Britain has grown since the 1990s. The main institutional factor explaining this change is government policy; as in the area of child- and eldercare in the voluntary sector, the welfare state has made decisive moves to foster and regulate caring and support relationships in civil society. The backing that public policy-makers have given to the formal voluntary sector has strengthened it while also changing its nature; by becoming more measurable and accountable it is now also more standardized and has lost informality.

The survey data suggests that the opportunities opened by this change in policy have been used by middle-class volunteers more; far fewer of those living in deprived areas have taken advantage of them. Thus, the increase in employment and in double-earner households summarized at the start of this chapter has not diminished the appetite for engagement in civil society of its well-integrated members, whereas it has done little to engage those already marginalized. The criticism that this type of public policy is therefore not addressed to those threatened by exclusion is borne out by this data.

At the same time public policies directed at established charities have not crowded out informal engagement; plenty of voluntary workers are active in all types of communities, and the data suggests that mutual support is as common in marginalized communities as it is elsewhere.

6.4. INFORMAL WORK IN THE CONTEXT OF THE WORK-WELFARE ARRANGEMENT OF THE UNITED KINGDOM

In the introduction to this chapter we asked how informal work develops in a liberal welfare regime with an employment structure where paid formal work is concentrated in two-earner households, and where a comparatively high share of households is economically inactive. We now turn to reexamine this question against the background of the four policy areas described above.

With regard to childcare, we have seen a significant shift in governments' policies. In the mid 2000s, households with children received greater support with formal childcare than such families did a decade before. The dominant political ideology has been in favour of supporting all parents in combining employment and childcare, potentially reducing the hours all households need to spend on informal care. However, because material support focused on education, poverty prevention, and on integrating the inactive into the labour force, the majority of households with children continue to carry substantial responsibility for care. More economically active mothers thus piece together flexibly the services they need and that the household is able to afford, generating more formal employment and informal forms of paid work in this area. Still, maternal informal care remains the central part by far, which is expressed by the facts that British women's part-time rates continue to be among the highest of the countries studied here and that the difference between male and female working hours is the biggest.

The main change in the area of informal eldercare has been a move away from large institutions, which has increased the amount of home-based care, and which gave those elderly entitled to public services greater choice over the type of service they wanted. However, these changes only affected relatively few elderly in need of care. The majority are still cared for on an unpaid basis, mainly by elderly spouses, some frail themselves, as well as by adult children, most of them female, who often struggle to combine employment and care responsibilities. These carers are thus in more need of support than the existing formal and informal paid services offer.

Comparative statistics on informal employment suggest that it only plays a minor role in Britain. From this perspective it seems indeed that the liberal labour market has crowded out this form of work. However, the qualitative studies of more and less affluent areas tell a different story. They show that those households most engaged in employment are also the most active providers and consumers of informal paid work. Deprived households only rarely use or provide informal employment to make ends meet; instead they rely on unpaid mutual support predominantly between relatives. If it is true that formal economic activity leads to demand for informal paid work we can assume that this type of work has expanded since the mid-1990s.

Looking at voluntary work, a similar pattern is apparent. Those most economically established are also most established in voluntary work, if we define it as work done under the umbrella of established institutions. This type of voluntarism has expanded, due to the boost the voluntary sector received from the Labour governments. If we broaden our definition to include individuals not affiliated institutionally, our volunteers become more numerous and diverse in background. From this perspective voluntarism can be found anywhere where neighbours or friends support each other, including in underprivileged areas.

Finally, reinspecting the different areas, what have been the main drivers of change? To be sure, policy-makers have intended to be among them. In particular the Labour governments' belief in Third Way politics and the 'social investment state', which aims to promote human capital and to enable citizens to be active members of society, rather than passive recipients of state benefits or services, is a visible force behind the post-1997 policies in all areas reviewed here (Lister 2003, 2006, 316; Williams 2004, 402). Childcare policies have focussed on labour-force activation and education; in the areas of eldercare and voluntarism stronger incentives have been introduced for citizens to choose and provide care and to develop community services. Informal employment has not been part of the social investment agenda, and thus the attempt was made to suppress it.

However, although these policies have contributed to bringing about some of the changes in informal work that we have seen, they have only been the main drivers in the area of formal voluntary work, as the changed opinions of volunteers testify. In the other areas, the decisions households make continue to be characteristic of a liberal welfare regime, where a low level of state support is typical, and in which most citizens have to rely on the market or the family for their welfare. In childcare, even though state support has increased, the private decisions of households with average incomes with economically active mothers have increased demand for formal and informal services; in eldercare the private decisions of spouses and children of the elderly to care on an unpaid basis guarantee the bulk of services in this area. Finally, informal employment develops despite government's determination to suppress it, because affluent households are keen to get a bargain.

NOTES

1. The authors thank Saniye Dedeoglu for her support in the fieldwork stage of this research, and Paul Bridgen and Heather Buckingham for helpful comments on an earlier draft of this chapter.
2. There is a debate about the degree to which this 'consensus' existed at all (see, e.g., Hall 1993; Hewitt 1992, 65–67; Pierson 1991, 130; Timmins 1996, 171).

3. In the mid-eighties, British social spending of GDP (19.6%) was already below that of the countries in this book with more developed welfare states: Denmark (24.2%), Germany (23.6%), and Finland (22.8%), and this gap remained. In fact, in 2000, three years after the end of the conservative reign, Britain's social expenditure of GDP was the lowest (19.1%) amongst the six countries (Table 1.1 Appendix).
4. The authors excluded student and pensioner households.
5. In 2003, for example, a weekly support through tax and benefits of about £90 was available to households with two children earning up to £300 a week; it was halved for households above that income (Cabinet Office 2002, 88; see also Hills and Waldfogel 2004, 773–775).
6. £117.18 in 2006, or 90% of the woman's average weekly earnings if this is lower.
7. Spending oscillated between 0.4 and 0.5 of GDP (OECD).
8. We conducted qualitative interviews with six handymen/gardeners and six cleaners/childminders in Southampton and with fifteen households in London and Southampton which employed informal workers.
9. Formal volunteering on a monthly basis increased by two per cent since 2001 but those who had volunteered in the last twelve months had increased from 27 per cent to 44 per cent in the same period (Department for Communities and Local Government 2006, 3).

REFERENCES

Annesley, C. (2003) 'Americanised and Europeanised: UK social policy since 1997' *British Journal of Politics and International Relations* 5(2):143–165.

Arber, S., and Ginn, J. (1993) 'Gender and inequalities in health in later life', *Social Science and Medicine* 36(1):33–46.

Arksey, H., and Glendinning, C. (2008) 'Combining work and care: Carers' decision-making in the context of competing policy pressures', *Social Policy and Administration* 42(1):1–18.

Barman, E. (2007) 'What is the bottom line for nonprofit organisations? A history of measurement in the British voluntary sector', *Voluntas* 18:101–115.

Bond, S., and Sales, J. (2001) 'Household work in the UK: An analysis of the British household panel survey 1994', *Work, Employment and Society* 15(2):233–250.

Bridgen, P., and Meyer, T. (2005) 'When do benevolent capitalists change their mind? Explaining the retrenchment of defined benefit pensions in Britain', *Social Policy and Administration* 39(4):764–785.

———. (2007) 'The British pension system and social inclusion', in T. Meyer, P. Bridgen, and B. Riedmüller (eds) *Private Pensions versus Social Inclusion? Non-state Provision for Citizens at Risk in Europe*, Cheltenham, UK, and Lyme, US: Edward Elgar.

Bryson C., Kazimirsky, A., and Southwood, H. (2006) National centre for social research, childcare and early years provision: A study of parent's use. Views and experience, Research Report RR723, National Centre for Social Research, Centre for Education and Skills, http://www.dfes.gov.uk/research/data/uploadfiles/RR723.pdf (accessed May 2008).

Cabinet Office (2002) *Budget Report,* London: HM Treasury, www.hm-treasury.gov.uk/media/4/1/Budget_2002.pdf (accessed 17 May 2008).

———. *The Future Role of the Third Sector in Social and Economic Regeneration: Interim Report.* London: HM Treasury, http://www.hm-treasury.gov.uk./media/9/8/pbr06_3rd_sector_428.pdf (accessed May 2008).

————. (2007) Jane Kennedy MP speech to Daycare Trust Conference, London, 14 November 2007, www.hm-treasury.gov.uk/newsroom_and_speeches/speeches/finsecspeeches/speech_fst_141107.cfm (accessed 17 May 2008).

————. (2008) *About Us*, London, http://www.cabinetoffice.gov.uk/third_sector/about_us.aspx (accessed 21st May 2008).

Clarke, J., and Newman, J. (1997) 'From the cradle to the grave: The crises of the post-war welfare settlements', *The Managerial State: Power, Politics and Ideology in the Remaking of Social Welfare*, London: Sage Publications, 1–17.

Clasen, J. (2003) 'Towards a new welfare state or reverting to type? Some major trends in British social policy since the early 1980s', *The European Legacy* 8(5):573–586.

————. (2005) *Reforming European Welfare States. Germany and the United Kingdom Compared*, Oxford: Oxford University Press.

Dahlberg, L., S. Demack, et al. (2007). "Age and gender of informal carers: a population-based study in the UK." *Health & Social Care in the Community* 15(5): 439-445.

Deakin, N. (2001) 'Public policy, social policy and voluntary organisations', in M. Harris and C. Rochester (eds) *Voluntary Organisations and Social Policy in Britain: Perspectives on Change and Choice*, Basingstoke: Palgrave.

Department for Communities and Local Government (2006) *2005 Citizenship Survey. Active Communities Topic Report*, London, www.communities.gov.uk (accessed April 2008).

DWP (2006) *NI17A—A Guide to Maternity Benefits*, London: Department of Work and Pensions.

Esping-Andersen, G. (1990) *The Three Worlds of Welfare Capitalism*, Cambridge: Polity Press.

Fernández, J.L., Kendall, J., Davey, V., and Knapp, M. (2007) 'Direct payments in England: Factors linked to variations in local provision', *International Social Policy* 36(1):97–121.

Glendinning, C. (2003) 'Breaking down barriers: Integrating health and care services for older people in England', *Health Policy* 65(2):139–151.

Glendinning, C., Halliwell, S., Jacobs, S., Rummery, K., and Tyrer, J. (2000) 'New kinds of care, new kinds of relationships: How purchasing services affects relationships in giving and receiving personal assistance', *Health & Social Care in the Community* 8(3):201–211.

Glyn, A. (2001) 'Inequalities of employment and wages in OECD countries', *Oxford Bulletin of Economics and Statistics* 63 (Special Issue):697–713.

Government Statistics Services (1999) *Labour Market Trends. Women in the Labour Market Results from the Spring 1998 Labour Force Survey*, London.

Gregg, P., and Wadsworth, J. (2001) 'Everything you ever wanted to know about measuring worklessness and polarization at the household level but were afraid to ask', *Oxford Bulletin of Economics and Statistics* 63(Special Issue):777–806.

Hall, P.A. (1993) 'Policy paradigms, social learning and the state. The case of economic policy-making in Britain', *Comparative Politics* 25(3):275–296.

Hall, P.A., and Soskice, D. (2001) 'An introduction to varieties of capitalism', in P.A. Hall and D. Soskice (eds), *Varieties of Capitalism: The Institutional Foundations of Comparative Advantage*, Oxford: Oxford University Press, 1–70.

Harris, M. (2001) 'Voluntary organisations in a changing social policy environment', in M. Harris and C. Rochester (eds), *Voluntary Organisations and Social Policy in Britain: Perspectives on Change and Choice*, Basingstoke: Palgrave.

Harris, M., Rochester, C., and Halfpenny, P. (2001) 'Voluntary organisations and social policy: Twenty years of change', in M. Harris and C. Rochester (eds),

Voluntary Organisations and Social Policy in Britain: Perspectives on Change and Choice, Basingstoke: Palgrave.

Hay, C. (1996) 'Narrating the crisis: The discursive construction of the "winter of discontent"', *Sociology* 30(2):253–277.

Hewitt, M. (1992) *Welfare, Ideology and Need: Developing Perspectives on the Welfare State*, Hemel Hempstead: Harvester Wheatsheaf.

Hills, J., and Waldfogel, J. (2004) 'A "third way"' in welfare reform? Evidence from the United Kingdom', *Journal of Policy Analysis and Management* 23(4):765–788.

HM Revenue & Customs (2007) *Paying for Childcare, IR115*, London, www.hmrc.gov.uk/leaflets/ir115.pdf (accessed 11 May 2008).

Information Centre (2007) *Community Care Statistics 2006. Home care services for adults, England*, Government Statistical Service, http://www.ic.nhs.uk/web-files/publications/ccs06homehelp1/HH1%20Pub.pdf (accessed May 2008).

Kavanagh, D. (1990) *Thatcherism and British Politics: The End of Consensus?*, 2nd ed., Oxford: Oxford University Press.

Kelly, J. (2007) 'Reforming public services in the UK: Bringing in the third sector', *Public Administration* 85(4):1003–1022.

Kendall, J. (2003) *The Voluntary Sector*, London: Routledge.

Kiernan, K., Land, H., and Lewis, J. (1998) *Lone Motherhood in Twentieth-Century Britain: From Footnote to Front Page*, Oxford: Clarendon Press.

Lewis, J. (1992) 'Gender and the development of welfare regimes', *Journal of European Social Policy* 2(3):159–173.

———. (2001) 'Older people and the health-social care boundary in the UK: Half a century of hidden policy conflict', *Social Policy and Administration* 35(4):343–359.

———. (2003) 'Developing early years childcare in England, 1992–2002: The choices for (working) mothers', *Social Policy and Administration* 37(3):219–238.

Lewis, J., Campbell, M., and Huerta, C. (2008) 'Patterns of paid and unpaid work in western Europe: Gender, commodification, preferences and the implications for policy', *Journal of European Social Policy* 18(1):21–37.

Lister, R. (2003) 'Investing in the citizen-workers of the future: Transformations in citizenship and the state under new labour', *Social Policy and Administration* 37(5):427–443.

———. (2006) 'Children (but not women) first: New labour, child welfare and gender', *Critical Social Policy* 26(2):315–335.

Lord Grabiner QC (2000) *The Informal Economy*, London: The Treasury, http://www.hm-treasury.gov.uk./media/0/0/74.pdf (accessed March 2008).

Low, N., Butt, S., Ellis Paine, A., and Davis Smith, D. (2007) *Helping Out: A National Survey of Volunteering and Charitable Giving*, London: National Centre for Social Research and the Institute for Volunteering Research, Cabinet Office/Office of the Third Sector.

Marchbank, J. (2000) *Women, Power and Policy: Comparative Studies of Childcare*, London: Routledge.

McKie, L., Bowlby, S., and Gregory, S. (2001) 'Gender, caring and employment in Britain', *Journal of Social Policy* 30(2):233–258.

Means, R., and Smith, R. (1998) *From Poor Law to Community Care*, Bristol: The Policy Press.

Meyer, T., and Pfau-Effinger, B. (2006) 'Gender arrangements and pension systems in Britain and Germany: Tracing change over five decades', *International Journal of Ageing and Later Life* 1(2):67–110.

Millar, J. (2000) 'Lone parents and the new deal', *Policy Studies* 21(4):333–345.

Milligan, C., and Fyfe, N.R. (2005) 'Preserving space for volunteers: Exploring the links between voluntary welfare organisations, volunteering and citizenship', *Urban Studies* 42(3):417–433.

Mohan, J., Twigg, L., Jones, K., and Barnard, S. (2006) 'Volunteering, geography and welfare: A multilevel investigation of geographical variations in voluntary action', in C. Milligan and D. Conradson (eds) *Landscapes of Voluntarism: New Spaces of Health, Welfare and Governance*, Bristol: Policy Press.

Morris, L. (1995) *Social Divisions: Economic Decline and Social Structural Change*, London: UCL Press.

Nickell, S. (2001a) 'Special issue: The labour market consequences of technical and structural change—Introduction', *Oxford Bulletin of Economics and Statistics* 63:617–627.

———. (2001b) 'Fundamental changes in the UK labour market', *Oxford Bulletin of Economics and Statistics* 63:715–736.

OECD (2002) *Labour Force Statistics*, Paris: OECD.

———. (2007) *Labour Force Statistics*, Paris: OECD.

———. *Social Expenditure Data Base*, Paris: OECD, http://www.oecd.org/statsportal/. Accessed May 2008.

Office of Public Sector Information (2003) *Community Care (Delayed Discharges etc.). Act, (2003)*, London, http://www.opsi.gov.uk/ACTS/acts2003/2003005.htm. (accessed 17 May 2008).

OFSTED (2003). Registered childcare providers and places in England, OFSTED.

———. (2006). Quarterly Childcare Statistics as at 31 March 2006, OFSTED.

ONS (2001) *Social Trends 34*, London: Office for National Statistics, www.statistics.gov.uk/downloads/theme_social/Social_Trends34/Social_Trends_34.pdf (accessed 11 May 2008).

———. (2002) *Population Trends*, London: Office for National Statistics.

———. (2005) *Labour Force Survey. Spring 2005*, London: Office for National Statistics, http://www.statistics.gov.uk/statbase/product.asp?vlnk=8292 (accessed 10 April 2007).

———. (2006) *Labour Market Review*, London: Office for National Statistics, www.statistics.gov.uk/statbase/Product.asp?vlnk=14315&More=n (accessed May 2008).

———. (2007) *Focus On Gender. October 2006*, London: Office for National Statistics, www.statistics.gov.uk/downloads/theme_compendia/fog2006/gender_summary.pdf (accessed 11 May 2008).

Pahl, R.E. (1984) *Division of Labour*, Oxford: Blackwell.

Papadopoulos, F., and Tsakloglou, P. (2002) 'Aggregate level and determining factors of social exclusion in twelve European countries', *Journal of European Social Policy* 12(3):211–225.

Pascall, G. (1999) 'UK family policy in the 1990s: The case of new labour and lone parents', *International Journal of Law, Policy and the Family* 13:258–273.

Paull, G., Taylor, J., and Duncan, A. (2002) *Mothers' Employment and Childcare in Britain*, IFS Reports, R64 ISBN: 978–1-903274–23–1.

Pierson, C. (1991) *Beyond the Welfare State? The New Political Economy of the Welfare State*, Cambridge: Polity.

Powell, J.L., and Edwards, M.M. (2002) 'Policy narratives of ageing: The rights way, the third way or the wrong way', *Electronic Journal of Sociology http://www.sociology.org/*.

Rake, K. (2001) 'Gender and new labour's social policies', *Journal of Social Policy* 30(2):209–231.

Randall, V. (2000) *The Politics of Child Daycare in Britain*, Oxford: Oxford University Press.

Rowthorn, R. (2000) 'Kalecki centenary lecture: The political economy of full employment in modern Britain', *Oxford Bulletin of Economics and Statistics* 62(2):139–173.

Scourfield, P. (2005) 'Implementing the community care (direct payments) act: Will the supply of personal assistants meet the demand and at what price?', *Journal of Social Policy* 34(3):469–488.

Smith, D.J. (1998) *The 1997 National Survey of Volunteering*, The National Centre for Volunteering, London, http://www.ivr.org.uk/researchbulletins/bulletins/1997–national-survey-of-volunteering-in-the-uk.htm (accessed 21 May 2008).

Spandler, H. (2004) 'Friend or foe? Towards a critical assessment of direct payments', *Critical Social Policy* 24(2):187–209.

Symonds, A., and Kelly, A. (eds) (1998) *The Social Construction of Community Care*, Basingstoke: Macmillan.

Taylor-Gooby, P. (2001) 'Welfare reform in the UK: The construction of a liberal consensus', in P. Taylor-Gooby (ed.) *Welfare State under Pressure*, London: Sage Publications, 147–170.

Timmins, N. (1996) *The Five Giants. A Biography of the Welfare State*, London: Fontana Press.

Ungerson, C. (1997) 'Give them the money: Is cash a route to empowerment?', *Social Policy & Administration* 31(1):45–53.

———. (2000) 'Thinking about the production and consumption of long-term care in Britain: Does gender still matter?', *Journal of Social Policy* 29(4):623–643.

———. (2004) 'Whose empowerment and independence? A cross-national perspective on 'cash for care' schemes', *Ageing and Society* 24:189–212.

Wanless, D. (2006) Securing good care for older people, King's Fund, London.

Williams, C.C. (2002) 'Harnessing voluntary work: A fourth sector approach', *Policy Studies* 23(3/4):247–260.

Williams, C., and Windebank, J. (1998) Informal employment in the advanced economies: Implications for work and welfare, London and New York: Routledge.

———. (2002a) 'Why do people engage in paid informal work? A comparison of higher- and lower-income urban neighbourhoods in Britain', *Community, Work and Family* 5(1):67–83.

Williams, C.C., and Windebank, J. (2002b) 'The uneven geographies of informal economic activities: A case study of two British cities', *Work Employment and Society* 16(2):231–250.

———. (2003) 'Reconceptualizing women's paid informal work: Some lessons from lower-income urban neighbourhoods', *Gender, Work & Organization* 10(3):281–300.

Williams, F. (2004) 'What matters is who works: Why every child matters to new labour. Commentary on the DfES green paper every child matters', *Critical Social Policy* 24(3):406–427.

Wincott, D. (2006) 'Paradoxes of new labour social policy: Toward universal child care in Europe's "most liberal" welfare regime?', *Social Politics* 13(2):286–312.

7 The Metamorphosis of Informal Work in Spain

Family Solidarity, Female Immigration, and Development of Social Rights

Lluís Flaquer and Anna Escobedo

INTRODUCTION

Spain is characterised by a widespread prevalence and social acceptance of informal work, not only in terms of both informal care work and informal employment, but also in terms of voluntary help amongst households. This feature accompanies a strong tradition of family solidarity in keeping with historically low rates of female employment, very low levels of public expenditure on family and children, and a relatively high degree of development of extended family forms. The traditional importance of the family in Spanish society is probably a reflection of a deep-seated mistrust of the state associated with a difficult and belated economic modernisation, a delayed transition to democracy as late as the end of the 1970s, and a problematic nation-building process resulting from long-standing cultural heterogeneity and complex territorial tensions. The lack of confidence in the state and the low level of legitimacy of public institutions is also evidenced by the persistence of clientelism in a number of social areas and a great amount of fiscal evasion and black economy.

Spain is a very good case with which to illustrate the shifting boundaries between formal and informal work: Recent contradictory developments show the metamorphosis of informal work as the response to the challenges posed by the changing economic system, evolving societal tensions, and new political and legal developments. As a result of these factors, the already problematic inclusion of Spain within current typologies—either for welfare regimes or family/gender arrangements—has been made even more difficult.

The purpose of this chapter is to provide a description of the specific extent and structure of informal work in Spain and to try to explain its peculiar features in the context of the specific arrangement of work and welfare in this country. In the first section of this chapter the arrangement of work and welfare in Spain is discussed. The second section deals with the development of formal employment and economic change. Finally, the third section presents the main features of informal work in Spain, especially focusing on policies and patterns, and giving an explanation with respect to family-based childcare, eldercare, informal employment and voluntary work.

7.1. THE ARRANGEMENT OF WORK AND WELFARE IN SPAIN

After the bloody Civil War of 1936–1939 and nearly forty years of dictatorship, Spain finally came to democracy with the approval of a new constitution in 1978. One of the legacies of Franco's authoritarian regime was a deep-rooted mistrust of the state and an intense depoliticising of everyday life; another was the state's avoidance of intervention in family matters.

The impact of the extended dictatorship was added to the former long-standing tradition of little confidence in a political system entirely controlled by the ruling elites, which allowed the people a very limited participation that was often channeled by social movements of premodern character, such as Carlism and Anarchism during the nineteenth and the first decades of the twentieth centuries. The traces of these past undemocratic experiences are still visible in a certain confusion in the perception of private and public interest, discredit of politics as a highly divisive concern, deficit in 'stateness' and weakness of the political system and civil society (Ferrera 1996; Subirats 1999). The values and attitudes underlying Spanish civic culture are expressed by scant affiliation with political parties and little interest in politics.[1]

One of the factors that largely explains the arrangement of work and welfare in Spain from the democratic transition period up the end of the 1990s is the inability to update or expand family-policy measures in contrast to other areas of social policy. Up until the death of Franco in 1975, conservative family policy, mainly consisting of cash benefits for large families, had been a dominant component of Spanish social provision and therefore was considered one of most prominent features of the authoritarian regime. The subsequent shunning of family policy can be interpreted as a strong backlash against the legacy of authoritarian policies. All relevant postauthoritarian political and social actors, wanting to distance themselves from Franco's pronatalist and antifeminist family policies, avoided policy-making in the field. They associated any family programme at all with the measures of former times (Valiente 1997).

This avoidance of measures to relate family and employment and to provide needed care services, along with certain structural factors, such as high rates of unemployment that will be discussed in Section 2, are the main reasons for the long prevalence of an arrangement of work and welfare based on the prominence of the family in welfare provision.

According to Esping-Andersen (1990, 1999), Spain is a 'conservative' welfare regime, but some writers have challenged his categorisation of

Southern European countries such as Spain or Italy (Leibfried 1992; Saraceno 1994; Ferrera 1996; Flaquer 2000; among others). In recent years, the notion of 'family/kinship solidarity' model has been proposed to characterise the Southern welfare regime, because in such countries strong intergenerational ties and intense kin solidarity along the life course are expected both within the household and between households (Naldini 2003). The presence in the Spanish population of strong family networks and of extended family forms has long been a bulwark against hardship as well as a convenient arrangement to help harmonise the demands of work and family, soften the consequences of the increasing rate of family breakdown, and diminish for adult children the cost of achieving economic and residential independence from their parents.

Household complexity allows an intergenerational exchange in both directions of family services and accounts for the importance of mutual help among close female kin living in different households. By complex households we mean those corresponding to family forms including as coresidents adult people other than nuclear family members. Complex households include very different kinds of situations and family forms: (a) Families with dependent children and (nondependent) older siblings still living in the household; (b) Complex one-parent families, that is, single parents with children living with their parent(s); (c) Couples with dependent children living with one or more grandparents. In 2002, the percentage of Spanish households made up of three or more adults with or without dependent children amounted to 41 per cent, whereas in the EU-15 this figure was 23 per cent on average. Although the average household size decreased from 3.6 in 1981–1982 to 3 in 2002, it is still larger than in the EU-15, where it decreased from 2.8 to 2.4 (Eurostat 2004).

Under the 'family/kinship solidarity' welfare regime, gender and family arrangements are not based so much on the male-breadwinner/homemaker model, but rather are influenced by the family economy model (Pfau-Effinger 2004). However, for many years, due to a number of circumstances (high rates of female unemployment, lack of childcare services, etc.), in the majority of couples only the man was employed. Here a distinction must be made between normative models and family organisation patterns. In Spain, the modernisation of the male-breadwinner family model was not a viable option because, both structurally and politically, it was in a very weak position and had no tradition (Pfau-Effinger 2005a and 2005b). This model, developed under Franco's rule when the share of industrial workers was small[2], was not actively supported in the democratic period as it was considered part and parcel of authoritarian family policy. In any case, widespread support (64 per cent) was recently expressed by women for an ideal family model with both partners employed during similar working hours and with childraising and domestic chores equally shared; alternative preferences scored very low (Table 7.1).

Table 7.1.   Preferences for Ideal Family Models in Spain, 2006

	. %	. (N)
A family in which both partners have employment with similar working times and in which childcare and domestic chores are equally shared	64.0	(6230)
A family in which the wife has a part-time job and she devotes more time than her husband to childcare and domestic chores	16.2	(1577)
A family in which the husband has a part-time job and he devotes more time than his wife to childcare and domestic chores	1.2	(118)
A family in which only the husband has a job and in which the wife devotes her time to childcare and domestic chores	13.9	(1357)
A family in which only the wife has a job and in which the husband devotes his time to childcare and domestic chores	0.5	(47)
Other	1.1	(111)
N.S.	2.4	(232)
N.C.	0.6	(60)
TOTAL	100.0	(9736)

Source: Survey on fertility and values in 21st-century Spain, Centro de Investigaciones Sociológicas (Question 615: There are many ways in which family tasks and responsibilities can be shared. I shall give you a few examples. If money were no problem, which of the following options would you choose? Women age 15 and over, Spain, 2006).

Of the countries covered in this volume, Spain has one of the lowest levels of social expenditure on the family and children (Tables 1.1 and 1.2 Appendix). In 2004 Spain devoted only 0.7 per cent of GDP to this spending area. This is the smallest percentage among the EU-25.[3] However, in the last few years the picture given by these data has become somewhat misleading because a part of the increasing Spanish family subsidies is not categorised as social expenditure. Middle-class parents get generous allowances for dependent children in the form of income-tax credit, and most formal childcare institutions are preprimary schools financed by educational authorities.

Our argument is that the arrangement of work and welfare based on the 'family/kinship solidarity' model seems now to be on the wane, despite the fact that many remnants of this pattern are still present in Spanish society. Two recent developments appear to challenge its continuation: the provision of care services by immigrant women, and the introduction of new social rights underpinning the care of dependent adults. Furthermore, a continuous expansion of early education and childcare services—supported by all political options though following different criteria—is following in the wake of increased maternal employment, particularly in the 2000s.

7.2. DEVELOPMENT OF FORMAL EMPLOYMENT AND ECONOMIC CHANGE

Low female activity rates were long one of the most prominent characteristics of the Spanish labour market. They were due to the policy legacies of the Franco regime, women's low educational qualifications, discouragingly high unemployment rates, and a virtual lack of public care services. This left much scope for the development of family-based informal care and undeclared work.

Since the late 1990s the evolution of employment has been quite positive (Tables 4.1 and 4.2, Appendix). The intense growth of female employment during the last two and a half decades is connected with the increase in the share of dual-earner couples among the Spanish population, with 44 per cent of couples working full-time in 2003, a figure very close to the EU-25 average (45 per cent). However, in a similar percentage of couples (43 per cent) only the man was employed, in contrast with a EU-25 average of only 29 per cent, and the share of couples in which the man was working full-time and the woman part-time was one-tenth of the total (versus two-tenths in the EU)[4].

Despite female part-time employment nearly doubling since 1992 and its particular rise since 2004, the Spanish rates lie in the middle range (Table 4.4, Appendix). Part-time employment tends to be unstable and mainly in low-qualification, poorly paid positions, which also explains why the rate of voluntary part-timers is so low in Spain. More than half of part-time work is temporary or informal, and job turnover is very high (CES 2002; EC 2007: Indicator 21.M2).

One of the most conspicuous characteristics of the Spanish labour market is the persistent duality of a well-protected core workforce on the one hand, and a mass of workers with fixed-term contracts and unstable working conditions on the other. There is a very pronounced segmentation with an insider core workforce benefiting from social rights and heavily protected against dismissal, contrasting with a mass of workers who have unstable contracts or are unemployed. This pattern is related to three different factors: shortage of employment, disparities between genders and generations, and the structure of the economy.

This pattern evolved from a situation of widespread unemployment in the 1980s and 1990s due to the overlapping of industrial and postindustrial transitions in different parts of Spain, together with a massive influx of women onto the labour market. The insider–outsider divide emerged as a result of an implicit compromise reached with the unions under threat of drastic deregulation measures aimed—with the idea of creating more jobs—

at making labour cheaper and more flexible. However, the widespread use of fixed-term contracts does not appear to have spurred an increase in permanent jobs (Bentolila and Dolado 1994; Rhodes 1997; Cousins 1999).

This is basically a gender and age divide, and it mirrors a generational gap between younger cohorts with fairly solid academic credentials and poorly educated older cohorts with an abiding influence wielded through mechanisms of social closure: Middle-aged male heads of the family earn the lion's share of the welfare-state benefits, and women, young people, virtually all entrants to the labour market, and immigrants bear the brunt of 'precarity' and unemployment. The high wages and job security enjoyed for years by (chiefly male) insiders is the reverse side of the coin of the exclusion affecting their sons, daughters, and wives (Cousins 1999; Esping-Andersen 1999).

Many gender and age disparities have remained or even grown. Unemployment rates among women are nearly double those of men (11.6 per cent versus 6.4 per cent), and young people are the most beset by both unemployment (18 per cent) and job instability (65 per cent have temporary employment)[5.] Similarly, the gender pay-gap most affects both extremes of the least and most qualified women, basically in the private sector (25 per cent, versus 4 per cent in the public sector in 2001) (Caprile and Escobedo 2003).

Casual work is prominent in the Spanish economy and is rooted in sectors such as tourism and construction but also in other sectors such as personal and household services. It is not only widespread in the private sector but also in public administration where fixed-term contracts have grown more usual in recent years.

Though since the beginning of the 2000s unemployment has drastically fallen, labour segmentation has not only persisted but a new divide between Spanish and immigrant workers has forcefully emerged. Typically, illegal immigrants work first in the informal economy until they succeed in attaining legal residency, upon which they enter the formal labour market where they predominate in farming, construction, and domestic services. Between 2000 and 2005 about three million immigrants arrived in Spain. In 1999 they only represented 2 per cent of the total workforce, in 2007 they accounted for 14 per cent of all employees contributing to Social Security.

Figure 7.1 illustrates the steep rise in the foreign population during the last decade. In 2007 foreign citizens were one-tenth of the population resident in Spain. Eight out of ten migrants are potentially active in the economy. As seen in the graph, the growth is mostly among people of prime age and their children, and it is expected that this will bring with it a considerable rejuvenation of the Spanish population.

7.3. MAIN FEATURES OF INFORMAL WORK

Informal work has long been very widespread, culturally embedded, and socially well accepted in Spain. However, since the beginning of the 2000s

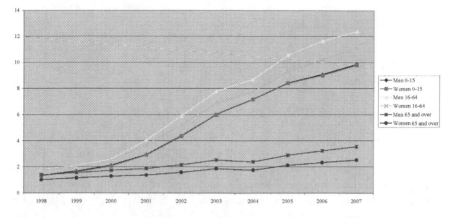

Figure 7.1. Percentage of foreign citizens among the Spanish population by sex and age groups in Spain, 1998–2007. Source: Own elaboration using data from the Spanish National Statistics Institute.

it has been experiencing a profound metamorphosis in its size, profile, and character. This is happening for various reasons. In the first place, the fast-growing employment rates of younger women are reducing the potential number of caregivers and challenging the sustainability of the welfare arrangement based on family solidarity. Secondly, in response to this a number of legal and policy developments are eliminating the older forms of informal work as care occupations are formalised and undeclared work situations legalised, though this does not hinder the development of new, different sources of informal work.

Up to the end of the 1990s the low level of female participation in the labour market made the great bulk of caregivers available for family-based informal work and mutual exchange of help among households. This is related to the educational divide between younger and older generations of women. As the surviving housewives approach retirement age, this divide is increasing. One of the ways in which a substantial part of the increased middle-class female participation has been made possible is through the growth of domestic service (*empleadas de hogar*). Many domestic servants are female immigrants who also provide care services (Parella Rubio, 2003; Solé and Flaquer 2005).

Informal family-based care is slowly but steadily decreasing in favour of new employment opportunities in the care sector. Nevertheless, formal leave-of-absence schemes for family-care purposes (parental leave or adult-care leave schemes) have still not been developed as a real option, as they are mostly unpaid and therefore rarely used.

Most informal employment is taken by irregular immigrants who work in labour-intensive economic sectors, but undeclared work is also common among natives. Finally, participation in charitable associations is rather low, and a great part of voluntary work is performed in the exchange of services among family households.

7.3.1. Policies, Patterns, and Explanation with Respect to Family-Based Childcare

7.3.1.1. Welfare-state Policies and Institutional Framework

Spaniards are having fewer children, and they tend to have them later in life, and the expectations placed on children and the quality of their care and education have risen. In the last two decades childcare has been progressively and steadily institutionalised, mainly in the realm of school and early educational programmes. At the same time family-based childcare is still very widespread, and it compensates for the shortcomings of state policies and regulations intended to reconcile the demands of family and work.

In 1990 compulsory education was mandated for those age 6 to 16. The pre-6 period was deemed noncompulsory 'early education', and the political goal was to ensure universal coverage with early childhood education for children from age 3 up. This target was reached at the end of the 1990s. Starting in 2004 the aim has been to support early education (age 3–6) through public funding either in publicly managed centres or in subsidised, nonprofit schools. (Spain has a significant share of subsidised private schools, often managed by Roman Catholic organizations.) School hours are 25 per week, but most centres provide care and meals for 9 to 17 hours.

For children under the age of three the situation is very different. Public funding has not yet been extended to this age group, except for publicly managed nursery schools and some nonprofit centres, but with a new education law in 2006 the government committed to extending public funding to 20 per cent of under-3-year-olds. Early childhood education (up to age 3) is increasingly perceived as a positive resource, and especially public-sector nursery schools are benefiting from more funds and good-quality standards, but the extension of its coverage is not keeping up with the increase in mothers' employment. The increasing gap between maternal employment and childcare coverage for the under-3s in regular early education has been instead filled by an increase in nonregulated childcare services and arrangements with child-minders, chiefly on an informal employment basis, and within family networks (especially involving grandparents).

Family day care, which constitutes one part of the public supply of childcare for the under-3s in most EU countries, is virtually nonexistent. Paid care at the child's own home performed by household assistants or child-minders, often on an informal employment basis, is much more common among families who can afford it. The laws which affect these caregivers, as household employees, are those regulating domestic service. There is neither public supervision nor regularly gathered data on this kind of childcare job.

Out-of-school services, that is, the care of school-aged children, have also been developing from the early 1990s onwards in connection with the growth of full-time maternal employment, given that school schedules often are not compatible with ordinary working hours and vacations. To cover the child-care needs of children when they are ill, outside of school hours, and during school holidays, a combination of family, public, and private resources has emerged. This combination consists of parents' work arrangements, grand-parents' help and also child-minders and household assistants. Municipali-ties and parents' school boards are also taking more and more responsibility for developing outside-of-school-hours care service offers.

Between 1992 and 2006 early childhood education coverage increased from 4 per cent to 17 per cent of under-3s (4 per cent for under-ones; 16 per cent of one-year-olds; 30 per cent of under-twos) in nursery schools (*escuelas infantiles 0–3*) providing care usually on a full-time basis, with 43 per cent in public and 57 per cent in private centres. In 2006, 47 per cent of under-3s were estimated to be in centre-based childcare on average 28 hours per week, including other socioeducational centres and nurser-ies not authorised by the educational administration; furthermore 29 per cent are cared for by paid or unpaid carers (including relatives) an average of 23 hours per week, and up to 54 per cent of under-3s had employed mothers[6]. In a comparative perspective the coverage of children 3 and older is nearly complete, but there is a medium-level coverage of children under 3 (Table 5.1, Appendix). The satisfaction with access to and qual-ity of childcare facilities is poor (about ten percentage points below the EU-25 average (European Commission 2005), which can be explained by the prominence of unsubsidised facilities and such not supervised by the educational authorities.

The regulation of leave-of-absence arrangements in Spain has been mod-ified many times since 1989, importantly in 1999 and 2007, mostly with the aim of improving coverage and related benefits. However, the practical impact is rather limited in that that parents still only have 18 weeks paid leave upon the birth of a child under normal circumstances (since March 2007 fathers can take two weeks) (see Table 7.2).

Furthermore, the effects of the intended improvements to the Spanish laws have been limited by job instability: Although most of the laws were mainly conceived within a context of stable working contracts, these days more than one-third of young adults have only temporary or unstable jobs. The fact that parental leave and the work-time reduction for childcare are not paid is an additional factor which hinders their use, even by those who have steady jobs. Because most families with young children usually have high mortgage payments (the rental housing market is minimal in Spain, accounting for less than 15 per cent of all housing arrangements), they can-not afford to reduce their earnings, except for short periods. In temporary and irregular employment situations, many employees do not feel empow-ered to develop strategies to reconcile the demands of work and family time or even to make use of the opportunities provided by current regula-tions. In irregular or temporary employment certain job guarantees such as parental leave or family sick leave simply do not apply.

Table 7.2. Statutory Leave-of-Absence Arrangements for Working Parents for Family Reasons in Spain, 2007

Maternity leave

Sixteen weeks paid at 100% of previous earnings by social security. The mother can transfer the last ten weeks of the maternity leave to the father. Ten weeks can also be redistributed over twenty weeks at part-time. Contributory requirements are to be currently paying social security contributions and to have contributed at least the equivalent of 180 full-time days in the last seven years. Contributory requirements have been softened for part-time mothers and young mothers under 26; since 2007 there is also a new, flat-rate forty-two-day maternity benefit for employed mothers who do not qualify for the contributory one. There is a small work-time reduction (feeding leave) of one-half or one hour per day until the child is nine months old, to be paid by the employer. Since 2007 it is possible to consolidate this reduction in work time as an extension of maternity leave by some weeks (usually two to three weeks).

Paternity Leave

Since March 2007, the two previously provided days of paternity leave have been supplemented with thirteen additional days (the new law foresees extending paternity leave to four weeks within a six-year period). It is paid at 100% of earnings by social security except for the first two days which are paid by the employer. The paternity leave can be used during or after the end of maternity leave. With an employer's consent, it can be used full- or part-time.

Parental leave

An unpaid leave scheme that can be taken until the child is three. The person on leave is considered inactive and excluded from the part of the social protection schemes related to employment contributions. During the first year, the same job position and workplace are maintained, and the period counts towards social security rights. After the first year, the job protection applies to a job of the same category. There is also an **unpaid work-time reduction** of between one-half and one-eighth of the usual work-time of a guardian of a child under age eight or a disabled child. It is an individual entitlement.

Leave to care for a sick child

Two days (four days if travelling is required) [child] sick-leave are paid by the employer only in case of severe illness, accident, or hospitalisation. It is an individual right that can be used by both parents.

Leave to care for a sick relative

An unpaid leave scheme (similar to the unpaid parental leave) of a maximum of two years for taking care of a severely ill relative (up to second degree of consanguinity or affinity, which includes children, parents, parents-in-law, partners, and siblings). The person on leave is considered inactive, but up to one year of leave counts towards social security rights. There is also an **unpaid work-time reduction** of between one-half and one-eighth of the usual work time. It is an individual entitlement.

7.3.1.2. The Specific Features of Informal Childcare

In 2001, 17 per cent of adults performed childcare on a daily basis (25 per cent of adult women, of which 59 per cent devoted more than 40 hours per week), and the brunt of informal childcare fell mainly on the 30–44 age group[7]. In comparative terms the percentage of women looking after children in Spain falls in the middle range of the countries studied in this volume. Data indicate that informal childcare decreased slightly from 1996 to 2001, both in terms of the proportion of population involved in it on a daily basis, and in terms of the number of hours per week. The proportion of adults caring for children daily decreased by two percentage points. On the other hand, the proportion of those spending more than 40 hours per week on childcare decreased in favour of those spending less than this amount of time (which is an intensity of care more compatible with paid employment). According to the Spanish survey on time use (2002–2003), 11.2 per cent of men and 18.6 per cent of women were directly involved in childcare, with a daily average duration of 1:27 and 2:11 hours, respectively[8]. In 2004, 14.6 per cent of children under 3 were looked after by informal carers without pay, with an average number of 22.5 hours per week.[9]

Finally, between 1995 and 2005, maternity leave coverage (16 paid weeks) increased from 31 per cent to 65 per cent of all children born. The coverage of unpaid parental leave (up to the child's third year) is very low inasmuch as in 2005 registered leaves only accounted for around 7 per cent of the newborns, or 2 per cent of the under-two age group, and were taken in 30 per cent of the cases for less than three months, and in 90 per cent of the cases for less than one year (Escobedo 2007).

7.3.1.3. Family-based Childcare—Explanation

Until the second half of the 1990s low female activity rates, especially in women of older generations, meant plenty of available time for potential caregivers to perform informal family-based childcare. This possibility was enhanced by the large share of childcare, especially in the many extended family households in which a grandmother was present. The growth of female employment, coupled with the gradual disappearance of the older generation, has encouraged the rise of new childcare arrangements. Part of the problem has been solved by the increase of immigrant household employees, either under formal contract or in undeclared work, some of whom help with childcare under the supervision of an active mother. Furthermore, the public funding given to early education of children age 3–6 years—not obligatory schooling although free of charge—has meant nearly 100 per cent enrollment for this age. The pending issue now is childcare for children under 3 years. Despite the fact that, legally, it is considered early childhood education, its provision is only in part publicly subsidised, and the growth in the number of places, though steady, is slow. The largest part of the demand is nevertheless met by the market for private childcare facilities, which are expensive and of low quality (Síndic de Greuges 2007).

In Spain more than three-quarters of public expenditure on childcare and early education services per child is on preprimary education (OECD 2003). Early education services rather than day-care facilities have been developed as a result of Spanish women's preference for working full-time and the historical tradition of pedagogical reform movements supporting this option. A substantial share of Spaniards think that women with children under school-age should work full-time (18.7 per cent). After Poland, this is the highest percentage in the countries studied in this volume. Similarly, only 37 per cent of respondents prefer that women with a child under school-age stay at home. This value is much lower than the percentage in Poland, Great Britain, West Germany, or Finland (Table 7.1, Appendix). This attitude is probably also connected with the failure to develop paid parental leave schemes in Spain (Escobedo 2007).

The main activity of nearly half of the women looking after children without pay in Spain is homemaking. This is the most extreme figure in Europe (Kilpeläinen 2005). The fact that most informal carers are housewives or retired women—instead of women working part-time as in other European countries—is associated with the existing divide between the older and younger generations of women.

7.3.2. Policies, Patterns, and Explanation with Respect to Family-Based Eldercare

7.3.2.1. Welfare-state Policies and Institutional Framework

In the wake of the earlier universalisation of health care in 1986, the 'Law on the Promotion of Personal Autonomy and Care for Dependent Persons' (Spanish Parliament 2006) established in 2007 a new social right: the universal right to public benefits for all dependent Spanish citizens. This was one of the Socialist government's top agenda items and the fourth pillar of the Spanish welfare state. By dependency the Act means the permanent state in which persons for reasons of age, illness, or disability, or the lack or loss of physical, mental, intellectual, or sensory autonomy, require the care of another person or persons or significant help to perform basic activities of daily living or, in the case of people with mental disabilities or illness, other support with the aim of increased personal autonomy. Most of these persons are elderly.

The new act defines the framework for a national system of care services and benefits, based on universal coverage for residents according to different levels of dependency, and on cooperation between state, regional and local levels together with market-based and third-party nonprofit-sector cooperation. The implementation of this law, from 2007 to 2015, will create about 300,000 jobs in the care sector, and it is expected that by 2015 national public expenditure on services for the elderly and people with disabilities will increase to about 1 per cent of GDP (Tables 1.4 and 1.5, Appendix 1).

As long as public formalised services are not available to all entitled residents, cash benefits, training, and respite care schemes will be provided to formalise the employment of housewives who are already the main informal carers or to formally employ personal assistants. Both measures are oriented towards formalizing informal care and increasing employment rates, which is the Spanish national priority. The two main areas under discussion have been, first, the financing of the new social protection schemes under the law (general taxation, contributions to social security, and percentage of copayments by service users) and secondly, the contents of the new schemes, particularly the balance between services and cash-for-care benefits.

Formal, regulated eldercare has been growing steadily, as care service coverage increases, albeit starting from very low rates. For example, in 2002 public home-help services covered 3 per cent of the Spanish population over age 65 (2 per cent in 1999). There were a total of 239,761 places in residential care (both public and private) all over Spain. Coverage was 1.4 per cent in publicly funded places and 3.4 per cent in both public and private places in 2002. Remote assistance services covered 1.5 per cent of the Spanish population over age 65. Day-care centres covered 0.3 per cent of the elderly, half of the centres were in the public sector. Supervised public housing (*viviendas públicas tuteladas*) was very scant, with 4,280 places in 2002. Except for senior citizen clubs (38 per cent of the elderly frequent such social centres), elderly social care services were mainly used by people over the age of 80. Therefore, given the gender structure of the elderly population, they are used mostly by women.

Some Spanish regions did introduce in the 1990s experimental schemes to economically support eldercare by family members, offering a small cash sum per month to families living with and caring for dependent elderly. These are usually not universal entitlements but programmes subject to budget availability. They do not compensate for the loss of wages of an informal caregiver who takes a leave of absence from employment, but were rather conceived as compensation for housewives taking on an extra burden within the context of a male-breadwinner household.

Finally, each employee may take up to two years of leave (*excedencia por cuidado de un familiar*) or have working hours reduced by between one-eighth and one-half to take care of a dependent relative due to severe illness, disability, accident, or old age (See 'Leave to care for a sick relative' in Table 7.2). The leave or reduced hours are unpaid. Workers taking leave are credited with social security contributions, which affect pension accounts, health coverage, and new leave entitlements, for the first year of this full-time or part-time leave. Introduced in 1999, the unpaid family leave to care for ill relatives was extended in 2007 from one to two years in the free-market sector and three years in the public sector, and social protection was added for one year. From mid-2007 the informal carer on leave will be able to receive a cash benefit of 487 euros per month if the leave is associated with the care of a person with officially certified high-level dependency.

7.3.2.2 The Specific Features of Informal Eldercare

The amount of family-based eldercare is slowly increasing due to the ageing of the population. Spain is projected to have the oldest population in the world by 2050, with a median age of 55 (United Nations 2001). From 1970 to 2000 the population over age 65 doubled and made up 17 per cent of the total population. The over-80 age group has increased the most. About one-third of the senior population has some disability, versus one-tenth in the general population. It has been estimated that in 2005 there were 1.125 million people with moderate to severe dependency, and that by 2020 this group will have increased to 33 per cent—nearly 1.5 million residents (IMSERSO 2005).

According to European Community Household Parcel (ECHP) data, in 2001 eldercare on a daily basis involved the work of 5.5 per cent of Spanish adults (8 per cent of adult women, of which 42 per cent devoted more than 40 hours per week). Informal eldercare responsibilities are concentrated in the 45–64 age group, followed by the group of 65 and over.[10] In comparative terms, this would be at medium level (Table 6.1, Appendix 3).

A detailed survey conducted in 1994 mapped informal eldercare as follows: 4–5 per cent of Spanish adults performed eldercare, of these 83 per cent were women and 17 per cent men; their average age was 52; 50 per cent were housewives; 22 per cent were employed (36 per cent part-time); 15 per cent were pensioners; and 13 per cent were in other situations; 52 per cent were daughters of the dependent elderly; 16 per cent were partners, 13 per cent were children-in-law; 7.5 per cent were sons; and the rest had other relationships (IMSERSO 1995). Ten years later the survey was repeated and shows that the sociodemographic profile of the Spanish elderly's main informal carers had remained quite stable, except that their average age had slightly increased, as did the presence of employed women (from 19 to 25 per cent of female informal carers) and of male pensioners (from 46 to 54 per cent of male informal carers). The typical profile of the Spanish informal carer in 2004 was a married housewife, about age 53 and with primary school education (IMSERSO 2005).

The sluggish development and scarcity of formal services for the elderly and other dependent adults contrasts with the rapid growth of informal employment in the household service sector. The sharp increase in immigration, especially female immigration from Spanish-speaking countries, can be explained by this growth in demand for household help. Of course these employees also perform other tasks such as childcare and household chores, but qualitative research indicates that eldercare is a very important part of the work of this group of employees. In Spain, eldercare is perceived as something that can be done by most adult women, whereas childcare requires further qualifications.

The leave to care for a relative was more symbolic than useful up to 2007, as it was unpaid and included scant guarantees of reemployment (except for public servants). Estimates based on a sample from Social Security registers indicate that between 2001 and 2005 around 11,000 periods of unpaid leave to care for a relative were registered, on average for two months. Leave takers were women in 82 per cent of the periods, and men in 18 per cent; in 20 per cent of the cases the beneficiary was repeating the leave. The yearly use trebled between 2001 and 2005 (Escobedo and Navarro 2007).

7.3.2.3. Family-based Eldercare—Explanation

The greater household complexity of Spanish society facilitates eldercare. It is relatively more common in Spain than in other European Union (EU) countries for an elderly widowed parent to live with one of his or her adult children. In Spain there is a very clear-cut preference for frail elderly people to be cared for at home. In 1998 more than two-thirds of respondents said that in case an elderly father or mother living alone could no longer manage, they would invite him or her to live with them (or with their siblings). This very high positive response level expresses a clear-cut preference that contrasts with the results from other countries (Table 7.2, Appendix). However, an update of this same question seven years later showed that this preference had greatly diminished, to less than half the respondents (42 per cent), although Spain (together with Poland) is still an outlier within the group of countries studied in this volume (European Commission 2005, 83). This value pattern probably accounts to a large extent for the great prevalence in Spain of extended family forms.

According to Eurostat projections, in 2010 Spain will be the European country with the fewest elderly people living alone, and it is expected that one-third of those over the age of 80 will live with one of their children. Although this greatly reduces the risk of poverty amongst the elderly living alone, it places a greater burden on adult women who perform the role of informal caregivers.

At the present stage of implementation of the 'Law on the Promotion of Personal Autonomy' (Spanish Parliament 2006), it is difficult to forecast what the final consequences will be for the Spanish welfare model. Although the recognition of care for dependents as a social right is undoubtedly an important sign of progress, some uncertainties remain. It is not yet clear to what extent care for dependents will be publicly funded, externalised onto the market, or familialised, as there are doubts whether the rise of nonprofessional carers is a transitory expedient to meet heavy demand, or is here to stay.

7.3.3. Policies, Patterns, and Explanation with Respect to Informal Employment

7.3.3.1. Informal Employment—Regulation and Institutional Framework

In Spain, informal employment and the shadow economy was very important in the 1980s and early 1990s, when unemployment and recession were acute. Since 1984, and in particular in 1994, a variety of labour-market reforms have aimed to increase labour-market flexibility. In conjunction with intense economic growth they produced steep growth in employment in the second half of the 1990s.

The problem of informal employment and the shadow economy has been addressed from various perspectives, but mainly in relation to unemployment and labour-market policy, inspection, and social security administration (CES 1999). There are comparatively weak incentives to make the transition from informal work to formal employment (unemployment benefit coverage is low and leave-of-absence benefits for family reasons are scant), but recently a set of measures has been devised to promote self-employment by improving its working conditions and benefits.[11]

Some experts have claimed that in Spain flexible or unstable employment has replaced nondeclared work. However, from 1998 onwards nondeclared work has once again risen steeply with the increasing presence of illegal immigrants, as substantial numbers of them could not legalise their situation. This growth has taken place in the same sectors which traditionally fostered low-qualified nondeclared work. Because current immigration policies aim both to formalise and to limit illegal immigration, the extent to which this will mean a decline in undeclared work caused by regulations aimed at restricting migration remains to be seen. It is more likely that curbing the undeclared employment of irregular immigrants will come about as a result of the current economic slowdown.

7.3.3.2. Main Features of Informal Employment

Undeclared work in Spain follows a Southern-European pattern consisting of the predominance of low-qualified, informal jobs among young people, adult women who often work at home or in domestic service, and illegal immigrants. It is also especially prevalent among part-timers and the self-employed. Therefore, this kind of undeclared work can be characterised as the 'poverty-escape' type. Low-qualified, undeclared work is quantitatively and qualitatively most relevant in sectors of low productivity and competitiveness and in companies typically operating in local markets. After the conversion during the 1990s of part of this informal employment into casual yet formal employment, a new, significant influx of immigrants from non-EU countries has generated a new source of informal employees.

More highly qualified undeclared work also exists, especially as second jobs or among some professionals in combination with formal work (for example in personal services and household repair), but there is little evidence of it because of a lack of research.

The 1998 a European Commission (EC) Communication on undeclared work estimated that the shadow economy in the EU amounted to 7–16 per cent of GDP, or 7–19 per cent of declared employment, and it situated Spain in the medium-high group (EC 1998). Other estimates were higher: 23 per cent in 1996–1997 (Schneider and Enste 2000) or 21 per cent of declared gross added value in 2000 (Alañón and Gómez 2003).

The estimates of informal employment are various and depend above all on what is understood as informal employment: Does it mean just not contributing at all to social security or does it include a a wider variety of irregularities related to social security contributions? They also vary with the population covered. According to a survey on living and working conditions performed by the Ministry of Economy and Finance, in 1985 informal employment in a broad sense involved the labour of between 15 and 22 per cent of the employed Spanish population. This figure fell to 14 per cent in 1993, probably due to an increase in temporary employment (1993 FOESSA survey in Juárez 1994). A direct estimate in 1997 resulted in 10 per cent of adults having some irregularity in terms of social security and a similar share were reported to perform some kind of undeclared work.[12]

Since 2000 informal employment has increased once again. It appears that undeclared work has slightly increased in the last few years despite the extraordinary 'regularisation' process that in 2005 gave legal status to about half a million immigrants. A recent measurement in 2006 has estimated the share of undeclared work out of total employment to be 12.3 per cent (González and Sánchez 2007).

As in Spain, informal employment has been usually associated with low qualification; the rate of informal employment decreases with educational attainment. The higher rates of informal employment are at the beginning and end of working life. These days informal employment is also more clearly related to illegal immigration.

New sectors which also have significant rates of informal work have emerged in the field of personal and care services: childcare, out-of-school care, and eldercare (Departament de Treball 1999). The 'regularisation' process in 2005 discussed earlier in this section gives to a certain extent a picture of informal employment in Spain, at least of the part of it more apt to emerge from the shadows. It revealed a high degree of illegal work in domestic service (34 per cent of total applicants), construction (21 per cent), agriculture (15 per cent), hotels and restaurants (10 per cent), retail trade (5 per cent), textile (3 per cent), and others (12 per cent) (MTAS 2005). We estimate that, at the end of 2006, 31.1 per cent of immigrant men and 34.3 per cent of immigrant women were working informally (CES 2007).

7.3.3.3. Informal Employment—Explanation

A relatively high tax burden on formal employment and a quite low level of social protection within a historical context of high unemployment and some degree of mistrust of public institutions and taxation create together a cultural context which contributes to legitimating undeclared work.

The regulation of formal and informal work is greatly affected by the social protection system. The Spanish tax structure places a relatively greater burden on formal employment (especially the considerable social security contributions employers or self-employed must pay), which explains most undeclared employment. In some cases employers hire workers in the underground economy who are willing to accept earnings below the minimum wage, whereas in others both workers and employers obtain important savings in taxes and social security costs (González and Sánchez 2007). With employers' social security contributions amounting to nearly one-fourth of total labour costs, Spain, among the countries in this volume, has the highest tax burden on wages for employers (Table 2.4, Appendix).[13] Another factor often mentioned in relation to the difficulty of creating jobs is the steep cost for employers of redundancy payments.[14]

The segmentation of the labour market prevalent in Spain is a concomitant of informal employment. A number of studies have shown the connection between part-time work, rate of temporality, and job instability and rates of undeclared work. An analysis of the different Spanish regions as units shows a particularly strong correlation between the rates of temporality and undeclared work (González and Sánchez 2007).

7.3.4. Policies, Patterns, and Explanation with Respect to Voluntary Work

7.3.4.1. Regulatory Framework and Policies Towards Voluntary Work

The development of volunteer work in Spain is marked by the advent of democracy as late as 1978 and the influence of the Roman Catholic Church within the sector. A growing interest in volunteer work has been reflected in both legislation and research. In 1996 a state law on volunteerism was passed, and most regional governments have also developed their own regulations in this area (García 2003).

Since 1987, the Ministry of Labour and Social Affairs has promoted the emergence of this Third Sector by means of grants financing various projects carried out by foundations and associations for 'purposes of social interest'. These resources are generated by 0.7 per cent of income tax revenues allocated by the taxpayers themselves, who can also choose to devote this percentage to the Catholic Church.[15]

7.3.4.2. Main Features of Voluntary Work

Various indicators confirm that in Spain the amount of organised voluntary work is comparatively small. More than seven out of ten Spaniards declared that they are not members of any organisation. This score is 20 percentage points above the EU-25 average. Only 15 per cent of respondents said that they participate actively in organisations or do voluntary work. This value—half the EU-25 average—is the lowest among the countries studied in this volume (European Commission 2005).

A time-use survey conducted in 2002–2003 indicated that informal grassroots voluntary work as well as community participation are much more prevalent than voluntary work in the framework of nonprofit and nongovernmental organizations: Of the 13 minutes daily average per adult (16 minutes for women and 11 minutes for men) spent in voluntary work, only one minute took place within formal organizations. Similarly, 6.7 per cent of respondents did voluntary work as informal help in other households, but only 0.6 per cent of them did it on behalf of organizations.

Voluntary work is not evenly distributed amongst the population. Membership in voluntary associations grows with educational attainment, so the group with the highest educational attainment has twice the membership of the least educated group (42 per cent versus 21 per cent). Membership is evenly distributed among adults under 65 but decreases in the elderly. Voluntary work is not only gendered but is also concentrated within a small group, as in fact only 7.6 per cent of adults perform on average 2 hours and 15 minutes of volunteer work per day. Informal help for other households account for most of the voluntary work performed in Spain: 10 out of 16 minutes on average per day for all adult women and 6 out of 11 minutes per day for all adult men. The remainder, 5 minutes for women and 4 minutes for men, was devoted to informal participation, such as in church activities[16].

Little information is available on quantitative trends in volunteer work in Spain. According to ECHP data published by the Spanish National Statistics Institute, there is no evidence that membership in volunteer associations increased between 1996 and 2001. Rather, their numbers seem to be rather stable. We estimate that voluntary work probably increased during the 1980s and 1990s, an increase linked to a rise in the number of voluntary associations and the development of democracy. Nevertheless we do not know to what extent this still holds true for the early 2000s.

In Spain, the Third Sector comprises a total of more than 253,000 nonprofit organizations, of which 6,000 are foundations and 175,000 associations. The main organizations involved in voluntary work are Caritas and the Red Cross. *Cáritas Española* was established in 1947 as an official confederation of charity organizations of the Roman Catholic Church in Spain. About 65,000 people work for *Cáritas* as volunteers (Cáritas Española 2005). Another prominent welfare and charitable voluntary organisation is the *Cruz Roja Española* (Spanish Red Cross) with about 677,000 members, about 172,000 volunteers, and about 10,000 formal employees (Cruz Roja Española 2004).

Within the framework of a Comparative Nonprofit Sector Project led by the Johns Hopkins Center for Civil Society Studies (Salamon and Sokolowski 1999), comparative indicators have been developed for many countries, including Spain. According to these estimates, in 1995 the Spanish nonprofit sector employed about 475,000 people in full-time equivalents, corresponding to 4.5 per cent of nonagricultural employment. Volunteer work amounted to the equivalent of 254,000 full-time jobs (or 2.2 per cent of nonagricultural employment). The distribution of volunteers by sectors was as follows: 29 per cent in the field of social services; 22 per cent in culture and recreation; 12 per cent in education and research; 11 per cent in civic engagement and advocacy; 8 per cent in environmental conservation; 7 per cent in health care; 5 per cent in development and housing; 4 per cent in international activities; and finally 2 per cent in professional organizations and unions. In terms of expenditure, it accounted for 4 per cent of GDP. Furthermore, the entire Third Sector involved about 3 million people (between 5–9 per cent of the adult population), of which one million volunteers devoted more than four hours per week. The state administration contributed one-third of voluntary organizations' receipts by means of grants, and the rest was provided by membership dues, fees, and other contributions. Sociocultural activities and community participation accounted for 39.5 per cent of voluntary work, some form of teaching for 29 per cent, and care services for dependent people, 26.5 per cent (Ruiz Olabuénaga 2000).

7.3.4.3. *Voluntary Work—An Explanation*

A paradox emerges when we confront the low incidence of voluntary work in Spain with its valuation. Nearly eight out of ten Spanish citizens (77 per cent) declare that it is important in their lives. This percentage is the highest among the countries covered in this book and 18 percentage points above the EU-25 average (European Commission 2005). Whatever may be the interpretation of this surprising result, it indicates that in Spain there is great scope for the growth of voluntary work.

An attempt at an explanation of this paradox is that low membership levels of Spaniards in associations do not necessarily reflect a weak orientation to voluntary work. However, it is true that in Spain a lack of civil commitment—associated with strong disaffection with political and religious organisations that in other parts of the world usually channel and structure voluntary activities—results in low rates of practice of organised voluntary work. Although Spanish citizens have medium-level confidence in churches and religious organisations (Table 3.3, Appendix), their valuation of religion is very low,[17] and the participation of the faithful in the

Roman Catholic Church has traditionally been markedly passive.[18] Similarly, the disaffection with politics and labour unions is great.[19]

It has been suggested that the low level of practice of voluntary work is a corollary of the weakness of civil society. However, this is a contested issue, and various interpretations of this feature have been provided (Subirats 1999; Ruiz Olabuénaga 2000). In fact, what appears as civic disengagement may be the result of the development of soft forms of family-based sociability, such as family-centred networks, peer-groups, and the persistence of the *fiesta* culture (Pérez-Díaz 2002).

The distinction between bonding (or exclusive) and bridging (or inclusive) social capital seems relevant to illustrate the structure of voluntary work in Spain. Bonding social capital refers to strong ties among family members, friends, or tightly structured ethnic or religious groups. Bridging social capital refers to weaker social networks that can enable broader interaction and provide opportunities to develop social interaction that benefits individuals. Bonding capital produces a remarkably smaller amount of generalised trust than bridging capital. The countries with Mediterranean welfare regimes exhibit the average highest degree of bonding social capital and the lowest scores of bridging capital (except for postsocialist societies) (Kääriäinen & Lehtonen 2007). One possible interpretation for this is that in Spain bonding social capital is crowding out bridging social capital so that a considerable part of voluntary work takes place in unorganised family and community networks.

Finally, other factors that may be connected with the scant occurrence of voluntary work are the educational and generational gap among the Spanish population as a result of a belated modernisation process and the frequent prevalence of longer daily work hours.

7.4. CONCLUSIONS

In this chapter we have analysed the dynamic relationships between formal and informal work in Spain and focussed especially on recent developments in the 2000s. We started from the assumption that, in order to understand the nature and the characteristics of informal work, it is important to see its evolution in the context of changes in gender and family arrangements on the one hand, and in the welfare-state configuration on the other, and within the framework of new value orientations. As the main underlying factors in the character and features of informal work we also take into consideration the extent and the profiles of their different types, the relationships between formal and informal work, and the dynamics of these relationships. Four main areas of informal work have been examined in depth: family-based childcare; family-based eldercare; informal employment, and voluntary work.

In the recent evolution of the shifting relations between formal and informal work three different stages have been distinguished. Up to the end of the 1990s, the structure of the welfare regime roughly corresponded to the expectations attached to traditional gender roles, and therefore both areas mirrored each other; from the early 2000s onwards a new development appeared, especially among the middle classes, consisting of the provision of child and eldercare by female immigrants; and finally, the 2004 election of a Socialist government brought about the growth of early education facilities and the recognition of new citizenship rights empowering people to assume the care of dependent adults.

In the first stage, the extent and profile of different types of informal work in Spain depended to a great extent on a welfare regime based on family and kinship solidarity, which basically consisted of allocating care responsibilities to household members and restricting to very low limits public expenditure on benefits and services for families. It is this profile of low-level social protection for families and limited development of public care services for young children and the elderly that is connected with a long prominence of family-based informal care within and among households.

However, the gradual increase of female activity rates made these arrangements no longer sustainable. One of the ways widespread full-time employment and family life could be reconciled was through the provision of care services by immigrant women. There appears to be a close correlation between the growth of female labour-market participation and the increase of employed women in domestic service. Nevertheless, family-based care provision by immigrants did not really challenge the gender division of labour within the household and can therefore be construed as an adaptation of traditional arrangements to new circumstances.

The needs of middle-class households to which migrant carers respond reflect a deficit in the public system of care services and a lack of adequate social policies to reconcile the demands of employment and family life. Since 2004, the new Socialist government, and before that, other various regional administrations, have tried to develop suitable policies including a public network of educational and care institutions. In particular, the growth of early education and care, and the 2006 'Law on the Promotion of Personal Autonomy and Care for Dependent Persons' (Spanish Parliament 2006) stand out. These developments, based on the introduction of new social rights, could be a more serious challenge to the welfare model based on family solidarity, but the outcome is not yet clear. It remains to be seen if public involvement in early childhood education and care for children under 3 will develop as it did for children aged 3–6 and whether the full implementation of the 'Law on the Promotion of Personal Autonomy' will bring more formalisation of the care sector and more professionalisation of carers. This will depend on the incentives given by government policies, and the interplay of policy developments and people's preferences will shape future orientations and trends.

Undeclared work is a deeply seated phenomenon in the Spanish economy. The breadth and profile of informal employment depends to a great extent on the progress of immigrant legalization and the acquisition of social citizenship, but some rigidities in the employment system—employers' high social security costs or heavy redundancy settlements that discourage the creation of formal employment—may contribute to its permanence. However, the widespread acceptance of paid informal work among the Spanish population is key to its prevalence. Finally, the low incidence of voluntary work in organizations can be explained by the extensive informal family and community networks in Spanish society and by the widespread popular disaffection with traditional political and religious organizations.

NOTES

1. Only 3.6 per cent of Spanish citizens are affiliated with political parties. This is the lowest percentage among the countries studied in this volume (Eurobarometer 56.1, Q.18.12, 2001). On the other hand, 49 per cent of Spaniards declare that they never discuss political matters with friends. This extreme figure contrasts with much lower percentages reported for other countries (16 per cent for Germany, 17 per cent for Denmark, 22 per cent for Finland, 30 per cent for Poland, and 35 per cent for the UK (Eurobarometer 67, QA1, 2007).
2. In 1976, shortly after Franco's death, the share of industrial workers in the total workforce was only 27.4 per cent.
3. Eurostat data.
4. Percentages of couples aged 20–49 in which at least one partner has a job (elaboration with Eurostat data for 2003 by Aliaga, 2005).
5. Young people = 16–24 age-group (INE data for 2006).
6. Data based on the EU-SILC 2006, published by the Spanish Ministry of Education (2007) *Las cifras de la Educación en España. Estadísticas e Indicadores*. www.mec.es: Table D1–5 which differentiates the employment situation of the mother (employed, employer, unemployed, or inactive).
7. The following estimates are based on data from the ECHP Panel produced by the Spanish National Statistics Institute.
8. The sample universe consists of the Spanish population age 10 and over (INE, 2004a).
9. Data from EU-SILC 2004 published by the Spanish Ministry of Education.
10. Data from ECHP published by the Spanish National Statistics Institute.
11. Ley 20/2007, de 11 de julio, del Estatuto del Trabajo Autónomo (BOE del 12 de julio de 2007).
12. A Spanish survey on attitudes and behaviour in relation to the shadow economy conducted by the *Centro de Investigaciones Sociológicas* in 1997 (CES 1999).
13. In Spain the financing of the welfare state is disproportionally based on employers' contributions to Social Security. In 2001, these accounted for 53 per cent of total receipts, in contrast with only 39 per cent for the average EU-15. In the last few years this share has tended to increase (Eurostat data on Social Protection Expenditure and Receipts).
14. Spain has the highest redundancy payment in a selection of EU countries. A white-collar worker age 40 made redundant after ten years of service on an annual salary of 30,000 €, redundancy payments can vary from 7,692 € in the UK, 10,000 € in Germany and Finland, 15,000 € in Denmark, and 38,196 € in Spain (Formosa 2003).

15. Until 2007 this percentage was much lower: 0.52 per cent.
16. Results from the Spanish time-use survey, 2002–2003. Sample universe: Spanish population age 10 and over (INE 2004a).
17. Only one-third of Spaniards say that religion is important in their lives (34 per cent). This figure is about twenty percentage points below the EU-25 average (52 per cent) (Special Eurobarometer 273 on 'European Social Reality' 2007).
18. 86.9 per cent of respondents in a recent survey had never belonged to a parish association (CIS Barometer No. 2749 January 2008).
19. 92.6 per cent of Spaniards have never belonged to a political party, and 79.5 per cent have never belonged to a labour union (CIS Barometer No. 2749 January 2008) (See note 1).

REFERENCES

Alañón Pardo, A., and Gómez de Antonio, M. (2003) 'Una evaluación del grado de incumplimiento fiscal para las provincias españolas', *Papeles de Trabajo* Núm. 9/03, Madrid: Instituto de Estudios Fiscales: http://www.ief.es/

Aliaga, C. (2005) 'Gender gaps in the reconciliation between work and family life', *Statistics in Focus 4/2005*, Luxembourg: European Communities.

Bentolila, S., and Dolado, J.J. (1994) 'Labour flexibility and wages: Lessons from Spain', *Economic Policy* 9(18):53–99.

Cabra de Luna, M.A. (ed.) (1998) *El tercer sector y las fundaciones de España hacia el nuevo milenio: Enfoque económico, sociológico y jurídico*, Madrid: Escuela Libre/Fundación ONCE.

Caprile, M., and Escobedo, A. (2003) 'Overcoming barriers to equal pay in Spain: Monitoring gender mainstreaming', in L. Magnusson, L. Mosesdottir, and A. Serrano (eds) *Equal Pay and Gender Mainstreaming in the European Employment Strategy*, Brussels: European Trade Union Institute, 199–246.

Cáritas Española (2005) *Memoria 2003* [Annual report available online at http://www.caritas.es/ (accessed 21 October 2005).]

CES (1999) *La economía sumergida en relación a la Quinta Recomendación del Pacto de Toledo*, Colección Informes 2/1999, Madrid: Consejo Económico y Social.

———. (2002) *Memoria sobre la situación socioeconómica y laboral España 2001*, Madrid: Consejo Económico y Social.

———. (2007) 'Las mujeres inmigrantes en España', *Cauces. Cuadernos del Consejo Económico y Social* 2(Otoño): 24–30.

Cousins, C. (1999) *Society, Work and Welfare in Europe*, London: Macmillan.

Cruz Roja Española (2004) *Memoria 2004*, Annual report, http://www.cruzroja.es/ (accessed 21 October 2005).

Departament de Treball (1999) *Llibre blanc dels nous filons d'ocupació a Catalunya*, Barcelona: Generalitat de Catalunya.

EC (1998) *Communication on Undeclared Work*, European Commission.

———. (2007) *Indicators for monitoring the Employment Guidelines including indicators for additional employment analysis—2007 Compendium*, http://ec.europa.eu/employment_social/employment_strategy/pdf/2007compendium_en.pdf.pdf.

Escobedo, A. (2007), 'Spain', in I.P. Moss and K. Wall (eds), *International Review of Leave Policies and Related Research 2007*, Employment Relations Research Series No.80, Department of Trade and Industry, UK, 246–259, http://www.berr.gov.uk/files/file40677.pdf.

Escobedo, A., and Navarro L. (2007) 'Perspectivas de desarrollo y evaluación de las políticas de licencias parentales y por motivos familiares en España: Informe de resultados de la Muestra Continua de Vidas Laborales', (unpublished final report of a research funded by the Spanish Social Security Institution on Parental Leave in Spain).
Esping-Andersen, G. (1990) *The Three Worlds of Welfare Capitalism*, Cambridge: Polity Press.
———. (1999) *Social Foundations of Postindustrial Economies*, Oxford: Oxford University Press.
European Commission (2005) Special Eurobarometer 223 on 'Social capital'.
Eurostat (2002) *The Social Situation in the European Union 2002*, Luxembourg: Office for Official Publications of the European Communities.
———. (2004) *Living Conditions in Europe—Statistical Pocketbook. Data 1998–2002. Edition 2003*, Luxembourg: Office for Official Publications of the European Communities.
Ferrera, M. (1996) 'The 'southern model' of welfare in social Europe', *Journal of European Social Policy* 6(1):17–37.
Flaquer, L. (2000) 'Is there a southern European model of family policy?', in A. Pfenning and T. Bahle (eds) *Families and Family Policies in Europe. Comparative Perspectives*, Frankfurt a.m./New York: Peter Lang, 15–33.
Formosa, D. (2003) 'European employment conditions', London: Mercer Human Resource Consulting.
García, A. (2003) 'El voluntariado: recursos y normativas', in M. Montagut (ed.) *Voluntariado: La lógica de la ciudadanía*, Barcelona: Ariel, 125–168.
González Gago, E., and Sánchez, L. (2007) 'Article on undeclared work from SYSDEM correspondent: Spain', European Employment Observatory.
IMSERSO (1995) *Cuidados en la vejez. El apoyo informal*, Madrid: Ministerio de Asuntos Sociales.
———. (2005) *Libro Blanco sobre la Atención a las Personas en Situación de Dependencia en España*, Madrid: Ministerio de Trabajo y Asuntos Sociales, http://www.seg-social.es/imserso/dependencia/libroblanco.pdf.
INE (2004a) Encuesta de empleo del tiempo 2002–2003, Press Release. Madrid: Instituto Nacional de Estadística
———. (2004b) Cambios en la composición de los hogares, Press Release.
Juárez, M. (ed.) (1994) *V Informe sociológico sobre la situación social en España: Sociedad para todos en el año 2000*, 2 vols, Madrid: Fundación Foessa.
Kääriäinen, J., and Lehtonen, H. (2007) 'The variety of social capital in welfare state regimes: A comparative study of 21 countries', *European Societies* 8(1):27–57.
Kilpeläinen, R. (2005) 'Formal and informal work in Europe', Preliminary Findings Based on the European Community Household Panel (ECHP) Data, Discussion Paper No. 8, University of Hamburg.
Leibfried, S. (1992) 'Towards a European welfare state: On integrating poverty regimes into the European community, in Z. Ferge and J.E. Kolberg (eds) *Social Policy in a Changing Europe*, Frankfurt am Main and Boulder, CO: Campus Verlag-Westview Press, 245–279.
MTAS (2005) Balance del proceso de normalización de trabajadores extranjeros, Press Release. Madrid: Ministerio es Trabajo y Asuntos Sociales.
Naldini, M. (2003) *The Family in the Mediterranean Welfare States*, London & Portland, Ore.: Frank Cass.
OECD (2003) OECD Family Database. Paris: OECD.
———. (2007) 'Economic survey of Spain, 2007', *Policy Brief*, January 2007.
Parella Rubio, S. (2003) *Mujer, inmigrante y trabajadora: La triple discriminación*, Rubí: Anthropos.

Pérez-Díaz, V. (2002) "From civil war to civil society: Social capital in Spain from the 1930s to the 1990s", in R.D. Putnam (ed.) *Democracies in Flux: The Evolution of Social Capital in Contemporary Society*, Oxford: Oxford University Press, 245–287.

Pfau-Effinger, B. (2004) *Development of Culture, Welfare States and Women's Employment in Europe*, Aldershot: Ashgate.

———. (2005a) 'Development paths of care arrangements in the framework of family values and welfare values', in B. Pfau-Effinger and B. Geissler (eds) *Care and Social Integration in European Societies*, Bristol: Policy Press, 21–45.

———. (2005b) 'Welfare state policies and the development of care arrangements', *European Societies* 7(2):321–347.

Rhodes, M. (1997) 'Spain', in H. Compston (ed.) *The New Politics of Unemployment: Radical Policy Initiatives in Western Europe*, London: Routledge, 103–122.

Ruiz Olabuénaga, J.I. (ed.) (2000) *El sector no lucrativo en España*, Bilbao: Fundación BBVA.

Salamon, L.M. and Sokolowski, S.W. (1999) *Global Civil Society. Dimensions of the Nonprofit Sector*, The Johns Hopkins Comparative Nonprofit Sector Project, Baltimore, MD: The Johns Hopkins Center for Civil Society Studies.

Saraceno, C. (1994) 'The ambivalent familism of the Italian welfare state', *Social Politics* (Spring):60–82.

Schneider, F., and Enste, D.H. (2000) 'Shadow economies: Size, causes and consequences', *Journal of Economic Literature* 38:77–114.

Síndic de Greuges (2007) School Enrolment for children 0 to 3 in Catalonia. Extraordinary report of the Ombudsman in Catalonia, http://www.sindic.cat/ficheros/informes/53_EscolaritzacioOa3anys.pdf.

Solé, C., and Flaquer L.(eds) (2005) *El uso de las políticas sociales por las mujeres inmigrantes*, Madrid: Instituto de la Mujer.

Spanish Parliament (2006) Ley 39/2006, de. 14 de Diciembre, de Promoción de la Autonomia Personal y Astención a las personas en situación de depeudencia. Madrid: Baletin Oficial del Estado.

Subirats, J. (1999) 'Introducción', in J. Subirats (ed.) *¿Existe sociedad civil en España?: Responsabilidades colectivas y valores públicos*, Madrid: Fundación Encuentro, 19–36.

United Nations (2001) *World Population Prospects, the 2000 Revision, Highlights*, Population Division Department of Economic and Social Affairs.

Valiente, C. (1997) 'The rejection of authoritarian policy legacies: Family policy in Spain (1975–1995)', in U. Ascoli et al. (eds) *Comparing Social Welfare Systems in Southern Europe, Florence Conference*, vol. 3, MIRE: Paris, 363–383.

8 Formal and Informal Work in a Transition Country
The Case of Poland

Aleksander Surdej and Ewa Ślęzak

INTRODUCTION

In Poland as in other European countries the social science discourse on work focusses predominantly on aspects of work associated with formal employment and work in the shadow and/or black economy. Other aspects of informal work typical for our approach are presently framed in scientific debates on care, reciprocity, and volunteering.

However even with this traditional perspective on work, the various aspects and dimensions of work mentioned above are additionally embedded in the context of the systemic transformations that Poland has been going through since the end of the 1980s. Before the transformations began, Poland—according to B. Deacon (2000, 156–160), following the work of G. Esping-Andersen (1990, 2002)—was regarded as representative of the communist welfare regime, characterised by a social contract which guaranteed all citizens rights to employment, equal access to education and health services, and hardly any differences in pay levels between various socioprofessional groups. The prices of goods and services were heavily subsidised, in particular prices of food, transport, and housing.

The postcommunist socioeconomic transformations, described as policy-induced, multidimensional changes, were accelerated by the impact of growing economic openness and globalization. The economic policies of late 1980s were initiated as economic reforms aimed at inserting the market mechanism into the socialist system. Following them, from 1990 on, comprehensive transformations towards market economy commenced (Kolodko 1999).

The above has taken place in the context of an unstable political environment characterised by shifts in policies at least every four years since 1989. The result has been many noncohesive, if not contradictory, decisions of politicians and policy-makers in many spheres of public policy and the welfare state—the labour market, health care, social security insurance etcetera.

In light of the above, in this chapter we aim to analyse and explain the particular structures of informal work in postcommunist Poland. Its main research questions are:

- What have been the specific features of informal work in Poland since 1989?
- How can these be explained in the context of the specific arrangement of work and welfare in Polish society?

In the first section of this chapter, we explain the arrangement of work and welfare in transitional Poland. Our emphasis is on the role of socioeconomic transformations and changes in related public policies, especially in the sphere of formal employment. Then we characterise various forms of informal work typical for our approach. The chapter ends with some conclusions and the outlook for the future of informal work in Poland.

8.1. THE ARRANGEMENT OF WORK AND WELFARE IN POLAND: BACKGROUND REMARKS

The major change which has taken place in Poland since the late 1980s can be described as a shift in responsibility for the provision of social welfare from the state to families. The growing role of informal social care has been indicated as one of the most distinct features in this shift, which was initiated by politicians and policy-makers of different political backgrounds, left-wing and right-wing, conservative and liberal and ex-communists.

Since 1989, social policy, and welfare arrangements in general, in Poland have been going through a number of far-reaching, intentional and nonintentional changes. Surely Poland can be said to be moving away from the 'communist welfare state', characterised by guaranteed employment, state provision of social services, and extensive institutional support offered to citizens (Deacon 2000) towards a 'transitional' welfare regime.

This 'transitional' regime possesses some elements typical of the communist, in fact socialist, past, and other elements have a more liberal (Narojek 1986) and continental character (Golinowska 2002). This shows that there is no agreement among scholars and policy-makers as to the present type of welfare regime. Rather than calling it transitional, one should call it a hybrid regime, with various elements of the types pointed out by G. Esping-Andersen (1990, 2002).

With regard to social care, the transition has been facilitated by the fact that in the socialist period formalised care services existed predominantly in the sphere of childcare (kindergartens), whereas formal eldercare was of residual significance.[1]

Decidedly, changes in the sphere of social policy have been guided by the principle of subsidiarity, which overtly conveys to citizens the ideas that the state will no longer support citizens in need and that the state and its institutions are the source of help of last resort.

Large-scale socioeconomic transformations continue to increase the range and severity of risks faced by citizens. Growing uncertainty about the future and decreasing economic security have contributed to fall in the Polish birthrate, which in 2005 was one of lowest in the European Union (EU) and the lowest among the countries analysed.

Under communism the Polish family model was a traditional one— men centred their activity on providing for the family, whereas women focussed on caring functions. Despite ongoing social changes, the Polish family model remains predominantly traditional (Szatur-Jaworska 2000, 96; Worach-Kardas 1997, 23). Still, several factors contribute to the changing division of roles among men and women in Polish households, pushing both genders towards more equal shares of housework and responsibility for earning income. These include an increase in educational attainment, women's growing professional aspirations, and the rising number of divorces.

On the other hand, many Poles highly value and many still live in an extended (intergenerational) family (Szatur-Jaworska 1997; Synak 2003). This form of accommodation includes living in the same household (whether in flats or houses) or living nearby and maintaining strong contact with parents and grandparents. Poles believe that strong ties in such extended, intergenerational families are the major source of economic guarantees for their elders, who in turn prove their usefulness to the family by helping with care of grandchildren and performing various types of housework (Szatur-Jaworska 2000, 31). The assistance of grandparents is also important when parents cannot find jobs with work-time arrangements that facilitate reconciling job and family obligations.[2] Thus, one of the main characteristics of familial relations in Poland one should list is the reciprocity-based exchange of services within the extended family.

8.2. THE DEVELOPMENT OF FORMAL EMPLOYMENT AND ECONOMIC CHANGE

Before we analyse the aspects of formal employment in given periods, we briefly discuss economic change, as it composes the background for the changes on the labour market that have taken place since the 1990s.

The socialist economy of Poland, as in Hungary, was not a monolithic, state-owned economy. The state allowed its citizens a relatively broad range of economic activities; for instance, private farmers retained approximately 80 per cent of farmland, and private firms played a significant role in retail trade and construction. Yet these private economic activities were regarded as supplementary, albeit increasingly important, to the activities of the state (public) sector. In fact socialist ideology and government control of the economy limited their possibilities for growth.

From the mid-1980s onwards the socialist state started to loosen control over economic activities and slowly encouraged small enterprise start-ups. As a result, the number of private companies increased by almost 200,000, reaching 572,000 in 1988. In the same period the Parliament passed a 'revolutionary' law on economic activities proclaiming freedom of enterprise and simplifying the administrative requirements for business activity (23 December 1988). After 1989 the number of enterprises increased by 50 per cent in response to the changing economic policy and gradual democratisation announced by the state. Decreasing control over the economy encouraged the growth of a large informal economy which was ready to take up any opportunities brought by approaching liberalisation reforms.

Despite claims to the contrary, the program of postcommunist economic transformations launched in January 1990 was not comprehensively designed and precisely implemented but was instead based on some rather crude policy concepts and general ideas about the direction of changes. One dominant assumption was the belief in the need for shock therapy characterised by a broad scope and rapid pace of economic changes which would set off a process of 'creative destruction'. Initially the government conceived a 'negative' policy consisting of not impeding and not acting, and the idea of building an adequate institutional and legal framework for the market economy came to policy-makers only in the mid-1990s.

Throughout the 1990s the pivotal idea in economic and social policies was to shift responsibility for citizens' lives and well-being from the state and its administrative agencies to individuals. Politicians emphasised that individuals and their families would be expected to take advantage of new opportunities, cope with emerging challenges, and deal with threats. In a typical formulation it was stressed that democratisation had granted political and civil freedoms, whereas economic liberalisation had opened up many opportunities for people to start their own businesses. These can be regarded as the most distinct features of the postcommunist state under transformations affecting the lives of individuals.

Further changes in the structure of the Polish economy are expected. The most important shift will regard the movement of the workforce out of agriculture, as a modernised agriculture cannot keep employing more than a quarter of the labour force. Although a part of the redundant workforce can be absorbed by the growth of service economy in rural areas, the majority of young people born in rural families will move to cities (not necessarily in Poland), in search of jobs. On the basis of sociological research (Pfau-Effinger 2004) we can expect that the diminishing role of the peasant economy will have strong impact on women's employment, culture, and the welfare state in Poland.

Surely the transformations have resulted in individuals being faced with a number of changes, which not only positively but also adversely affect their lives. One of the most severe challenges has been the labour-market situation. In the late 1980s the labour-market participation rate fell dramatically, but it started picking up again following Polish EU accession. Thus in 2007 the employment rate was 57 per cent, having increased from 51.2 per cent in 2003. By comparison, the employment rate in 2006 was

54.5 per cent in Poland and had fallen behind the EU average; that is, in the EU-15 it was 66.2 per cent, and in the EU-25, 64.8 per cent. The decreasing labour participation rate affected women more than men. In 2006 the employment rate of women amounted to approximately 48 per cent, having fallen even more behind the EU-15 average of 58.7 and the EU-25 average of 57.5 per cent (GUS, 2007).

The planned communist economy was characterised by serious labour shortages. Transition to a market economy reversed the situation, as full employment, a feature typical of all communist economies, ceased to exist. Unemployment emerged and became the most severe social and economic problem. In 1990 unemployment was at a high 6.5 per cent, then skyrocketed to 14.9 per cent in 1995, and continued to grow, reaching 16.1 per cent in 2001 and 19.4 per cent in 2004. The labour-market situation started to stabilise following European Union (EU) accession in 2004, and by mid-2007 unemployment fell to 12 per cent and was at 9.6 per cent by the end of 2007. Women suffered more from the rise in unemployment than men as, once having had children, they were encouraged to withdraw from the labour market.

For grandparents, childcare is an opportunity to actively participate in the lives of their children and feel needed. Later on they can expect help from their children, as formal eldercare facilities in Poland are underdeveloped and insufficiently supported by the state. In 2005 less than 20 per cent of women age 55 to 64 were formally employed. This trend continued until 2007, when the rate was 19.4 per cent. In 2006 the employment rate for women in Poland was 19 per cent, whereas in the EU-15 it was 36.9 per cent and in the EU-25, 35 per cent. The employment rate of older persons in 2006 amounted to 29.7 per cent in Poland, while in the EU-15 it was 45.3 per cent and in the EU-25, 43.7 per cent (GUS 2007). This means a large pool of relatively young pensioners who, not being in formal employment, are informally activated by family-care duties. The integration of extended families has been historically facilitated by three factors: low mobility of Poles, large rural population, and apartment shortage. These factors are slowly losing their importance, and that will affect the lives of families.

The inflexibility of working time arrangements (more than half of working women say they cannot take a day off when they need to) and lack of part-time employment forces women to face a choice: whether to be employed and forgo family, or not be employed and care for their children.

The share of part-time employed in Poland has been slowly growing; however in 2005 it amounted to approximately 9 per cent for men and 16 per cent for women—significantly lower than in the EU-15. It is very likely that the accelerated economic growth and reallocation of labour from industry to services will increase the supply of part-time jobs, flexible employment, and self-employment. Yet, the Polish government uses employment laws to block labour-market flexibility rather than promote modern solutions.

To conclude this part of the analysis, socioeconomic transformations have generated large-scale changes in the economy, contributing first to fundamental changes to the formal sphere of work, which have then led to change in the nature of informal work in the emerging market economy. We elaborate on this in the following sections.

8.3. MAIN FEATURES OF INFORMAL WORK IN POLAND

The changes described in welfare arrangements and in the functioning of the labour market have affected the relationship between formal and informal work in Poland as observed in specific areas of informal work such as childcare, eldercare, informal employment, and voluntary work. We stress here that informal employment is a phenomenon which cuts across other dimensions of informal work, emerging in the area of care work and even voluntary work.

Both informal work and an informal economy existed under the socialist economy, and in fact both flourished. But with the transition to the market economy informal work and informal employment in particular have undergone major qualitative changes. The informal economy under socialism was nurtured by market shortages, which explains well the higher prices of goods and services offered informally. Market transformations improved the availability of goods and services in the official markets, hence goods and services produced in the informal economy became cheaper than those provided through regular markets. The change in the economic system has also changed the nature of informal employment: It is no longer illegal activity, such as smuggling goods in short supply; it is more often now the provision of cheaper services to individuals and households without taxes, social security contributions, or the observance of strict employment requirements. It would be too simplistic to argue that high taxes and high social security contributions are the main factors generating and explaining informal work in Poland. The fact that care work, both childcare and eldercare, has been predominantly informal work carried out within the household economy or in community networks, has equally to do with cultural values, labour-market regulations, and social welfare arrangements.

Care work within households can be called hidden work as it is not accounted for in national statistics and sometimes not even perceived as work by working persons who may regard it as their moral duty towards relatives. This has been to a large extent the dominant way of thinking about caring activities in Poland. But the social perception of in-house care has started to change, and this calls for adequate policy responses.

During the whole of the 1990s, social policy did not properly address child- and eldercare, as the issue was perceived as belonging to the internal sphere of families. Only when it became evident that the country faced the huge problems of low labour-market participation and a low fertility rate did a debate on family policy emerge. Even then it focussed on ways to foster higher fertility rather than encourage the professional aspirations of women, offer more mother-friendly work arrangements, or link fertility and working careers. Until recently, caring functions have been performed within families (chiefly by women), but slowly we are observing the rediscovery of the possibility that a high level of labour-market participation of women is not inimical to having more children. Hence one can expect policy developments which will increase the level of care formalisation.

8.3.1. Policies, Structures, and Explanation with Respect to Family-Based Childcare

8.3.1.1. Welfare-state Policies and Institutional Framework

The conceptual approach used in this volume enables the researchers to consider care activities as a part of both formal and informal work. The analysis of ways in which childcare is provided in the country help to identify welfare arrangements specific to a given country and society.

The forms of recommended childcare in Poland are still very much inspired by the teachings of the Catholic Church and the traditional value system. There is not much space left for the influence of state-formulated and implemented family policy. Policy-makers and politicians, as members of society, are inclined to follow traditional values and church 'recommendations'.

Not surprisingly most people continue to see the family as the best place for childcare activities (Golinowska 1996, 21). Tension arises only—and we return to this—when public attention focusses on ways to boost the rate of employment and increase fertility rates, often neglecting women's career prospects.

Although childcare still remains women's duty, a significant and observable change in this regard is taking place. Only between 40 and 50 per cent of men, that is, fathers, declare the involvement in childcare activities on a regular basis (Golinowska 1996, 21–22). Though one could argue that this number is not very low, it still proves that regular childcare activities rest in mothers' hands.

Despite the increasing engagement of men in childcare, women are the main source of care, organising and providing care whether they work or not (Kotowska, Sztanderska, Wóycicka 2007). In general men, as husbands or partners, declare support for women working; however they do not match this support by increasing their commitment to care activities, hence leaving women with the double burden of work and care.

The situation on the labour market however discourages women from taking care leaves, and they often worry when taking obligatory maternal leave. Women can take paid maternal leave of 16 weeks at the birth of the first child, 18 weeks at the second and subsequent children, and unpaid childcare leave lasting up to three years but covered by state-paid social contributions. Available statistical data show that the number of women benefiting from unpaid, optional childcare leave has been steadily decreasing. The main cause of this is that childcare leave causes career discontinuity, and women wanting to advance professionally or even just maintain their current positions cannot afford to stay home long.

To sum up, the state is pushing the responsibility for childcare in the direction of the family. At the same time, the prospect of the ageing society is forcing policy-makers and politicians to consider actions to enhance women's interest in childbearing. Yet, as the state in its family policies and pro-family programs focusses on incentives to encourage childbearing, it somehow forgets that families need support throughout the whole period from early childhood up to university education. Moreover the complex situation of the labour market and male-dominated, motherhood-unfriendly labour regulations discourage women from having more children. Surely more action on the part of the state will be required and is to be expected.

8.3.1.2. Extent and Structures of Informal Childcare

General Structures

Empirical data show that 15.7 per cent of women in Poland care for their children on their own, with no support from their partners; 67.6 per cent share care duties with a husband or partner; and 42.8 per cent get help from other family members, mainly grandmothers. Childcare is woman- and family-centred, as only 2.3 per cent of families hire external child-minders, 1.0 per cent send their children to a day nursery, and 18.1 per cent to kindergarten. In the case of older children, 10.8 per cent of women leave their children in organised school care after classes (GUS 1997).[3]

Institutionalised childcare is rare for children of preschool age throughout the country because of the underdeveloped public infrastructure, but also because Polish families believe that family-centred childcare is better for children and more efficient. Empirical research shows that when in need of childcare, parents opt first for family- or relative-based care (Firlit-Fesnak 1995, 8).

Not surprisingly, childcare usually takes place in the family setting, and public opinion is not pressing for the state to develop public full-day care facilities (mainly day nurseries, but also kindergartens). This common attitude is justified by the prevailing notion of the 'good childhood', that is, a childhood spent in the family, among loving and caring parents, grandparents, relatives, or even with a trusted and friendly child-minder, but not a childhood spent in a 'cold' institution.

The Relationship Between Formal Employment and Informal Childcare

This cultural ideal, as noted, is under strong pressure from the labour market and its changes. Furthermore one can expect a rediscovery of institutionalised childcare services in coming years, contrasting with their falling number since the 1990s (see Table 8.1). The shrinking of institutionalised childcare has been taking place in the context of the fertility rate decrease—from 2.03 children per woman in 1989 to 1.243 in 2005.

Public childcare institutions, besides being few particularly in rural areas, have become rather expensive, as nursery fees in public establishments have significantly risen, creating a financial barrier to poorer families. In particular, so-called jobless households, that is, families with both parents unemployed, suffer the most, as of mid-2003 the costs of public kindergarten amounts to as much as 35 per cent of the unemployment benefit and is not subject to a state subsidy. Such families have been forced to withdraw their children from public care facilities for this reason.

8.3.1.3. Explanation of the Main Features of Family-based Childcare in Poland

Poles maintain strong ties with their relatives within extended families, usually comprised of adult children with their parents and grandparents and including aunts and uncles. Such family networks create organisational bases for the intergenerational exchange of services, particularly care services and for the support of working women with dependent children. The help of external carers is considered a second-best option, and institutional care facilities are regarded as the care form of last resort. Most external carers, including external child-minders, are employed informally, without any written employment contract or taxes being paid.

The traditional childcare provision creates an area of potential conflict with reference to women and their place in the modern Polish economy and society. Increasingly, women are torn between their willingness to have

Table 8.1.   Formal Childcare Facilities in Poland (1990–2004)

	Nurseries		Kindergartens	
	Total	Number of places for 1000 children aged 0–3	Total	Number of places for 1000 children aged 3–6
1990	116,500	42	856,600	328
1995	68,400	23	773,200	356
2000	52,800	20	685,400	388
2004	45,900	20	644,100	416

Source: GUS Statistical Yearbook, various years.

children and care for them and their desire to have a job and to return to work after having children without endangering their career prospects.

Family-centred intergenerational reciprocity based the exchange of care services plays an important role in Polish society. Only migration (or emigration), when children leave the place of their origin, undermines these bonds of exchange. Elderly parents living in the same house with children and grandchildren tend to feel a moral duty towards grandchildren and are willing to engage in childcare.

Yet that might change because, as noted by Czekanowski (2003), there has been an observable trend towards 'distance intimacy'—more and more elderly people seeking to enjoy their private lives without intrusion or an excessive interest in their children and the rest of their families. This phenomenon can be seen as a signal of the diminishing role of intergenerational households and the diminishing scale of help provided by and returned to grandparents.

8.3.2. Extent and Patterns of Eldercare in Poland

8.3.2.1. Welfare-state Policies and Institutional Framework

Not unlike other European Union societies, Poland is affected by negative demographic trends. According to the most recent forecasts, the population will drop from 38 million in 2003 to less than 36 million by 2030, and in the same period the number people over 65 will double, approaching 25 per cent of the population (GUS 2003). This fact alone will cause serious problems and calls for adequate forms of eldercare service provision from the state. Yet no serious action is being taken by the state and its institutions.

At the turn of the twenty-first century eldercare facilities hosted less than one per cent of people over 65. Yet, with increased labour mobility, fewer people will be able to take care of their parents and relatives, and there are signs that the quantity and forms of institutionalised care for the elderly are insufficient.

Public organisations and voluntary associations have been working to improve organisational forms of eldercare. Examples of innovation in this sphere include:

- in-house care facilities designed for round-the-clock care of the ill or disabled elderly;
- family social assistance houses organising 24-hour care shared by three to eight persons;
- day-care houses with assistance in meeting the elderly's shelter, food, and education needs;
- nurse-guardians;
- medical centers assuring 24-hour help to the chronically ill not needing hospitalisation;
- hospices as a form of custody over irrecoverable patients (Perek-Białas 2003).

On a limited scale the Polish government has encouraged the adoption of new, semiformal forms of eldercare, such as elderly persons living in their own private apartments adapted at public expense, with a nurse and social worker making regular regular visits. However this solution is rarely applied as it is deemed too costly. In this context Szatur-Jaworska (1997) observes:

> In general, the issue is to stop worrying about an insufficient number of openings in assistance homes and the huge list of people waiting to get into them. Just the reverse—we should try to keep the largest possible number of senior citizens in their own apartments. This option is also much cheaper.

The only existing incentive consists of a tax deduction on all private expenditures related to nursing, home-provided healthcare, and relevant services for heavily handicapped and disabled people (including the elderly disabled). In the long run, one may expect the state attempts to formalise care work, yet at the moment the interests of informal care providers seem bleak.

The growing need for eldercare in ageing societies has important consequences for all countries in Europe. The Polish government in preparing for the future has proposed to introduce special eldercare insurance to help finance eldercare. According to the 2007 Health Ministry proposal, all employees would pay a contribution of 0.5 per cent of their salaries for eldercare and rehabilitation purposes. It has not, however, been precisely formulated who and which services would be entitled, and this is crucial for societal approval of such a new social tax. After the November 2007 elections the new government abandoned the idea, possibly because it is uncertain what the impact of such a measure would be on the formalisation or informalisation of eldercare. The threat of the ageing society forecasted by demographers and gerontologists calls for governmental action. Though a public debate has begun, no serious actions have been yet undertaken.

8.3.2.2. Extent and Structures of Informal Eldercare

For the time being the problem of eldercare is taken care of and internalised by Polish families, as the number of elderly people requiring external help is relatively low. Recent data show that 4.3 per cent of people aged 70 or older are completely unable to care for themselves, and 37.8 per cent have some limitation (Czekanowski 2003). When their children cannot help them, the elderly can usually count on the help of more distant relatives and eventually on public social assistance.

Family care of the elderly seems to be the only care present in rural areas. There, institutional care is almost morally condemned, as rural communities are much less secularised than urban ones, and life is strongly influenced by the Catholic Church (Piczura 2003).

The relative virtues of family eldercare are well known, but the real dilemma consists in the trade-off between labour market participation and the woman-centred model of family eldercare. Strong empirical indications show that family is an important value for Poles. From their early years children learn about their future responsibilities towards their parents in old age. Later it is natural for them to help or care for their frail elderly parents and relatives out of a feeling of obligation to 'pay back' all the help they received.

In cases of conflict between moral ideals and the ability to meet them when, for instance, a family wants to care for their elderly on its own but due to time constraints cannot cope and eventually decides to use an external informal carer or institutional care, the first choice of Poles is to keep their parents at home and hire an external carer. But this solution is expensive. Placing the elderly in an institutional care facility is the second-best solution but often difficult to realise due to the limited number of such facilities and available places.

8.3.2.3. Explanation of the Main Features of Family-based Eldercare in Poland

The solutions presented have a number of different benefits and consequences for the relationship between formal and informal work. Family-based care may be supplemented with the work of informal carers who as a rule are not formally or legally employed. The use of formally employed carers is rare, as their services are expensive in Poland. Financial incentives to encourage the employment of formal workers, which could also contribute to further improvement of the employment situation; but such financial support of family-based care hardly exists.

The above-discussed solutions present rather a blurred picture of eldercare in Poland. At first sight one can see that no real governmental incentives supporting the family exist. Its family policy places full responsibility for the elderly within their families, strongly suggesting that the provision of care and nursing services for them is a family moral obligation (Hryniewicz 2001). The policy-makers and politicians seem to view caring for the elderly as a family duty (most often the duty falling on women). They, similar to the rest of society, share the conviction that this is also the most economically efficient and humane solution.[4] Unfortunately the context of the approaching ageing society calls for devising other solutions to support families in the care of their elderly.

8.3.3. Extent and Patterns of Informal Employment

8.3.3.1. Informal Employment—Policies and Institutional Framework

An analysis of the informal economy and informal employment in the period of the socialist economy shows phenomena concentrated in areas of cross-border trade of goods, black-market trade in foreign currencies, jewelry, food, household repairs (Sowa 1990), and in the production and distribution of alcoholic beverages. At present informal employment is observed in various sectors of the economy, most frequently in construction, transport, retail, and wholesale trade, areas characterised by a high seasonality of activities (e.g., construction) or by the domination of small enterprises which rapidly expand or contract depending on local economic conditions. Thus informal employment as well as the informal economy have undergone profound changes since the period of systemic transformations.

Though there are administrative checks and financial penalties for informal employment, the penalties are not linked to the level of turnover or seen as a serious negative social phenomenon. Rather, people consider it as a way to compete with and cheat the greedy tax institutions. It is not surprising that informal employment also takes place in existing enterprises. According to the State Labour Authority (PIP), informal employment is common; for instance in 1992 PIP found that in the city of Lodz approximately 20 per cent of firms employed labour without formal registration. PIP inspectors also estimated that approximately 50 per cent of unemployment-benefit recipients worked illegally (Zarychta 1994, 21–22).

8.3.3.2. Informal Employment—Extent and Structures

Whether one analyses the pretransition or posttransition period, both informal economy and informal employment remain difficult to measure, or even to estimate, due to serious methodological problems.

Existing data show an increase in the extent of the informal economy from 15.7 per cent in 1989 to 23.5 per cent of GDP in 1991 (Kaufmann and Kaliberda 1996). Other authors using the electricity-consumption method estimate that the informal economy at the beginning of the 1990s oscillated between 17.7 and 20.3 per cent of Polish GDP (Johnson et al. 1999). The size of the informal economy in Poland in 1994–2004 remained between 17.2 and 14 per cent, while exhibiting some anticyclical movements (MPiPS 2007, 169).

Taking into account various estimations of the extent of the informal economy the number of people working in the informal sector have ranged from 2,199,000 in 1995 (Kloc 1998, 29) to 1,317,000 in 2004 (MG 2007, 178). Table 8.2 shows the scale of informal employment in the shadow economy in various sectors. The scale of informal employment in healthcare does not take into account informal carers, as they are often regarded by families not as external employees, but as family members.

The extent of the informal economy can also be analysed from the perspective of its users, such as by exploring the extent of its use in Polish households. Data show that the range of goods and services provided to households by the informally employed is rather broad: In the mid-1990s it

Table 8.2.   The Extent of the Informal Economy According to Sector in 2002 (in %)

Sector	Share of hidden turnover	Share of illegally employed
Manufacturing	17.1	14.0
Construction	26.0	27.3
Retail and wholesale trade	21.3	18.7
Hotels and restaurants	13.8	15.8
Transportation	20.9	22.2
Education	12.1	12.5
Healthcare	12.7	5.5
Total	20.2	18.6

Source: ASM—The Centre for Market Research and Analyses for the Polish Confederation of Private Entrepreneurs, data taken from Szwałek, K., Ostrożnie z wybielaniem. Raport specjalny: szara strefa (Special report: The shadow economy), in Business Week—Polish edition, 2003, no. 8, 13.

comprised house construction (11.9 per cent); house renovation and repair (42.9 per cent); car repair (18.6 per cent); tailoring and shoe repair (7.5 per cent); cleaning and childcare (4.4 per cent); tutoring (4.4 per cent); room rental for tourists (6.4 per cent); and flat or garage rental (3.9 per cent). The broad scope of informally supplied goods and services has been confirmed by subsequent studies (Kałaska and Witkowski 1996, 186) which indicate the existence of cultural factors, such as a low level of trust in public institutions or a low level of civil culture, which explain the wide approval of informal employment. For most Poles it is common practice to buy without fiscal receipts at bazaars or straight from the trucks of producers, as well as to informally employ child-minders or household helpers.

8.3.3.3. Explanation of Specific Features of Informal Employment in Poland

One should not however overstress the role of cultural factors in explaining the frequency of the use of informal work. Individuals decide to buy goods and services in informal markets or employ labour informally because they always search for a cheaper supply and seem not to perceive the existence of a link between the microrationality of their choices and certain negative aggregate effects of the informal economy. In a similar vein, entrepreneurs often employ off-the-books labour not only to evade taxes and social security contributions, but primarily to avoid the growing regulation of employment. Red tape and the heavy bureaucratic burden, together with low levels of trust in government and public administration, are the factors which most stimulate informal employment in Poland.

Who are the people working in the informal economy? The data show a high incidence of informal employment among youth and increasing incidence among those age 45–59. The latter tendency can be explained by pointing to the widespread practice of pre-retirement—the average Polish worker retires approximately 7 years earlier than the statutory age of 65.

Empirical research shows that almost 60 per cent of informal workers are those already employed, which indicates the coexistence of formal employment and often illegal moonlighting. These are individuals who perform additional work and hide part of the income from taxation. More than 10 per cent of the total informal workforce consists of retirees. The unemployed also make up a substantial share of informal workers, accounting for almost 16 per cent.

What encourages people to take up informal employment? Informal workers and their motives are diverse. Research identifies people who prefer to remain informally employed and work much less time rather than work full-time and receive similar income, and others who would be willing to take up any official job but cannot find any.

Many informal workers, especially those already employed and pensioners, see informal employment as a way to increase their income. For the unemployed, unregistered work is the main source of income, and the decision to engage in it stems from the lack of any other way to earn a living. The level of unemployment in Poland has been high throughout the 1990s and at the beginning of this century. As much as 80 per cent of the unemployed do not receive any unemployment benefit, which makes them eager to take up any paid work, including informal jobs.

Table 8.3.   Reasons for Undertaking Informal Employment in Poland (1995–2004) (in %)

Item	1995	1998	2004
Insufficient income	34.7	33.6	26.5
Inability to find registered work	21.5	23.3	36.0
High taxes discouraging registered work	13.3	10.9	7.5
Employer-imposed informal employment in exchange for higher salary	8.9	10.6	10.3
High social security contributions discouraging registered work	8.8	9.4	12.0
Threat/Risk of losing some social [security] entitlement[s]/benefits by taking registered work	5.7	5.3	4.3
Life or family situation	4.8	4.5	3.2
Unwillingness to undertake stable employment	0.7	0.9	0.3

Source: National Statistical Office, various years.

8.3.4. Extent, Patterns, and Explanation of Voluntary Work in Poland

8.3.4.1. Policies and Legal Framework

Following the conceptual framework of this volume, one notices the emerging phenomenon of the growing contribution of voluntary work to generating the welfare of modern societies. However the development of voluntary work has also deeply important consequences for the relationship between formal and informal work.

Voluntary work is a phenomenon of democratic societies characterised by a developed civic culture. It is no wonder that under communist rule voluntary social activities were channeled into state-controlled social organisations, and the only voluntary social activities were those conducted under the aegis of the Catholic Church. With the change of the political system in 1989 we have been observing the rebirth of the voluntary sector and voluntary work in Poland.

Yet, not many noteworthy actions were undertaken by the state until the early twenty-first century when, on 24 April 2003, the 'Law on Public Benefit and Volunteering' was enacted. Five years later it is still a main policy instrument regulating formal voluntary work and activating a strong 'third sector' in Poland.

8.3.4.2. Extent and Structures of Voluntary Work in Poland

At present voluntary work in Poland takes two forms: as organised (formal) activity carried out via nongovernmental organisations (NGOs), and as unorganised and spontaneous activity which takes place in social and community networks.

The existing empirical research predominantly deals with organised and formal voluntary work and shows that the number of volunteers in Poland is approximately 1.6 million or 5.4 per cent of the adult population. Yet if only those who regularly perform voluntary work are considered, this number falls to 331,000 or approximately 1.1 per cent of the adult population. According to other surveys there has been an increase in the number of people performing voluntary work or in individual involvement in NGO-based voluntary work, from 2 million in 1990 (Pietrowski and Maciula 1999) to almost 3.3 million in 2002. Dąbrowska and Gumkowska (2002) have estimated the number of NGOs at 42,000 and the size of formally employed persons in them at 96,000. About 47 per cent of NGOs involved volunteers in activities focussing on the provision of social services.

Besides the above, employed people see voluntary work as an addition to professional activities. Voluntary work is performed by various groups, but employed persons outnumber those in other groups. Research finds that the next most numerous volunteers are pensioners and students. The unemployed account for 12 per cent of the total number of volunteers, and housewives or househusbands and professionally inactive people volunteer the least. In addition, approximately 16.2 per cent of volunteers possess a diploma of higher education, and 16.5 per cent declare an active religious practice. The data show no gender divide with regard to voluntary work, but women participate in voluntary activities slightly more than men do: 11.9 per cent of women opposed to 10.1 per cent of men. However, men claim to dedicate more time to voluntary work than women: In 2002 men declared spending an average of 57 hours on voluntary work during one year; women declared 46 hours. Empirical research leads to the conclusion that in Poland the level of involvement in voluntary activities depends on age, location, education and socioprofessional position, religiosity, and wealth. The most active in voluntary work are young people aged 18–24 (38 per cent); people who live in rural areas (39 per cent); people with university degrees (46 per cent); managers and intelligentsia (57 per cent); and those who are economically better off.

Available data, some presented above, do not allow saying with great precision how many and how regularly Poles participate in voluntary work. But we can estimate that the true share must lie between 5.4 and 12 per cent of the adult population.

Such imprecision of data stems from the fact that the greatest part of it is based on self-declarations, and Poles would like to appear more involved in voluntary work as it is socially appreciated behavior and different researchers apply different definitions of voluntary work (or sometimes no explicit definition at all).

8.3.4.3. The Explanation of the Specific Structures of Voluntary Work in the Context of the Work-welfare Arrangement in Poland

There is an obvious link between voluntary work and childcare and, especially, eldercare, as many nongovernmental organisations play a central role in the delivery of services important to the well-being of particularly the elderly, children, and those suffering from health problems. They deliver direct help to elderly and other vulnerable persons and help with money if a person in need cannot afford to pay for care services. The voluntary work of Poles is concentrated mostly in church- or education-related and charity-oriented voluntary activities (Dąbrowska and Gumkowska 2002).

Voluntary work is an important way of expressing altruistic and community-oriented attitudes. The motivations of volunteers depend on their personal life situations and other characteristics, such as religiosity, education, age, or place of origin. The most important motive for voluntary work is the feeling of obligation. In Poland, however, altruistic motives seem not as important to volunteers as instrumental motives are; this is probably the effect of the diffusion of a pragmatic style of thinking about the individual and society characteristic of contemporary societies.

The participation of Poles in voluntary work, particularly unorganised work, can be explained by cultural factors and strong social norms such as helping others, a spirit of community in the Polish identity and national values, empathy for the poor, and support for the egalitarian distribution of goods (Kisiel 1999, 23–28). Those who do not volunteer (75 per cent) view voluntary work as an activity that 'steals' their time and resources from their families, who are said to be their priority. But some people perform voluntary work without knowing it, probably.

8.4. CONCLUSIONS

The description and analysis presented above shows that the relationship between formal and informal work is changing as a result of a number of complex and interlinked factors. From them we can identify the following reasons for the changing extent and character of informal work in Poland:

- The systemic transformations in the country induced radical economic and social changes overturning previous forms of economic and social organisation, sometimes without swiftly creating new ones. The postcommunist economic transformations increased informalisation of work by limiting the state's welfare responsibilities and inducing labour-market adjustments.
- The Polish welfare state has been redimensioned, and its institutional structure has been dramatically changing since 1989. Before that, the socialist state had developed and maintained public childcare institutions to support the dual roles, particularly of women, as both employees and mothers. However, as shown, in a tight labour market, many women have been forced out of the labour market or influenced to limit their career aspirations and build their lives around their responsibilities towards the welfare of their families. Politicians do not seem to understand the relationship between the labour-market situation and the extremely low fertility rate.
- State welfare transfers, so important in the socialist system, were largely reduced (or redirected to support the poor and unemployed) or eliminated, hence the observed fall in the number of state-supported care facilities.
- Tight labour market conditions force mothers to seek alternative forms of childcare, often of an informal or reciprocal character involving various extended family members (parents, in-laws, or more distant relatives). If they decide to employ strangers, they usually opt for informal employment for reasons of cost and then try to create informal, family-like bonds with such carers.
- The approaching threat of the ageing society and growing emigration of young people will force these to seek alternative forms of care for their frail elderly parents. Policy-makers alerted by scholars seem to be beginning to understand that families will not be able to manage eldercare without the support of the state.

- Informal employment is becoming an important topic of debate among politicians and policy-makers, who point to its negative impact on the economy and the need for citizens to be given incentives to be employed formally.
- Voluntary work is becoming an important aspect of the public debate on civil society for its role in bridging various social groups and building social cohesion.

Thus, it would be wrong to believe that the relationship between formal and informal work in Poland has been shaped exclusively by postcommunist transformations. Poland has been also affected by universal social and demographic changes. These—domestic and foreign, specific and universal—factors have also led to a rising awareness of policy-makers and subsequent radical shifts in public policies, particularly on social, education, health care and similar issues, leading to increased reliance on the market and family in the provision of social welfare.

Last but not least, citizens hope for and expect more family-friendly incentives and policies that will help families respond to the responsibilities placed on them by the state and the challenges of contemporary society, particularly in the sphere of care. Cultural characteristics indicate that policy makers are right to stress the fundamental role of the family. But they seem not yet to have taken fully into account that families may not succeed without the appropriately organised support of the state. The necessary changes in governmental action are still ahead of us.

NOTES

1. It should be remembered that Polish society was young, rural, and family-centred.
2. Although the shortage of job offers at a time of high unemployment (2000–2005) was the main reason women gave to explain their employment inactivity (approx. 50 per cent of responses from women age 30–39), the second reason was the impossibility of balancing work and family obligations (22.4 per cent of responses from women age 30–39)—see Matysiak 2007.
3. More than one option was available.
4. Some authors such as Szatur-Jaworska (1997) argue that home-based eldercare 'topped up' with additional services is more efficient than institutional care.

REFERENCES

CBOS. (2001) *Kondycja polskiego społeczeństwa obywatelskiego*, Biuletyn CBOS.
———. (2002) *Przemiany grupowej aktywności społecznej Polaków w latach 1998–2002*, Biuletyn CBOS, Warszawa, luty.
Czekanowski, P. (2003) 'Rodzina w życiu osób starszych i osoby starsze w rodzinie' [Family in the lives of the elderly and the elderly in the family], in B. Synak (ed.) *Polska starość*, Gdańsk: Wydawnictwo Uniwersytetu Gdańskiego.

Dąbrowska, J., and Gumkowska, M. (2002) *Wolontariat i filantropia w Polsce*, Raport z badań 2002, badanie wykonane przez SMG/KRC w dniach 15 października do 4 listopada 2002, na reprezentatywnej grupie 1000 dorosłych Polaków, 3w*001.

Deacon, B. (2000) 'Eastern European welfare states: The impacts of the politics of globalisation', *Journal of European Social Policy* 10(2), Thousand Oaks: Sage Publications.

Esping-Andersen, G. (1990) *The Three Worlds of Welfare Capitalism*, Cambridge: Polity Press.

———. (2002) *Why We Need a New Welfare State*, New York: Oxford University Press.

Firlit-Fesnak (1995) Polityka społeczna w świadomości społecznej, Warszawa: Elipsa.

Frątczak, E. (1987) Wybrane uwarunkowania i konsekwencje procesu starzenia się ludności Polski, Warszawa: Szkoła Główna Planowania i Statystyki.

Golinowska, S. (1996) 'Zawodowa i domowa praca kobiet. Polska i kraje Europy Środkowej i Wschodniej' in *Polityka Społeczna*, vol.8, Warszawa, sierpień.

———. (2002) 'Europejski model socjalny i otwarta koordynacja polityki społecznej', *Polityka Społeczna* 11/12.

GUS [Główny Urząd Statystyczny] (1997) Opieka nad dziećmi i młodzieżą— organizacja czasu wolnego, Warszawa.

———. (2007)Aktywnosc ekonomiczna ludnosci, available at: http://www.stat. gov.pl/gus/45_2189_PLK_WAI.htm.

Hrynkiewicz, J. (2001) 'Rodzina i Społeczeństwo', in Z. Strzelecki and A. Ochocki (eds) *Polska a Europa. Procesy demograficzne u progu XXI wieku*, pod red., Rządowa Rada Ludnościowa, Warszawa: RCSS.

———. (2001) Rola Kościoła w kształtowaniu polityki prorodzinnej i proopiekunczej, Mimeo.

Johnson, S., Kaufmann, D., and Pablo Zoido-Lobatón (1999) *Corruption, Public Finances and the Unofficial Economy*, Washington, World Bank Policy Research Working Paper No. 2169.

Kałaska, M., and Witkowski, J. (1996) 'Praca na czarno', *Kontrola Panstwowa* 1/1996.

Kaufmann,D., and Kaliberda, A. (1996) 'Integrating the unofficial economy into the dynamics of post socialist economies: A framework of analyses and evidence', [in:] B. Kaminski (ed.) *Economic Transition in Russia and the New States of Eurasia*, Londyn: M.E. Sharpe.

Kisiel, P. (1999) 'Społeczne uwarunkowania przedsiębiorczości—postawy społeczne wobec przedsiębiorczości', in J. Targalski (ed.) *Przedsiębiorczość a lokalny i regionalny rozwój gospodarczy*, Krakow: Wyd. AE, 23–28.

Kloc, K.: (1998) Szara strefa w Polsce w okresie transformacji, Raporty CASE Centrum Analiz Społeczno-Gospodarczych, Warszawa.

Kolodko, G.(1999)Od szoku do terapii: ekonomia i polityka transformacji, Warszawa Poltekst.

Kotowska, I.E., Sztanderska, U., and Wóycicka, I. (eds) (2007) Aktywność zawodowa i edukacyjna a obowiązki rodzinne w Polsce w świetle badań empirycznych, Warszawa: Scholar.

Matysiak, A. (2007) Indywidualne przesłanki zwiększenia aktywności zawodowej, w, in I.E. Kotowska, U. Sztanderska and I. Wóycicka (eds) (2007) Aktywność zawodowa i edukacyjna a obowiązki rodzinne, Wydawnictwo: Scholar.

Ministerstwo Gospodarki (MG) (2007) Zatrudnienie w Polsce w 2006 roku, Warszawa: MGiP.

Ministerstwo Pracy i Polityki Spolecznej (MPiPS(2007) Zatrudnienie w Polsce w 2006 roku, Warszawa: MPiPS.

Narojek, W. (1986) *Perspektywy pluralizmu w upanstwowionym spoleczenstwie. Ocena sytuacji na podstawie polskich kryzysow*, Londyn: Aneks.
Perek-Białas, J. (2003) *Active Ageing in Poland: Issues, Institutions, Policy, 2003*, Unpublished Report from Project on Overcoming Barriers and Seizing the Opportunities for Active Ageing Policy under the 5th FP, Poland (mimeo).
Pfau-Effinger, B. (2004) *Development of Culture, Welfare States and Women's Employment in Europe*, Aldershot: Ashgate.
Piczura, E. (2003) Starzenie się społeczeństwa jako narastający problem we współczesnym świecie: na przykładzie wybranej społeczności lokalnej, praca dyplomowa Instytut Socjologii UJ: Kraków.
Pietrowski, D., and Maciuła, M. (1999) Od chaosu do ustawy, in Roczniak nr 7.D. Pietrowski, M. Maciuła, Od chaosu do ustawy, w: Roczniak nr 7, s. 10–11.
Poliwczak, I. (2003) 'Zatrudnienie w niepełnym wymiarze czasu pracy' in *Polityka Społeczna*, vol. 7, lipiec.
Salamon, L.M., Sokolowski, S.W., and Anheier, H.K. (2000) *Social Origins of Civil Society: An Overview*, Working Papers of the Johns Hopkins Comparative Non-profit Sector Project, no. 38, Baltimore: The Johns Hopkins Center for Civil Society Studies.
Sowa, K. (1990) Gospodarka nieformalna. Uwarunkowania lokalne i systemowe, Rzeszow: TNOiK.
Synak, B. (ed.) (2003) *Polska starość*, Wydawnictwo Uniwersytetu Gdańskiego, Gdańsk.
'Sytuacja społeczno-zawodowa kobiet w 1994' in *Informacje i opracowania statystyczne*, Warszawa: GUS.
Szatur-Jaworska, B. (1997) *Warsaw Voice*, April 13, 1997 No 15 (442).
———. (2000) *Ludzie starzy i starość w polityce społecznej*, Wyd. Warszawa: ASPRA-JR.
Worach-Kardas, H. (1997) 'Współczesna rodzina w polityce społecznej', in *Polityka Społeczna*, vol. 9, Warszawa: Wrzesień.
Zarychta, H. (1994) 'Szara strefa rynku w Polsce. Część II', *Praca i Zabezpieczenie Społeczne*, Warszawa: PWE.

Part III

Comparative Perspective

9 Formal and Informal Work in European Societies

A Comparative Perspective

Birgit Pfau-Effinger, Per H. Jensen, and Lluís Flaquer

INTRODUCTION

Unlike the previous chapters, our objective in this chapter is to draw cross-national comparisons rather than provide country-specific in-depth analysis, with the aim of assessing how cross-national differences can be explained. We introduce a systematic internationally comparative perspective on informal work and the way in which it relates to formal employment. Under what conditions is work in European societies organised in an informal form, and under which circumstances is the same type of work organised as formal employment? How can cross-national differences in relation to the extent and structures of informal work be explained? Four main areas of informal work have been examined in depth: family-based childcare; family-based eldercare; informal employment; and voluntary work (see Jensen et al. in this volume).

In the first section of this chapter (section 9.1.), we outline the findings with respect to the specific extent and structures of informal work in each country. We show that the differences can only to a rather limited degree be explained by differences in the type of the welfare state according to the 'welfare regime' approach by Esping-Andersen. In section 9.2, we explain why specific activities are organised as informal, semiformal, or formal work in the specific context of the arrangements of work and welfare of the different countries. Section 9.3 provides an overview of some main changes that are occurring with regard to informal work and in the arrangements of work and welfare that are framing the development.

9.1. CROSS-NATIONAL DIFFERENCES IN RELATION TO INFORMAL WORK

In many Western European countries, we witnessed in the last two decades an overall process of formalisation of work, epitomised, for instance, as an increase in (formal) female labour-force participation rates. In effect, women have less time for housework and care responsibilities, which may have contributed to increasing the demand for formal care and generating an increase in demand for publicly provided care based on formal employment. In some countries, processes of an informalisation of care work also took place in part, particularly in the Central and Eastern European countries, as represented in our study by Poland. During the transformation process, the sector of public, formal childcare was to a large extent cut down, and the task of care was shifted to a substantial degree to the family, where it is mainly provided as informal family care in the extended family network. Table 9.1 provides an overview of the role of informal work in the six countries included in this book.[1]

Table 9.1.   The Extent of the Different Forms of Informal Work and Formal Care in the Countries Included in the Study

	DK	FI	BRD West	BRD East	UK	ES	PL
Formalisation of childcare (1)	High	High	Medium	High	Low	Medium	Low
Formalisation of eldercare	High	High	Medium	Medium	Low	Low	Low
Semiformal forms of child-care	Low	Medium	High	Medium	Low	Low	Low
Semiformal forms of elderly care (2)	Low	low	High	High	Low	Low	Low
Informal family childcare (3)	Low	Low	High	Low	High	High	High
Informal family eldercare (4)	Low	Low	Medium	Medium	High	High	High
Undeclared work in general	Medium	Low	Medium	Medium	Medium	High	High
- poverty-escape type	-	-	+	+	+	+	+
- moonlighting type	+	-	+	+	+	-	-
Voluntary work	Medium	Medium	Medium	Low	High	Low	Low

(1) For children below school age
(2) Paid care in the framework of welfare-state programmes such as paid parental leave, elder-care, insurance
(3) By part-time working mothers, grandparents, or relatives
(4) By relatives

As can be seen from Table 9.1, the welfare state has made important steps towards fostering and regulating care in several of the countries that were included in the study. However, there are still considerable differences concerning the share of formal, semiformal and informal family care from a comparative perspective. Besides informal and semiformal childcare and eldercare, the other forms of informal work that we had included in the study, namely voluntary work and undeclared work, also differ considerably between the countries included in the study. The citizens of the different countries organise themselves in voluntary work in civil society to differing degrees, and they are also involved in informal employment outside the sector of formal employment to differing extents.

From a comparative perspective, the share of *formal care* is particularly high for childcare in Denmark, Finland and East Germany. It is of a medium size for childcare in West Germany, Great Britain, and Spain, and low in Poland. The distribution in relation to the extent of formal eldercare is somewhat different, in that its share is high in Denmark and Finland, medium in Germany, and low in the other countries.

The demand for paid care can also be met by *semiformal* forms of care,[2] such as childcare by parents in the context of paid welfare state programmes such as paid parental leave schemes, or eldercare within specific welfare-state schemes. This is an important form of care, particularly for young children and for elderly people in Germany, and to some degree also in Finland in the field of childcare. Additionally, several options for *informal family care* are available. First, motherhood and wage work may be reconciled by means of *part-time work* (Germany and the UK) or by engaging *grandparents* or *relatives* in unpaid care obligations (Spain and Poland).

A huge variety of human activities can be performed as formal or informal work—be it paid or unpaid. Thus, some parts of paid work are organised as *informal employment* or *undeclared work*. This means that workers or users/employers are not prepared to declare them to the public authorities and pay taxes and/or social security contributions. The extent of undeclared work is relatively low in Finland, of medium size in Denmark, Germany and Great Britain, and high in Spain and Poland. Concerning cross-national differences in relation to undeclared work, we stress the argument that at least two different forms of undeclared work should be distinguished, namely the 'poverty-escape type' and the 'moonlighting type', because they develop according to very different logics. The poverty escape type of informal work may be viewed as a struggle for subsistence in a labour market with no job openings and meagre welfare benefits. It is therefore also a particularly precarious form of informal employment compared with the undeclared 'moonlighting', which is about earning an extra income in addition to the 'ordinary' wage income (see also Jensen et al. in this volume). The extent of the poverty-escape type of informal employment is particularly low in Denmark and Finland. The poverty-escape type as well as the moonlighting type of informal employment are of approximately medium extent in Germany and Great Britain, whereas the poverty-escape type clearly predominates in Spain and Poland, where the extent of the moonlighting type is relatively small.

This study shows that there is a functional equivalence between different forms of informal work. Informal family care, for instance, may take the form of *informal employment* or *undeclared work* if it is provided by persons who are hired and paid for this purpose. In this case, it is part of what we call the poverty-escape type of informal employment, insofar as it is organised in private households. Its share is particularly high in Spain, where immigrant women provide care services in the form of undeclared work, medium in Germany and Great Britain, and low in the other countries of the study.

Similarly, activities can be organised as *voluntary work* or as informal employment. Voluntary work is an activity providing social services for people in need or an activity which strengthens social bonds in civil society, as in the fields of sports and culture. Also in this respect, there are considerable differences between the countries which were included in the study: The extent of voluntary work is relatively high in Great Britain, medium in Denmark, Finland and West Germany, and relatively low in East Germany, Spain, and Poland (see Table 9.1). Informal care work can also be organised as voluntary work, which is, for example, partly the case in eldercare in Great Britain (see Meyer and Baxendale in this volume).

Limitations in the Explanatory Power of the Welfare-regime Approach

In several cases, the findings from the comparison of the extent of informal work in different European countries are in line with the results that one would expect using the 'welfare regime' approach of Esping-Andersen (1990, 1999) and its extension by two more regime types, that is, the 'Latin rim' and the 'post-communist'. From a comparative perspective, the share of *formal childcare* and *formal eldercare* is particularly high in the countries with a social democratic welfare regime, Denmark and Finland, even though some differences also exist between these countries. The share of formal childcare is, however, medium in West Germany in the context of a conservative welfare regime, where one would expect a low size, and is even high in East Germany, although one would expect a low size in a conservative welfare regime. Moreover, the extent of formal eldercare is medium in both parts of Germany. The extent of formal childcare is relatively low in Great Britain, as in Poland, even though one would expect a relatively high rate of formal care in the form of formal employment provided by the market in the liberal welfare regime of Great Britain. In Spain, although it is classified as a Latin rim welfare state which strongly relies on the provision of welfare within the family, the extent of formal childcare is medium, in contradiction to the low level that one would expect. The extent of formal eldercare is low in Great Britain, Poland, and Spain, despite the fact that one might expect at least a medium-sized extent of formal eldercare, based on market provision, in the liberal welfare state of Great Britain.

There is no coherent pattern concerning the relationship of welfare regime types and differences in terms of the share of *semiformal care*. In the social democratic welfare states, its relative size is low in Denmark and medium in Finland. Even within the same welfare state type in Germany, substantial differences exist in this respect between West and East Germany, with the share of semiformal care work being high in the West and only medium in the East, whereas its share in eldercare is high in both parts of Germany. In the liberal welfare state of Great Britain, the share of semiformal care work is low in childcare as well as in eldercare. Its share is also low in Spain and Poland.

There is also no clear picture with regard to the relationship of the extent of *informal unpaid family care* with the welfare regime type. The share of informal family care is clearly low in the countries with social democratic welfare regimes such as Finland and Denmark, as one would expect. In contrast to what one would expect, it is also low in East Germany in the context of a conservative welfare state, whereas it is of medium size in terms of eldercare and high in terms of childcare in West Germany. In Great Britain, its extent is high, even though one would expect considerable parts to be covered by formal employment in market-based organisations. It is also high in Spain and Poland.

We also analysed the relationship between *undeclared work* and the welfare regime type. If we follow the argument put forward by neoclassical economists (e.g. Schneider and Enste 2000), one would expect the share of undeclared work to be particularly high in welfare states with high taxes and/or social security contributions. Therefore, we would expect the share of undeclared work through which people aim to circumvent paying tax and social security contributions to be particularly high in the social democratic welfare regime type. With regard to the liberal welfare state, on the other hand, it might be assumed that the share of undeclared work is low, as taxes and social security contributions are low, and people therefore do not escape to informal forms of employment. One would also expect the share of informal work to be medium in the conservative welfare regime, which would then match with the extent of taxes and social security contributions, which are also of a medium size from a comparative perspective. In the Latin rim welfare state, and often also in the postsocialist welfare state, the taxes and social security contributions that the citizens have to pay are often particularly low. Therefore, one might assume that the share of undeclared work would also be particularly low in such countries.

However, the ways in which the extent of undeclared work and the welfare regime type interact partly contradict what one would expect following the explanation based on neoclassical economics. The share of undeclared work is relatively low in the social democratic welfare regime type, of medium size in the liberal welfare state as well as in the conservative type, and particularly high in the Latin rim and postsocialist regime type. The extent of the poverty-escape type of undeclared work is even particularly low in the social democratic welfare regime type, medium in the conservative welfare state, and high in the Latin rim and the postsocialist type. The relationship between the extent of the moonlighting type of undeclared work and the welfare state type is a little different. It is low to medium in the social democratic welfare regime, where one might expect a high share, but also low in the Latin rim and the postsocialist regime type, as well as in the liberal welfare regime. It is of medium size in the conservative regime type.

With regard to *voluntary work*, if one applies Esping-Andersen's approach, it might be assumed that strong welfare states are crowding out voluntary work, as strong welfare states such as the social democratic regime type tend to offer comprehensive public social services. The results show the opposite: Voluntary work is medium to high in the countries that have social democratic welfare states. Its extent differs within the same conservative welfare state of Germany between medium in West Germany and low in the East. Its share is rather low in the Latin rim and the postsocialist welfare states, but high in the liberal welfare regime of Great Britain.

Altogether, the findings show that the welfare regime approach does not provide a satisfactory theoretical framework to explain cross-national differences in the extent of the different types of informal work.

9.2. EXPLANATION OF THE DIFFERENCES IN THE CONTEXT OF THE DIFFERING 'ARRANGEMENTS OF WORK AND WELFARE'

Main Assumptions in Relation to the Explanation of Cross-national Differences

As was outlined in Chapters 1 and 2 of this volume, the 'welfare regime' approach of Esping-Andersen provides a useful starting point for the explanation of cross-national differences in the degree to which informal work is used in different European societies. However, according to our argument, only some parts of the approach can be used for explanation. The explanatory framework must be extended, and the broader institutional, cultural, sociostructural, and economic context of the respective society should be included. We therefore use the approach of the 'arrangement of work and welfare' which was introduced by Pfau-Effinger (in this volume) in order to identify the specific societal context that shapes the extent and structures of informal work and examine how it is linked with formal employment.

The *arrangement of work and welfare* is constituted by the overlapping of mainly two different societal arrangements:

- The *welfare arrangement*, which is constituted by the level of decom-modification according to Esping-Andersen (1990, 1999) and the underlying cultural values; the stratifying nature of welfare state poli-cies, according to Esping-Andersen (1990, 1999), and the relationship of the population with the welfare state, indicated by the strength of the civil society and the degree of trust in the state.
- The *work and family arrangement*, which is constituted by the wel-fare-state institutions and policies that are directed at the family, care, and employment; their stratifying nature in terms of gender; and the cultural values and models surrounding the relationship of family, care, and employment.

Accordingly, we expect that the specific welfare arrangement, and the ways in which it overlaps with the arrangement of work and family in each soci-ety, contribute to explaining why work is organised in informal and for-mal forms to differing extents in different societies, and why the structures of informal work are also different. The argument is emphasised that an arrangement can be contradictory in itself, or contradictions may exist in the ways in which the welfare arrangement on the one hand and the arrange-ment of work and family on the other frame the behaviour of individuals and social groups in relation to informal work and formal employment.

Explanation of cross-national Differences in the Organisation of Care Work

According to our assumption, the differences in relation to *childcare work* among the countries in the study can be explained to a substantial degree by the dominant cultural model of the family upon which the 'arrangement of work and welfare' is mainly based in a society, and the degree to which the welfare state supports this family model.

From the country chapters, it has emerged that in the different countries included in the study, mainly three different cultural models of the family are dominant. Using the classification model based on dominant cultural family models, it is possible to distinguish a 'male breadwinner/female part-time carer model', which is dominant in West Germany and Great Britain, a 'dual breadwinner/extended family care model' in Spain and Poland, and a 'dual breadwinner/state care model'[3] in Denmark, Finland, and East Ger-many (Flaquer and Escobedo; Jensen and Rathlev; Jolkkonen et al.; Surdej and Slezak; Meyer and Baxendale; Pfau-Effinger and Sakač Magdalenić, all in this volume).

The realisation of the dominant family model(s) is supported by the respec-tive welfare state in a country to differing extents. The realisation of the dual-breadwinner/external care model is strongly supported by the welfare states in Denmark and Finland, which have established extensive rights for children under six to receive care. In Finland, in addition, relatively generous schemes for parental leave were also established. The welfare state in Germany only supports the realisation of the male breadwinner/female part-time carer model to a limited extent, as the hours of childcare provided per day are not sufficient even for parents with part-time jobs, and only part of the parental leave is paid. The welfare state also supports the realisation of a different cultural family model, a dual-breadwinner/state care model, which is dominant in East Germany. In this area of Germany, childcare is relatively comprehensive for children over three and is usually provided on a full-time basis. Childcare is also provided for children under three to a higher degree. This is mainly also due to the policies of the *'Neue Laender'* and the municipalities in East Germany, which are oriented towards this family model. However, public provision of care for children under three is still limited and does not really match the demand in the population. The welfare states of Spain and Poland to a large extent tolerate the dual- breadwinner/extended family model that is dominant in these countries, but they do not actively support the family in its caring function. The support is rather passive, tacit, or implicit (Flaquer 2002).

According to Table 9.2, the differences in the specific patterns of formal care work and the diverse forms of informal care work in the field of childcare in the different countries can, to a considerable degree, be explained by the dominant family model upon which the respective arrangement of work and family is based and the degree to which the welfare state supports the respective model.

In those countries in which a male breadwinner/female part-time carer family model is dominant in the work-family arrangement, the extent of formal childcare is relatively low if the welfare state only supports the realisation of this family model to a limited degree, as in Great Britain. It is of medium size if the welfare state supports the realisation of this family model to a medium degree, as in West Germany. On the other hand, if a dual-breadwinner/extended family model is dominant, and the degree to which the state supports this family model is low, or it is only a passive support, then the extent of formal care is low, as is the case in Poland, and in eldercare in Spain, or it is at most medium, like childcare in Spain. Also in this case, the extent of semiformal family care is particularly low, and the extent of informal family care by parents or relatives is particularly high. This is the case in Poland and Spain.

The picture is somewhat different in countries in which a dual-breadwinner/external-care provider model is dominant as the cultural basis of the work-family arrangement, as in Denmark, Finland, and East Germany. In Finland and Denmark, the welfare state strongly supports the realisation of this model. However, there are some differences. Welfare state policies in Denmark strongly support the full and full-time integration of parents into formal employment after a relatively short period of maternity and parental leave. It provides a comprehensive public infrastructure in relation to childcare (Jensen and Rathlev in this volume). The case is approximately

Formal and Informal Work in European Socities 201

Table 9.2. The Societal Organisation of Care Work in Childcare in the Context of the Dominant Cultural Basis of the Work–Family Arrangements and the Degree to which this is Supported by the Welfare State

Dominant cultural basis of the work-family arrangement	Relative support that is given by the welfare state to the dominant family model of the arrangement of work and welfare		
	Strong/active support	*Medium/active support*	*Low/passive support*
Male- breadwinner/female part-time career model		**West Germany** Mixture of -formal childcare: medium -semiformal childcare: high -informal parental care: high	**UK** Mixture of -formal childcare: low -semiformal childcare: low -informal parental care: high
Dual- breadwinner/extended family care model			**Poland** **Spain** Mixture of -formal childcare: low to medium -semiformal childcare: low -informal family care: high (parents and relatives)
Dual-breadwinner/external care model	**Denmark** **Finland** -formal childcare: high -semiformal childcare: low-medium -informal parental care: low	**East Germany** -formal childcare: high -semiformal childcare: low-medium -informal parental care: low	

the same in Finland, where every child under six has a social right to public or publicly financed childcare. In both welfare states, the quality of public childcare is high. However, in Finland, the welfare state has also established the option for parents to take a relatively long period of paid parental leave until children are three years old. In this respect, parents have a 'real choice' between formal public childcare and semiformal family care for their young children. Although the take-up rates in relation to paid parental leave are about 50 per cent, and parental leave of mothers—who are the main persons using this option—is in most cases only a couple of months after maternity leave, the average amount of time for which mothers of young children stay at home and provide semiformal family care after the birth of a child is considerably higher in Finland compared with Denmark (Jolkkonen et al. in this volume).

Table 9.3 shows that it is also possible to a substantial degree to explain the differences in the specific patterns of formal care work and the diverse forms of informal care work in relation to *eldercare* in the different countries through the interaction of the dominant cultural values regarding family care for elderly people and the degree to which the welfare state supports this model in the context of the arrangement of work and family.

The countries in which the role of family care is relatively highly culturally appreciated differ with regard to the degree to which family care by relatives is supported by the welfare state. Accordingly, the dominant patterns in relation to formal and informal eldercare are also different. In both Poland and Spain, the extent of family care is altogether high. Nevertheless, whereas in Poland formally and semiformally provided care levels are low, in Spain, the levels of these two forms of care are growing as a result of the shift of support by the welfare state away from the dominant cultural values. In those countries in which the welfare state supports family care to a relatively strong degree, such as Germany, it is provided in semiformal form to a relatively high extent, whereas in countries with a weak role of the welfare state towards the family, it is mainly provided in an informal form. Although family care in Germany receives a high cultural appreciation, the welfare state has also established a strong option to decide in favour of publicly financed eldercare by service agencies in the private households or publicly financed residential care. Frail elderly people are taking up this option much less than is possible, but the share of formal care is at least medium in Germany (see Pfau-Effinger and Sakač Magdaleni´cin this volume).

The pattern is different in countries in which the societal appreciation of family care is relatively low and the welfare state is given a relatively strong role in the area of eldercare, such as in Denmark and Finland. Here, a relatively high degree of eldercare is formalised and publicly provided. The share of semiformal or informal family care is comparatively low. It should also be considered that in these countries, the need for eldercare is much more broadly defined. Eldercare is understood as any kind of support for elderly people in their everyday life. Even taking into consideration

Table 9.3. The Societal Organisation of Eldercare in the Context of the Main Cultural Values in Relation to Eldercare and the Degree to Which This is Supported by the Welfare State

Main cultural values in relation to eldercare	Relative support that is given by the welfare state to the dominant cultural values related to eldercare in the arrangement of work and welfare	
	Strong/active support	*Low/passive support*
High cultural appreciation of family care	**Poland** Mixture of -formal care: low -semiformal care: low -informal care: high	**Spain** Mixture of -formal care: low but growing -semiformal care: low but growing -informal family care: high
Medium cultural appreciation of family care	**Germany** Mixture of -formal care: medium -semiformal care: high -informal family care: medium	**UK** Mixture of -formal care: low -semiformal care: low -informal family care: high
Low cultural appreciation of family care	**Denmark** **Finland** -formal care: high -semiformal care: low -informal family care: low to medium	

this broad definition, the welfare state provision of formal care is relatively high. In the other countries, the definition of the need for care of elderly people is much more restricted to the physical dimension of care. Therefore, a comprehensive provision of formal care means something different, and there is a much higher degree of provision of formal care in Denmark and Finland than in the other countries (see Jensen and Rathlev in this volume; Jolkkonen et al. in this volume).

Explaining Differences in Undeclared Work and Voluntary Work in the Context of Different Arrangements of Work and Welfare

According to the main assumptions upon which the approach of the 'arrangement of work and welfare' is based, the extent and structures of *undeclared work* and *voluntary work* can be explained to a substantial degree by the specific profile of the welfare arrangement on the one hand and the underlying cultural values on the other. However, it is argued here that there is not a uniform type of *undeclared work*, and there are different explanations for the differing types of undeclared work.[4]

The extent of the poverty-escape type of undeclared work strongly relies on the availability of a workforce who are in a situation where they feel forced to accept work under particularly precarious and uncertain conditions. Some types of companies, mainly small companies in decentralised sectors of the economy (Williams and Windebank 1998), may always be interested in this type of undeclared work, but they only can realise their interest if such a workforce exists. Another precondition may also be the existence of private households that are interested in employing workers in undeclared work, either for housework, such as cleaning and the like, or

Table 9.4.   Undeclared Work in the Context of Different Types of Welfare Arrangement

	Different types of welfare arrangement				
Extent of undeclared work	*Social democratic*	*Conservative*	*Liberal*	*Latin rim*	*Postsocialist*
Undeclared work in general	Low (Finland) Medium (Denmark)	Medium (Germany)	Medium (Great Britain)	High (Spain)	High (Poland)
- poverty-escape type	Low	Medium (Germany)	Medium (Great Britain)	High (Spain)	High (Poland)
- moonlight-ing type	Low (Finland) Medium (Denmark)	Medium (Germany	Low (Great Britain)	Low (Spain)	Low (Poland)

for childcare and eldercare, or else for different kinds of craftwork, such as construction and repair. This was also shown in different chapters of this book. The respective workforce can exist in a situation of high unemployment rates, together with a relatively low level of decommodification of the unemployed, or if a broad part of formal employment does not offer an income above the poverty line. The labour supply for undeclared work can also be based on a broad group of immigrants who are not allowed to be commodified because they do not receive a work permit, but for whom the degree of decommodification is also low and does not guarantee benefits above the poverty level.

In addition, some elements of the arrangement of work and family in a society may contribute to the explanation, for example if the state is only given a relatively weak role regarding the family and therefore does not provide adequate support to the family household. In this case, the employment of servants on the basis of undeclared work may be used mainly also by affluent middle-class families to fill the gaps. Another precondition in this case is that the employment of household staff in general is culturally accepted (Solé and Flaquer 2005).

These conditions differ relatively systematically with the type of welfare arrangement. The conditions that create this type of workforce exist to a rather low degree in the social-democratic welfare arrangements of Denmark and Finland. Here, the welfare state is based on a high level of decommodification, and a migration policy that avoids the development of a group of poor immigrants without work permits. The welfare state support for the family is high, and undeclared work in private households is rather rarely accepted in the population. The interaction of these factors contributes substantially to explaining why the share of the poverty-escape type of undeclared work is very low in these countries (see also Jensen and Rathlev in this volume).

In Germany and Great Britain, the extent of the poverty-escape type of undeclared work is of medium size. It is mainly also used by affluent middle-class households for cleaning, but also for childcare and eldercare in order to solve problems that emerge because the provision of public childcare and eldercare is low. This has much to do with the lower level of decommodification of unemployed people in both countries, which creates a group of poor unemployed people, and the fact that a group of poor immigrants without work permits exists as a consequence of the specific type of migration policy. On the demand side, mainly in private households, it is also relevant that the welfare state provision of the family does not match with the needs of the families and that there is a relatively high degree of acceptance in the population for employing household servants in undeclared work (Meyer and Baxendale in this volume, Pfau-Effinger and Sakač Magdalenić in this volume).

The share of the poverty-escape type of undeclared work is relatively high in the Mediterranean welfare state of Spain as well as the postsocialist welfare state of Poland. This is mainly because in these welfare states, the decommodification level is relatively weak, and particularly in Spain, there is also a large group of immigrants without a legal status and without work permits. In Spain, the employment of immigrants on the basis of unde-clared work is also a main measure taken by private households from the middle classes to bridge the discrepancies between the need for childcare and eldercare and the relatively limited support of the family in this respect (Flaquer and Escobedo in this volume).

The factors that can explain the extent of the moonlighting type of unde-clared work are different. What is important here is that a relatively afflu-ent middle class exists that can afford to hire professionals or craftsmen for work in the fields of IT, construction and repair, for private households, and that these tasks are the main fields in which this type of undeclared work is performed. Another precondition is that in part, people do not accept the obligation to pay tax, which itself has a great deal to do with the level of trust in the welfare state. These preconditions exist mainly in the conservative welfare state of Germany, which is a country with a broad and relatively affluent middle class where the degree of distrust in the state is relatively high (see Tables 3.1. and 3.4., Appendix 2). However, the moon-lighting type of undeclared work also plays a relevant role in Denmark, where it is also of medium extent. This can mainly be explained by the fact that the obligation to pay taxes is very comprehensive and covers all kinds of mutual help in social networks; at the same time taxes, in this field of mutual help in particular are not well accepted in the Danish population.

With regard to *voluntary work*, one might assume that strong welfare states are crowding out voluntary work if one applies Esping-Andersen's approach, as strong welfare states, such as the social democratic regime type, tend to offer comprehensive public social services. However, it has been shown that the empirical evidence does not support this assump-tion. Rather, it has been demonstrated that the 'other side' of the respec-tive arrangement of work and welfare, which includes the traditions of self-organisation of the citizens in civil society, should also be considered. Cross-national differences in terms of the extent of voluntary work can be substantially explained by differences relating to such traditions. In coun-tries such as West Germany and Great Britain, but also in Denmark and Finland, the self-organisation of the citizens in civil society, and accord-ingly also in voluntary work, has a long tradition. This is a main reason why the extent of voluntary work is medium or high in these countries. The extent of voluntary work is relatively low, by contrast, in East Ger-many and Poland, as well as in Spain. In the former socialist states of East Germany and Poland, this can mainly be explained by the fact that the socialist states hindered the development of autonomous activities of the citizens in civil societies to a large degree and therefore substantially weakened the civil society. The relatively low extent of voluntary work can be seen as a legacy of these times (Jensen and Rathlev; Jolkkonen et al.;

Pfau-Effinger and Sakač Magdalenić; Meyer and Baxendale; Flaquer and Escobedo; Surdej and Slezak; all in this volume). As in Poland, in Spain, the low practice of voluntary work is associated with a legacy of Francoism. In both countries, especially in the last stages of their authoritarian regimes, voluntary work used to take place in unorganised family and community networks, including underground Catholic Church associations. However, although the identity of the Poles came to be increasingly associated with the Catholic faith, in the last decades in Spain, the Catholic tradition has been increasingly eroded. This is one of the reasons why Spaniards these days participate so little in the activities of the Church, which in other countries often channels an important part of charitable concerns (Flaquer and Escobedo in this volume). It should also be mentioned that particularly in the field of voluntary work, comparative data are very rare.[5]

Conclusions in Relation to the Explanation of Cross-national Differences

It has emerged that the welfare regime typology by Esping-Andersen contributes to explaining cross-national differences in relation to the degree to which specific activities in European societies are organised into informal work or formal work. This relates mainly to the classification of welfare states on the basis of the 'level of decommodification', and in some parts in relation to the stratification impact of welfare state policies. However, it is also important to include in the analyses the general relationship of the citizens towards the state, which mainly encompasses the role of the civil society vis-à-vis the state, the degree of trust that citizens have in institutions, and the degree to which the citizens accept the obligation to pay taxes (Janoski 1998).

It is then also possible to explain differences within the same welfare regime type. Voluntary work in Denmark and Finland is a good example. Whereas voluntary work virtually does not exist in the field of social services in Denmark, it plays a substantial role in the Finnish welfare state. This is a remnant of the Finnish history, in which—different from Denmark—the welfare state and the ideas behind it were first developed in civil society, under the condition of a state that was the state of the occupying Russian society and not the Finns' 'own' state at the turn of the twentieth century. The civil society remained another strong power in the welfare system of Finland, a power it does not hold in Denmark.

The specific profile and cultural basis of the arrangement of work and family, and the strength of the role that is given the welfare state regarding the family, as well as the cultural family model/s upon which this arrangement is mainly based in a society, adds another important element to the explanation, particularly in the field of childcare and care of the elderly. It can also contribute to explaining why the rapid increase in labour-force participation of women in Spain was based on full-time employment, and the labour market integration of women in West Germany and Great Britain is mainly based on part-time work, even though until the start of the twenty-first century in Spain, very little public childcare existed for children under three years. Women in Spain are mainly oriented towards a dual-breadwinner/extended-family care model on a full-time basis for mothers of small children, which is shifting towards a dual-breadwinner/state-care model. Full-time employment of mothers is not seen as detrimental to children as long as they are cared for by other reliable adults under their mothers' supervision (Flaquer and Escobedo in this volume). This is different in West Germany and Great Britain, where people believe that a 'good childhood' consists of children being cared for by their own mothers in the family home for at least part of the day. Cultural differences also contribute substantially to explaining the differences in the behaviour of mothers in West Germany and East Germany towards waged work: Whereas women in West Germany nearly exclusively take up a period of three years of parental leave and work part-time afterwards, women with small children in East Germany decide in favour of a much shorter period of parental leave and work full-time afterwards. These differences can be explained in the context of differences in the cultural basis in the dominant arrangement of work and family in both parts of Germany. In West Germany, there is a longer tradition of a 'male breadwinner/female part-time carer model', but there is a longue durée in East Germany of a 'dual breadwinner/state care model' (Pfau-Effinger and Sakač Magdalenić in this volume).

In both Poland and Spain, the prevalence of the dual-breadwinner/extended family care model is very significant. According to Eurostat data, in these two countries the presence of extended family forms (households with three or more adults with or without children) is nearly double that of the EU-25 average. In Spain, however, this model seems to be on the wane, and there is an evolution towards the dual-breadwinner/state-care model, but this is not the case in Poland. In fact, transition processes are running in opposite directions, because whereas Poland used to exhibit a dual- breadwinner/state-care model in the past, Spain appears to be heading towards it. A second important difference between these two countries is that in Spain, 13.3 per cent of the total labour force is foreign-born and, by contrast, this percentage is insignificant in Poland (0.3 percent).

9.3. ONGOING CHANGE IN RELATION TO INFORMAL WORK IN THE ARRANGEMENTS OF WORK AND WELFARE IN EUROPEAN SOCIETIES

There is an ongoing trend towards a formalisation of childcare in those countries which lag behind—with the exception of Great Britain, where the state still leaves the task of childcare to the family or the market.

This policy trend can be explained to a considerable degree by the fact that at the cultural level, the value of gender equality is increasingly established as a fundamental basis of the 'European social model'. The lack of provision of public childcare even in those countries which are based on a part-time model of the employed mother and carer is seen as a substantial barrier to the realisation of this ideal. Furthermore, the discourse on the demand of globalisation for a highly qualified workforce, and the need that has been stressed for developing a 'social investment state' which invests strongly in the human capital of its workforce, contributed to a policy shift towards the extension of the educational system of the state to preschool children, as is the case in Germany. Concerns of the policy elites regarding low birthrates have also contributed to the policy shift towards an extension of social rights and public infrastructure relating to childcare (Pfau-Effinger and Sakač Magdalenić in this volume). However, such changes will only lead to an extension of formalised public childcare to the degree in which public childcare is accepted in the population. Therefore, it is, for example, not yet clear whether the trend in welfare state policies in Germany to extend the right to public childcare to children of the age of two years will lead to a comprehensive increase in the take-up rates of childcare by parents of children of this age in Western Germany.

Another development is that in all countries, at least in the Western European countries included in the study, there is a trend in welfare state policies towards extending two different types of social rights towards eldercare: social rights for frail elderly people to receive care, and social rights for relatives to give care to their frail elderly spouses or parents (see Knijn and Kremer 1997). The strengthening of social rights for elderly people to receive care was mainly based on an extension of public financing of eldercare in the private household by service agencies in several Western European welfare states that are included in the study. In Germany and Spain, social rights for relatives to give care were also extended in that schemes were established by which informal family care was transformed into semiformal, paid forms of family care.

In this context, the rapid change that is taking place in the Spanish welfare state is particularly interesting. The recent shift in policies towards education and care has initiated a new development towards formalisation of childcare and eldercare on the basis of public or publicly financed care services. From 2004, a new Socialist government, and from even earlier on, various other regional administrations, have tried to develop some of these policies including a public network of educational and care institutions. The growth of early education and care for children under three and the 2006 Law on the Promotion of Personal Autonomy and Care for Dependent Persons are particularly striking. These developments, based on the recognition of new social rights, could be a serious challenge to the welfare model based on family solidarity, but the outcome is not clear. It remains to be seen if public involvement in early childhood education and care for children under three will develop in a similar way as it did for children from 3–6, and whether the full implementation of the Dependency Act will bring more formalisation and more professionalisation of carers. This will depend on the kind of policy developments incentivised by the government, and the interplay between policy developments and people's preferences will mark the orientation of future trends. It seems that, concerning the cultural family model that is most popular in the population, a change is taking place from a 'dual breadwinner/extended family care model' towards a 'dual breadwinner/state care model' in which the welfare state is given a more prominent role for providing childcare and eldercare also at the cultural level (Flaquer and Escobedo in this volume).

Social rights that are related to care were also recently strengthened substantially in the field of eldercare (Flaquer and Escobedo in this volume). In Spain, a similar legislation to the German Nursing Care Insurance Law of 1996 has recently been introduced. The 'Law on the Promotion of Personal Autonomy and Care for Dependent Persons', which was introduced in 2007, has introduced several options between family care and in-house care services by agencies. Because the value of the moral obligation within the family to care for the elderly relatives is strong in these countries, and eldercare is mainly also provided by spouses or daughters who are themselves elderly people and often already retired, it can be expected that family care will also be important in the future in both countries, and a combination of family care and care by services will be more common than a substitution of family care by such care services.

There is another trend in welfare-state policies that might in part contradict the extension of publicly financed professional care services. This sector is governed to a growing extent by principles of efficiency and marketisation of the care services. Another trend in the public provision of social services is that this sector is increasingly governed by principles of efficiency and marketisation of the care services. It is a contested issue if these changes, for example by the introduction of 'cash for care systems', might contribute to an increase in informal forms of care work such as undeclared work (Bode 2004; Vabö 2006).

It emerged in general that undeclared work is often used by family households in order to solve their problems if public supply of childcare does not match their needs. When a workforce is restricted from earning incomes above the poverty line in formal employment, extensive use of undeclared labour for care purposes by the affluent middle classes often results. If welfare-state policies do not match the growing need for comprehensive public, or publicly financed, care services in the field of eldercare, the extension of undeclared work in the private households may be an unwanted side effect. Such tendencies already exist, for example, in Germany, Spain, and Great Britain, and, to some extent, also in Denmark (Flaquer and Escobedo; Jensen and Rathlev; Meyer and Baxendale; Pfau-Effinger and Sakač Magdalenić; all in this volume). Due to the ongoing 'greying' of the population, and because the publicly paid services by care agencies are far from comprehensive in Germany, Great Britain, and Spain, it can be expected that in future, undeclared work by immigrants from less affluent countries might be used in these countries to a growing extent.

A further trend that can be detected is a growth in voluntary work in many European countries. Welfare state policies in several countries have strongly promoted voluntary work. This was due on the one hand to the fact that it was detected on the basis of discourses about the value of 'social capital' (Putnam 1993) as a new source for strengthening social cohesion. On the other hand, it was also detected as a new source of unpaid work which could be used to extend the supply of social services on an unpaid basis, as do the Third Way policies of some social democratic parties, for example, the Labour Party in Great Britain and the Social Democratic Party of Germany (SPD) (Meyer and Baxendale in this volume; Pfau-Effinger and Sakač Magdalenić in this volume). Such policies aim in part to substitute unpaid informal care work within the family with unpaid voluntary work in the community and civil society. However, this may cause substantial problems in terms of personal continuity of the caring staff as well as crucial quality problems (Effinger and Pfau-Effinger 1999).

Altogether it is possible to detect a 'dual' development. There is an ongoing trend towards a formalisation of informal work in European societies. This by no means suggests that informal work is being increasingly eradicated. Rather, there is a trend towards the transformation of the traditional forms of informal work, mainly unpaid informal work provided by women in the family, into different and in part new informal or semiformal forms, such as semiformal care by parents or relatives in the framework of welfare-state programmes and voluntary work. Moreover, informal employment in the private household is increasingly used by parents or elderly people in need of care to solve problems in organising adequate care provision. It is also used by companies, at least in those countries in which a labour force exists which needs to gain an income outside of formal employment or which does not accept the obligation to pay tax.

A certain part of informal employment, above all in Spain and Poland, is indeed being reduced through modernisation developments, with the concern here being particularly with the "poverty escape" type, which is on the decline in these countries (Surdej and Slezak in this volume, Renooy et al. 2004). Moreover, policies that legalise the labour-market status of immigrants contribute to diminishing the share of this type of undeclared work. The Spanish government, for example, was successful in lowering the number of undeclared workers when it legalised the citizenship status of a great number of immigrants in 2005 (Flaquer and Escobedo in this volume).

However, even if several areas of undeclared work disappear in some countries in the course of modernisation, it often reemerges in changed forms in modernised economies and societies. In this regard, strong welfare states appear to be in a better position to keep its extent low than are weak welfare states. It seems that high minimum wages and social policies that are based on relatively generous unemployment benefits in general and are inclusive towards immigrants tend to crowd out parts of the poverty-escape type because they reduce the supply of workers who are seeking undeclared work (Jensen and Rathlev in this volume; Jolkkonen et al. in this volume).

NOTES

1. The table uses parameters such as 'high', 'medium', and 'low' to measure the differences among the six countries. These parameters should not be understood in absolute terms. High in relation to 'formalisation of child care' does not necessarily mean that coverage is close to 100 per cent. Rather, 'high', 'medium', and 'low' are relative assertions. 'High' in relation to "formalisation of child care" signifies that expenditures and coverage are substantially higher as compared to the other countries included in the book; 'medium' that expenditures and coverage are about average; and 'low' that coverage and expenditures are comparatively substantially lower than in the other countries. By the same token, 'high' in relation to 'informal family childcare' does not mean that informal family childcare is the only or predominant form of care. Rather, 'high' indicates that 'Informal family childcare' in a given country plays a relatively large role as compared to countries with 'medium' and 'low' extents of informal family of childcare.
2. The term 'semiformal' forms of work was introduced into the debate by Geissler and Pfau-Effinger (2005). It means that care is provided by family members or within social networks in the context of welfare-state programmes such that it is no longer informal, but has some formal features in that it is registered and may also be connected with some kind of pay and social security (see Chapter 1).
3. This is a specific variant of a 'dual breadwinner/external care model'.
4. For an extended classification model of types of undeclared work in European societies and an elaborated approach to the explanation of differences, see Pfau-Effinger (forthcoming).
5. In part, international comparative data sets on organisations of the nonprofit sector are available. However, it should be considered that work in nonprofit organisations is in many countries to a substantial degree mainly based on formal employment and not, as is sometimes assumed, exclusively on voluntary work.

REFERENCES

Bode, I. (2004) *Disorganisierter Wohlfahrtskapitalismus. Die Reorganisation des Sozialsektors in Deutschland, Frankreich und Großbritannien*, Wiesbaden: VS-Verlag.

Effinger, H., and Pfau-Effinger, B. (1999) Freiwilliges Engagement im Sozialwesen—Ausweg aus der Krise der Erwerbsgesellschaft und des Wohlfahrtsstaates?', in E. Kistler, H.-H. Noll, E. Priller (ed.) *Perspektiven gesellschaftlichen Zusammenhalts. Empirische Befunde, Praxiserfahrungen, Messkonzepte*, Berlin: Edition Sigma.

Esping-Andersen, G. (1990) *The Three Worlds of Welfare Capitalism,* Cambridge: Polity Press.

——. (1999) *The Social Foundations of Postindustrial Economies,* Oxford: Oxford University Press.

Flaquer, L. (2002) 'Political intervention and family policy in Europe and the USA: Family policy and the maintenance of the traditional family in Spain', in A. Carling, S. Duncan, and R. Edwards (eds) *Analysing Families: Morality and Rationality in Policy and Practice,* London: Routledge, 84–92.

Geissler, B., and Pfau-Effinger, B. (2005) 'Change in European care arrangements', in B. Geissler, and B. Pfau-Effinger (eds) *Care and Social Integration in European Societies,* Bristol: Polity Press, 3–20.

Janoski, T. (1998) *Citizenship and Civil Society: A Framework of Rights and Obligations in Liberal, Traditional and Social Democratic Regimes,* Cambridge: Cambridge University Press.

Knijn, T., and Kremer, M. (1997) 'Gender and the caring dimension of Welfare States: Towards inclusive citizenship', *Social Politics,* 3: 328–361.

Pfau-Effinger, B. 'Varieties of undeclared work in European societies', *British Journal of Industrial Relations* 3 (forthcoming).

Putnam, Robert D., 1993: Making Democracy Work: Civic Traditions in Modern Italy.(Princeton Press).

Renooy, P., Ivarsson, S., Wusten-Gritsai, O. van der, and Meijer, E. (2004) 'Undeclared work in an enlarged union. An analysis of undeclared work: An in-depth study of specific items', *European Commission,* http://europa.eu.int/comm/employment_social/employment_analysis/work/undeclared_work_final_en.pdf

Schneider, F., and Enste, D. (2000) *Schattenwirtschaft und Schwarzarbeit. Umfang, Ursachen, Wirkungen und wirtschaftspolitische Empfehlungen,* München: Oldenbourg.

Solé, C., and Flaquer, L. (eds) (2005) *El uso de las políticas sociales por las mujeres inmigrantes,* Madrid: Ministerio de Trabajo y Asuntos Sociales, Instituto de la Mujer.

Vabö, M. (2006) 'Caring for people or caring for proxy consumers?', *European Societies* 8(3): 403–422.

Williams, C.C., and Windebank, J. (1998) *Informal Employment in the Advanced Economy. Implications of Work and Welfare,* London: Routledge.

Appendix 1:
Social Expenditure as Percentage of GDP

Table 1.1. Total Social Expenditure as Percentage of GDP in Selected Countries and OECD Average for Selected Years, 1980–2003

Year	1980	1985	1990	1995	2000	2001	2002	2003
Denmark	25.2	24.2	25.5	28.9	25.8	26.4	26.9	27.6
Finland	18.4	22.8	24.5	27.7	21.3	21.4	21.9	22.5
Germany	23	23.6	22.5	26.6	26.3	26.3	27.0	27.3
Poland	–	–	15.1	23.1	21.2	22.4	23.0	22.9
Spain	15.5	17.8	20.0	21.5	20.4	20.2	20.2	20.3
United Kingdom	16.6	19.6	17.2	20.4	19.1	20.1	20.1	20.6
OECD–Total	15.9	17.6	17.9	19.9	19.4	19.7	20.3	20.7

Source: OECD Social Expenditure Database.

Table 1.2. Social Expenditure on Family and Children as Percentage of GDP in Selected Countries and OECD Average for Selected Years 1980–2003

Year	1980	1985	1990	1995	2000	2001	2002	2003
Benefits in kind								
Denmark	1.72	1.72	1.84	2.00	2.19	2.27	2.32	2.33
Finland	0.80	1.10	1.36	1.49	1.36	1.35	1.36	1.38
Germany	0.50	0.47	0.49	0.75	0.78	0.77	0.77	0.77
Poland	–	–	0.00	0.00	0.50	0.44	0.45	0.50
Spain	0.03	0.03	0.08	0.13	0.56	0.59	0.61	0.65
United Kingdom	0.52	0.45	0.39	0.49	0.71	0.77	0.80	0.75
OECD–Total	0.34	0.35	0.43	0.51	0.73	0.76	0.80	0.80
Cash benefits								
Denmark	1.07	0.89	1.41	1.84	1.49	1.49	1.53	1.62
Finland	1.06	1.46	1.86	2.56	1.70	1.64	1.59	1.59
Germany	1.82	1.29	1.20	1.17	1.16	1.13	1.18	1.17
Poland	–	–	1.72	1.08	1.03	1.07	1.09	1.00
Spain	0.44	0.24	0.24	0.29	0.30	0.29	0.29	0.39
United Kingdom	1.78	1.85	1.54	1.87	1.87	1.89	1.89	2.18
OECD–Total	1.29	1.24	1.26	1.30	1.21	1.23	1.26	1.32

Source: OECD Social Expenditure Database.

Table 1.3. Benefits for Families and Children by Benefit and Scheme Type as Percentage of GDP in Selected Countries (Eurostat 2004)

	EU-25	Denmark	Germany	Spain	Poland	Finland	UK
Income maintenance benefit in the event of childbirth	0.2	0.6	0.1	0.1	0.1	0.4	0.1
Periodic parental leave benefit	0.1	–	0.2	–	0.2	0.2	0.0
Family or child allowance	1.2	1.0	1.8	0.2	0.5	0.9	1.2
Other periodic cash benefits	0.1	0.0	0.1	0.0	0.1	0.1	0.0
Birth grant	0.0	–	0.0	0.0	0.0	0.0	0.0
Parental leave benefits lump sum	0.0	0.0	0.0	–	0.0	–	0.0
Other lump sum cash benefits	0.0	–	0.0	0.0	–	–	0.0
Cash benefits	*1.5*	*1.6*	*2.2*	*0.4*	*0.9*	*1.6*	*1.3*
Child day care	0.2	1.6	0.4	0.0	–	0.9	0.2
Accommodation	0.1	0.5	0.0	0.1	–	0.2	0.1
Home help	0.0	0.0	0.0	0.0	–	0.0	0.0
Other benefits in kind	0.2	0.2	0.4	0.2	–	0.2	0.1
Benefits in kind	*0.6*	*2.3*	*0.7*	*0.3*	–	*1.3*	*0.4*
Ratio cash/in kind	2.5	0.7	3.1	1.3	–	1.2	3.3
Nonmeans-tested benefits	1.5	3.7	2.2	0.3	0.3	2.9	1.3
Means-tested benefits	0.5	0.2	0.8	0.3	0.6	0.0	0.4
Ratio means-tested/nonmeans-tested	0.3	0.1	0.4	1.0	2.0	0.0	0.3
All family/children benefits	2.1	3.9	3.0	0.7	0.9	3.0	1.7

Source: Author elaboration based on Eurostat data (please note: some data are provisional or estimated).

Table 1.4. Social Expenditure on Old-Age Benefits in Kind as Percentage of GDP and OECD Average in Selected Countries for Selected Years, 1980–2003

Year	1980	1985	1990	1995	2000	2001	2002	2003
Denmark	2.31	2.21	2.23	2.14	1.72	1.75	1.81	1.83
Finland	0.48	0.65	0.73	0.87	0.80	0.85	0.87	0.92
Germany	0.16	0.19	0.20	0.35	0.20	0.19	0.20	0.20
Poland	–	–	0.00	0.00	0.00	0.00	0.00	0.00
Spain	0.04	0.04	0.17	0.19	0.21	0.21	0.21	0.22
United Kingdom	0.42	0.38	0.33	0.48	0.42	0.45	0.51	0.55
OECD–Total	0.31	0.31	0.39	0.46	0.48	0.50	0.52	0.54

Source: OECD Social Expenditure Database.

Table 1.5. Old-Age Benefits in Kind by Benefit and Scheme Type as Percentage of GDP in Selected Countries, 2004

	EU-25	Denmark	Germany	Spain	Poland	Finland	UK
Accommodation	0.2	0.1	0.1	0.2	–	0.4	0.3
Assistance in carrying out daily tasks	0.1	1.6	0.1	0.1	0.0	0.3	0.3
Other benefits in kind	0.1	0.1	0.0	0.0	–	0.3	0.0
All old-age benefits in kind	0.4	1.9	0.2	0.4	0.0	1.0	0.6
Means-tested benefits in kind	0.3	–	0.1	0.3	–	–	0.6
Nonmeans-tested benefits in kind	0.2	1.9	0.1	0.0	0.0	1.0	0.0
Ratio means-tested/ nonmeans-tested	1.5	–	1	–	–	–	–
All old-age benefits	10.8	11.1	12.0	7.9	10.8	8.6	10.7

Source: Author elaboration based on Eurostat data (please note: some data are provisional or estimated).

Appendix 2
Taxes, Social Contributions, and Labour Costs (OECD, Taxing Wages 2000–2004)

Table 2.1.   Income Tax and Social Security Contributions for an Individual at the Income Level of the Average Production Worker (APW) as Percentage of Labour Costs, 2000 and 2004

| | Income tax % | | Social security contributions | | | | | | Labour costs ($, PPP) | |
| | | | Employee % | | Employer % | | Total % | | | |
	2000	2004	2000	2004	2000	2004	2000	2004	2000	2004
Denmark	32.0	30.4	12.0	10.5	0.0	0.5	44.0	41.5	32789	37788
Finland	21.0	19.5	6.0	4.9	21.0	19.4	47.0	43.8	31215	37174
Germany	18.0	16.2	17.0	17.3	17.0	17.3	52.0	50.7	38945	42543
Poland	5.0	5.1	21.0	21.1	17.0	17.0	43.0	43.1	14100	17319
Spain	9.0	9.7	5.0	4.9	23.0	23.4	37.0	38.0	24655	29382
United Kingdom	14.0	14.5	7.0	7.8	9.0	9.0	30.0	31.2	30924	36159

Source: OECD (2002, 2004) Taxing Wages 2000–2001, Taxing Wages 2003–2004, available on-line at OECD Web site www.sourceOECD.org.
Note: Labour costs are provided in dollars with equal purchasing power.

Table 2.2.   Labour Costs for an Individual at the Income Level of the Average Production Worker, 2000 and 2004 ($, PPP)

	Labour Costs ($, PPP)	
	2000	2004
Denmark	32789	37788
Finland	31215	37174
Germany	38945	42543
Poland	14100	17319
Spain	24655	29382
United Kingdom	30924	36159

Source: OECD (2002, 2004) Taxing Wages 2000–2001, Taxing Wages 2003–2004, available on-line at OECD Web site www.sourceOECD.org.
Note: for a single individual at the income level of the average production worker (APW).

Table 2.3.   Income Tax and Social Security Contributions as Percentage of Labour Costs, 2000 and 2004

	Total Taxes %	
	2000	2004
Denmark	44	41.5
Finland	47	43.8
Germany	52	50.7
Poland	43	43.1
Spain	38	38.0
United Kingdom	30	31.2

Source: OECD (2002, 2004) Taxing Wages 2000-2001, Taxing Wages 2003–2004, available on-line at OECD Web site www.sourceOECD.org.
Note: for a single individual at the income level of the average production worker (APW).

Table 2.4.   Employer Social Security Costs as Percentage of Labour Costs, 2000 and 2004

	Employer %	
	2000	2004
Denmark	0	0.5
Finland	21	19.4
Germany	17	17.3
Poland	17	17.0
Spain	23	23.4
United Kingdom	9	9.0

Source: OECD (2002, 2004) Taxing Wages 2000–2001, Taxing Wages 2003-2004, available on-line at OECD Web site www.sourceOECD.org.
Note: for a single individual at the income level of the average production worker (APW).

Table 2.5.   Employee Social Security Costs as Percentage of Labour Costs, 2000 and 2004

| | *Employee %* | |
	2000	*2004*
Denmark	12	10.5
Finland	6	4.9
Germany	17	17.3
Poland	21	21.1
Spain	5	4.9
United Kingdom	7	7.8

Source: OECD (2002, 2004) Taxing Wages 2000-2001, Taxing Wages 2003–2004, available on-line at OECD Web site www.sourceOECD.org.
Note: for a single individual at the income level of the average production worker (APW).

Table 2.6.   Income Tax as Percentage of Labour Costs, 2000 and 2004

| | *Income tax %* | |
	2000	*2004*
Denmark	32.0	30.4
Finland	21.0	19.5
Germany	18.0	16.2
Poland	5.0	5.1
Spain	9.0	9.7
United Kingdom	14.0	14.5

Source: OECD (2002, 2004) Taxing Wages 2000–2001, Taxing Wages 2003–2004, available on-line at OECD Web site www.sourceOECD.org.
Note: for a single individual at the income level of the average production worker (APW).

Table 3.1.   "How Much Confidence Do You Have in the National Parliament?" (in %)

	Denmark	*Germany*	*UK*	*Spain*	*Poland*	*Total*
Complete confidence	2	2	1	5	1	2
A great deal of confidence	18	11	5	17	5	11
Some confidence	39	33	51	39	37	40
Very little confidence	28	34	35	25	32	31
No confidence at all	12	21	8	15	24	16
PDI (confidence minus no confidence)	-20	-42	-37	-18	-50	-34

Source: ISSP 1998 (Q12A, v20).

Table 3.2.   "How Much Confidence Do You Have in Business and Industry?" (in %)

	Denmark	Germany	UK	Spain	Poland	Total
Complete confidence	4	3	1	5	0	3
A great deal of confidence	33	18	9	22	6	18
Some confidence	46	48	68	42	54	52
Very little confidence	15	23	18	22	28	21
No confidence at all	2	8	4	10	12	7
PDI (confidence minus no confidence)	20	-10	-12	-5	-34	-7

Source: ISSP 1998 (Q12B, v21).

Table 3.3. "How Much Confidence Do You Have in Churches and Religious Organisations?" (in %)

	Denmark	Germany	U.K.	Spain	Poland	Total
Complete confidence	8	6	3	11	13	8
A great deal of confidence	24	15	14	23	27	21
Some confidence	37	29	45	29	41	36
Very little confidence	20	23	27	20	13	21
No confidence at all	11	28	12	18	7	15

Source: ISSP 1998 (Q12C, v22).

Table 3.4.   "How Much Confidence Do You Have in Courts and the Legal System?" (in %)

	Denmark	Germany	U.K.	Spain	Poland	Total
Complete confidence	16	5	2	4	3	6
A great deal of confidence	42	21	16	16	19	23
Some confidence	25	36	55	31	44	38
Very little confidence	12	23	20	28	20	21
No confidence at all	6	15	7	21	14	13
PDI (confidence minus no confidence)	40	-12	-9	-29	-12	-5

Source: ISSP 1998 (Q12D, v23).

Table 3.5.   "How Much Confidence Do You Have in Schools and the Educational System?"(in %)

	Denmark	Germany	U.K.	Spain	Poland	Total
Complete confidence	9	4	3	11	6	7
A great deal of confidence	47	30	20	44	31	34
Some confidence	35	45	61	31	51	45
Very little confidence	7	16	13	10	9	11
No confidence at all	1	5	2	5	4	3
PDI (confidence minus no confidence)	48	13	8	40	24	27

Source: ISSP 1998 (Q12E, v24).

Data provided by Jakob Rathlev, University of Aalborg, in the framework of the research project in the 5th EU Framework Programme 'Formal and informal work in Europe. A comparative analysis of their changing relationship and their impact on social integration' (FIWE).

Appendix 3
Data on Employment (OECD 1994–2006)

Table 4.1. Labour-force Participation Rates, Population Age 15–64, all (women)

	1994	1996	1998	2000	2002	2004	2006
Denmark	78.8	79.5	79.3	80.0	79.9	80.2	80.1
	(73.8)	(73.6)	(75.1)	(75.9)	(75.9)	(76.1)	(76.7)
Finland	72.0	72.5	72.4	74.3	74.5	73.7	74.7
	(69.1)	(69.9)	(69.7)	(72.1)	(72.8)	(71.9)	(73.2)
Germany	70.5	70.7	71.4	72.2	71.5	72.6	75.0
	(60.9)	(61.5)	(62.5)	(63.2)	(64.2)	(65.8)	(68.5)
UK	76.0	76.1	75.9	76.6	76.2	76.2	76.7
	(67.1)	(67.5)	(67.9)	(68.9)	(69.3)	(69.6)	(70.3)
Poland	68.4	66.9	66.1	65.8	64.8	64.2	63.4
	(62.1)	(60.5)	(59.7)	(59. 9)	(58.9)	(58.2)	(56.8)
Spain	62.4	62.0	64.4	66.7	67.1	69.7	71.9
	(46.3)	(47.0)	(49.9)	(52.9)	(53.7)	(57.7)	(61.1)

OECD: Employment Outlook, Paris: 2001, 2002, 2006.

Table 4.2. Employment Rates, Population Age 15–64, all (women)

	1994	1996	1998	2000	2002	2004	2006
Denmark	72.4	74.0	75.3	76.4	76.4	76.0	76.9
	(67.1)	(67.4)	(70.3)	(72.1)	(72.6)	(72.0)	(73.2)
Finland	59.9	61.9	64.0	67.0	67.7	67.2	68.9
	(58.7)	(59.4)	(61.2)	(64.5)	(66.1)	(65.5)	(67.3)
Germany	64.5	64.4	64.7	66.3	65.3	65.0	67.2
	(54.7)	(55.5)	(56.3)	(57.7)	(58.8)	(59.2)	(61.5)
UK	68.7	69.9	71.2	72.4	72.3	72.7	72.5
	(62.1)	(63.3)	(64.2)	(65.5)	(66.3)	(66.6)	(66.8)
Poland	58.3	58.4	58.9	55.0	51.7	51.9	54.5
	(51.9)	(51.8)	(52.2)	(48.9)	(46.4)	(46.4)	(48.2)
Spain	47.4	48.2	52.4	57.4	59.5	62.0	65.7
	(31.5)	(33.0)	(36.5)	(42.0)	(44.9)	(49.0)	(54.0)

OECD: Employment Outlook, Paris: 2001, 2002, 2006.

Table 4.3.   Unemployment Rates, All Women

	1994	1996	1998	2000	2002	2004	2006
Denmark	7.7	6.3	4.9	4.4	4.6	5.5	4.0
	(9.0)	(8.4)	(6.4)	(5.0)	(4.4)	(5.5)	(4.2)
Finland	16.8	14.6	11.3	9.8	9.1	8.9	7.8
	(14.9)	(15.0)	(12.1)	(10.6)	(9.1)	(9.0)	(8.1)
Germany	8.3	8.6	8.8	7.2	8.2	9.5	10.4
	(10.1)	(9.7)	(9.9)	(8.7)	(8.4)	(10.1)	(10.3)
UK	9.3	7.9	6.1	5.4	5.1	4.7	5.4
	(7.4)	(6.3)	(5.3)	(4.8)	(4.4)	(4.3)	(5.0)
Poland	14.4	12.3	10.2	16.1	19.9	19.0	14.0
	(16.4)	(14.3)	(12.6)	(18.4)	(21.2)	(20.2)	(15.1)
	19.5	17.8	15.0	11.1	11.1	10.6	9.2
Spain	(31.8)	(29.8)	(26.7)	(20.6)	(16.4)	(15.1)	(11.6)

OECD (2006) Employment Outlook, Paris: OECD, 247.

Table 4.4.   Maternal Employment Rates by Age of Youngest Child, Total Female Employment Rates, and Part-Time Employment Rates of Women Age 15–64 (OECD 2005–2006)

	Maternal employment rates by age of youngest child, 2005				*Total female employment rates, 2006*	*Part-time rate of women, 2006*
	0-16	*Under 3*	*3-5*	*6-16*		
Denmark	76.5	71.4	77.8	77.5	73.2	25.6
Finland	76.0	52.1	80.7	84.2	67.3	14.9
Germany	54.9	36.1	54.8	62.7	61.5	39.2
UK	61.7	52.6	58.3	67.7	66.8	38.8
Poland	46.4				48.2	16.3
Spain	52.0	52.6	54.2	50.9	54.0	21.4

Source: OECD 2007: Babies and Bosses: Reconciling Work and Family Life (vol. 5): A Synthesis of Findings for OECD Countries (www/oecd.org/els/social/family); Tables 1.1., 3.2.

Table 5.1. Participation Rates in Day Care and Preschool for Children under Six (OECD circa 2004)

| | *Enrolment in day care for the under 3s and preschool for 3 to 6* | | | |
	Under 3 years	*3 years*	*4 years*	*5 years*
Denmark	61.7	81.8	93.4	93.9
Finland	35.0	37.7	46.1	54.6
Germany	9.0	69.5	84.3	86.7
UK	25.8	50.2	92.0	98.2
Poland	2.0	26.1	35.7	46.2
Spain	20.7	95.9	100.0	100.0

Source: OECD Family Database, www.oecd.org/els/social/family/database, last updated 20/02/2008; PF11 3.3.2008.
For Germany and Poland, the reference year is 2001; for Finland, 2003; for Spain and UK, 2004, and for Denmark, 2005.

Table 6.1. Caring for the Ill, Disabled, or Elderly in the Home (Eurobarometer 2002)

	Denmark	*Germany*	*UK*	*Spain*	*Poland*	*Total*
Proportion of people of working age (16–65) caring for the ill, disabled or elderly in the home	5	15	11	11	18	12

Source: Eurobarometer 2002. Elaborated by EurLife: Database from European Foundation for the Improvement of Living and Working Conditions. Average is unweighted.

Appendix 4

Attitude Data in Relation to the Family, Mother's Employment, and Elderly Care (ISSP 2002 & Eurobarometer 1998)

Table 7.1.   Attitude Data in Relation to the Family and Mother's Employment (ISSP 2002)

Variable	Label of variable	West Germany (D-W)	East Germany (D-E)	Great Britain (GB)	Poland (PL)	Spain (E)	Denmark (DK)	Finland (SF)
Attitudes towards gender division of labour within the family v10	Both should contribute to household income	66.1%	91.2%	60.5%	75.2%	87.9%	77.2%	68.3%
v11	Mens job is work; womens job household	23.3%	14.7%	17.7%	43.5%	24.7%	13.6%	11.8%
v13	Men should do larger share of childcare	71.2%	66.8%	63.3%	75.9%	90.7%	63.6%	74.6%
Attitudes towards the relationship between employment of mothers and the well-being of their family resp. their children v5	Working mom: preschool child suffers	55.8%	32.7%	37.1%	55.0%	52.2%	32.4%	36.1%
v6	Working woman: family life suffers	47.8%	28.2%	35.7%	41.1%	55.3%	29.1%	21.5%
Attitudes towards the employment of mothers v15	Should women work: child under school age: work full-time + work part-time	48.0%	85.3%	43.8%	43.5%	63.0%	76.7%	60.2%
v15	Should women work: child under school age: work full-time	3.2%	17.3%	3.9%	19.9%	18.7%	15.5%	18.2%

v15	Should women work: child under school age: work part-time	44.8%	68.0%	39.9%	23.7%	44.3%	61.1%	42.0%
v15	Should women work: child under school age: stay at home	52.0%	14.8%	56.2%	56.5%	37.0%	23.3%	39.8%
Attitudes towards the financial support of parents by the welfare state v28	Working parents should: financial benefits	69.3%	88.2%	55.7%	52.7%	81.1%	61.1%	68.9%

The proportion in per cent that is given in the table refers to the proportion of respondents who "strongly agree" and "agree" in relation to the variables v5, v6, v10, v11, v13, v28: strongly agree + agree

Source: ISSP 2002: Family and Changing Gender Roles.

The data were weighted on the basis of the ISSP 2002 Study Description, 1-18, 49, 119.

Exact formulation of the questions in the questionnaire (Source Questionaire Family 2002 - http://www.za.uni-koeln.de/data/en/issp/codebooks/ISSP2002_source_quest.pdf)

R1. (1) To begin, we have some questions about women. To what extent do you agree or disagree ...?
(v5) b. A preschool child is likely to suffer if his or her mother works.
(v6) c. All in all, family life suffers when the woman has a full-time job.

R 2. (2) And to what extent do you agree or disagree...?
(v10) a. Both the man and the woman should contribute to the household income.
(v11) b. A man´s job is to earn money; a woman's job is to look after the home and family.
(v13) d. Men ought to do larger share of childcare than they do now.

R 3. (3) Do you think that women should work outside the home full-time, part-time, or not at all under the following circumstances?
(v15) b. When there is a child under school age.

R 6. (14) To what extent do you agree or disagree...?
(v28) a. Families should receive financial benefits for child care when both parents work.

Table 7.2.   Attitudes towards Eldercare (Eurobarometer 1998)

Q.36. – Let's suppose you had an elderly father or mother who lived alone. What do you think would be the best if this parent could no longer manage to live on his/her own? (One answer only; Accounts in percent).

	Denmark	Germany/ West	Germany/ East	Spain	Great Britain	Finland
1. Myself or one of my brothers or sisters should invite my father or mother to live with one of us	8.9	39.4	32.7	66.9	30.2	12.1
2. I or one of my brothers or sisters should move in with my father or mother	1.1	5.7	3.5	6.4	4.3	3.7
3. One should move closer to the other	9.0	12.3	15.0	3.1	12.9	6.9
4. My father or mother should move into an old people's home or a nursing home (M)	32.2	9.6	11.4	4.6	13.5	15.6
5. My father or mother should stay at home and receive visits there, as well as appropriate health care and services	43.2	21.9	25.6	8.9	24.4	51.6
6. It depends (spontaneous)	4.1	9.1	8.4	6.4	10.4	7.6
DK	1.5	2.1	3.5	3.7	4.2	2.5
Total	100	100	100	100	100	100

Source: INRA (EUROPE) EUROBAROMETER 50.1 – Autumn 1998.

Appendix 5
Data on Informal Employment (Various Sources)

Table 8.1. Incidence of Informal Employment

Country	Year	Amount (% GDP)	Source
Denmark	2001	5.5	Rockwool Foundation Study No. 10, questionnaire survey
Finland	1992	4.2	National Statistical Bureau
Germany	2001	4.5 16	Rockwool Foundation Study No. 10, questionnaire survey Schneider; IAB
UK	2000	2	Rockwool Foundation Study No. 10, questionnaire survey
Poland	2003	14	Renooy et al. 2004
Spain	2006	12.3 (Estimated share of undeclared work in total employment)	E. González and L. Sánchez (2007), Undeclared Work in Spain, European Employment Observatory

Source: Renooy et al. 2004, 7; Pedersen 2003; Schneider 2000; IAB 2002.

Table 8.2. Time per Week Spent in Informal Employment by Informal Employees Aged 18–66

Germany	8 hours 14 minutes
Denmark	5 hours 10 minutes
UK	3 hours 48 minutes

Source: Pedersen 2003, 105.

Contributors

Graham Baxendale is currently a PhD student at the University of Southampton, researching the regulation of sexuality in Britain. He took a degree in Politics and History at the University of Portsmouth and an MA in European Studies at the University of Reading.

Anna Escobedo is a researcher and Associate Lecturer at the Department of Sociology of the Universitat Autònoma de Barcelona (Spain). Her research focusses on the family, social change, and comparative social policy, with special emphasis on the work-life balance, the relationship between formal and informal work, parental leave and childcare, and professional developments in care work. She has participated in a wide range of national and European research projects in the field of social policy and the employment market. She is member of the International Network on Leave Policies and Research. Contact: Anna.Escobedo@ uab.cat; http://selene.uab.es/_cs_iphigenia/escobedo-eng.html

Lluís Flaquer is Professor of Sociology at the Universitat Autònoma de Barcelona. He took a degree in political science at the University of Paris' Institut d'Études Politiques and then he received his Ph.D. in law at the Universitat Autònoma de Barcelona. His current research topics include the changing structure of the family, new family forms, family policy, and child poverty. He was the director of the WELLCHI NETWORK on 'The well-being of children: The impact of changing family forms, parents' working conditions, social policy and legislative measures', financed under the 6th Framework Programme of the European Union (2004–2007). Contact: lluis.flaquer@uab.cat; http://selene.uab.es/_cs_iphigenia/flaquer-eng.html

Per H. Jensen is Professor of Social Policy, Centre for Comparative Welfare Studies, Aalborg University. His research is mainly focussed on citizenship, labour markets, and welfare states in a comparative perspective. More recently he has published a book on the causes and effects of early exit/retirement (2006), edited a book about the concept of welfare (2007), and coedited 'The Changing Face of Welfare' (2005).

Arja Jolkkonen is Senior Researcher at the Karelian Institute, University of Joensuu, Finland. She received her doctorate from the University of Joensuu in 1998. Her dissertation was on the labour-market strategies of women. Her current research interests focus on globalisation and local labour-market adjustment, the Finnish flexicurity model, and regional and occupational mobility of labour.

Riitta Kilpeläinen is a researcher working at the Karelian Institute at the University of Joensuu, Finland. She is a graduate student in labour-market studies and sociology, and her dissertation, on informal work and its significance on the individual life-course and labour-market history, will be partly based on the data and theoretical assumptions of the research project 'Formal and Informal Work in Europe'.

Pertti Koistinen is Professor of Labour and Social Policies at the University of Tampere, Finland. His research interests are labour and labour-market policies and comparative studies of European employment systems and social policies. Koistinen has published more than one hundred articles and ten books and monographs on social policies and labour markets. He is author of the university textbook *The Foundations of Labour Policies* (in Finnish), and coeditor of the book *Working Europe*. He has also contributed to two ETUI publications titled 'Manifesto Social Europe'. Other notable publications are *Labour Flexibility a Factor of the Economic and Social Performance of Finland in the 1990s, Mystery of Care and Care Relations* (in Finnish), the book article (as coauthor) 'Policies promoting employment and gender equality in the knowledge-based society', and (as editor) two forthcoming books: *Emerging Systems of Work and Welfare* and *Fading Borders of Work* (in Finnish).

Traute Meyer is a Reader in Social Policy at the University of Southampton. She has participated in international research projects in the area of pensions, informal, and care work and she is the coeditor of the *European Journal of Social Policy*. Most recent publications include: *PrivatePensions versus Social Inclusion?* (2007), and 'Class, gender, chance and the social division of welfare' (Ageing *and Society* 2008) (both with P. Bridgen).

Birgit Pfau-Effinger is full Professor of Sociology, holds the Chair for Social Structure Analyses, and directs the Research Centre for Globalisation and Governance at the University of Hamburg. She has taught at the Universities of Goettingen, Bremen, and Jena and been Visiting Professor at the Universities of Tampere, Barcelona, and Aalborg. Her special interests include theory and methods in the field of comparative sociology, the relationship of institutions and culture, social policy analysis, analysis of the family-employment relationship, informal work, childcare and long-term care, gender studies, and sociology of transformation. She has published widely at the national and international levels in these fields. She was coordinator of the EU 5th Framework research project on 'Formal and informal work in Europe' (FIWE).

Jakob Rathlev holds an MA in social science and is a part-time lecturer and PhD scholar at the Centre for Comparative Welfare Studies, Aalborg University. He is studying voluntary work and welfare-state interactions across different welfare regimes and furthermore has taken part in the Danish Election Study where he has published on generational differences in attitudes towards redistribution and new politics. He is also engaged in organising research activities within European social policy as secretary of the ESPAnet.

Slađana Sakač Magdalenić, is a PhD student and Research Fellow at the Institute of Sociology and the Centre for Globalisation and Governance, University of Hamburg, Germany. She graduated in sociology from the University of Bremen. She has previously worked within the 5th EU Framework Research Project on 'Formal and Informal Work in Europe' at the University of Hamburg. Her PhD research is on local economies and particularly the sociocultural context of economic activities in Central and Eastern Europe. Her main research interests are the sociologies of economy, work, and transformation, and the relationships between institutions and culture.

Ewa Ślęzak has received her PhD from the Cracow University of Economics, Poland. She has worked in a number of research projects including the 5th FP 'Formal and informal work in Europe: A comparative analysis of their changing relationship and their impact on social integration' (FIWE). Her research interests focus on public policies, in particular as they affect social inclusion, the learning society, and informal work. She is author of a number of articles in Polish and in English. A graduate of the Cracow University of Economics, she received additional academic training at the Central European University in Budapest, the Inter-University Centre of Studies for Social Theory, and the University of Limerick. Apart from purely academic work she has been active in the field of policy and project evaluation.

Aleksander Surdej is Professor of European Public Policy and head of the Department of European Studies of the Cracow University of Economics. An economist and sociologist, he graduated from the Cracow University of Economics, the Jagiellonian University, and the Johns Hopkins University. His research interests focus on the policies of social regulations (including higher education and R&D policies), on the methodology of public policy analysis, and on the political economy of postcommunist transformations in Central and Eastern Europe. He has authored and coauthored many articles, book chapters, and policy reports for English, Italian, and Polish academic publications and policy-research centres such as the World Bank and UNU WIDER. He was Fellow of the Royal Institute of Advanced Social Studies in the Netherlands, Jean Monnet Fellow at the EUI Florence, and grant-holder at the CEU in Budapest. Recently he has published a book in Polish, *Determinants of Legal Administrative Instruments in Regulatory Policies*. He is editor-in-chief of *Panstwo i rynek* (State and Market), the Polish-language internet journal devoted to public policy analysis available at www.pir.org.pl.

Index

Page numbers in *italics* denotes a table